Narratives
of
Resistance

D1522912

Narratives

of

Resistance

JAMAICA, TRINIDAD, THE CARIBBEAN

BRIAN MEEKS

THE UNIVERSITY OF THE WEST INDIES PRESS
Barbados • Jamaica • Trinidad and Tobago

The University of the West Indies Press
1A Aqueduct Flats   Mona
Kingston 7   Jamaica

04   03   02   01   00   5 4 3 2 1

CATALOGUING IN PUBLICATION DATA

Meeks, Brian.
   Narratives of resistance : Jamaica, Trinidad, the
   Caribbean / Brian Meeks.
   p. cm.
   Includes bibliographical references and index.
   ISBN: 976-640-093-8

   1. Radicalism – Caribbean, English-speaking.
   2. Nationalism – Caribbean, English-speaking.
   3. Stone, Carl. 4. Manley, Michael. 5. Jamaica –
   Politics and government. 6. Political indicators –
   Caribbean, English- speaking. 7. National United
   Freedom Fighters (Trinidad and Tobado). 8. Henry
   Rebellion, 1961.

   F2133.M434   2000   972.9 dc - 20

Book design by Robert Harris
Set in Adobe Garamond 11/15 x 27
Printed in Canada
Cover photograph by courtesy of the Jamaica Observer Ltd
(www.jamaicaobserver.com)

For Patsy and my children Seya, Anya and Neto

The following chapters are revised from previously published articles and reprinted with permission:

Chapter 1, "The Henry Rebellion, Counter-Hegemony and Jamaican Democracy", first published in *Small Axe*, no. 2 (September 1997): 39–62.

Chapter 2, "NUFF at the Cusp of an Idea: Grassroots Guerrillas and the Politics of the Seventies in Trinidad and Tobago", first published in *Social Identities* 5, no. 4 (1999): 1–25.

Chapter 4, "Carl Stone: Political Scientist as People's Tribune", first published in *Social and Economic Studies* 45, no. 1 (1996): 1–26.

Chapter 5, "Remembering Michael Manley: 1924–1997", first published in *Against the Current*, n.s., 12, no. 4 (1997): 28–33.

Contents

Preface

If there is a central thesis to this volume, it is this: Despite the social and economic crises of the recent past, despite the increased marginalization of the Caribbean and of its poor, there is embedded in the common resistance of the people the real, though still very tentative possibility of a social and political revival. Central to such a project, however, is the development of new modes of thought oriented towards recognizing and valorizing the social and political praxis of the subaltern. Until Jamaica and the rest of the Caribbean come to terms with the majority of its people and their history, until new modes of democracy, both national and transnational, are introduced to subvert the old, restrictive, hierarchical structures, the possibility of a popular renewal is likely to be frustrated.

Beyond this, the aims are threefold. First, unlike my earlier studies, which were more reliant on a comparative, Caribbean frame of reference, this one seeks to focus (though not exclusively) on the Jamaican matrix. This is done to better grasp the nature of the social and political dimensions of what is elsewhere described as a moment of "hegemonic dissolution".[1] Second, it seeks to probe the notion of hegemony and to explore contemporary forms of social, political and intellectual resistance to this hegemony as it is manifested in Jamaica, Trinidad and elsewhere in the Caribbean. And third, there is an effort to implicitly introduce elements of an alternative methodology. There is an attempt, launching off from Antonio Gramsci, James Scott and others, to weave a path between the behaviouralist/institutionalist traditions of West Indian social sciences and, later, mechanistic Marxist approaches. This is evident not only in the approach to the analysis of history and data but, hopefully, to the style of writing itself. A concerted attempt is made to depart from the international aid agency approach of 'consultancy' writing, which has gradually gained ascendancy in Caribbean social sciences, to a less obfuscating, more transparent approach to narrative.

While doing an earlier study on Caribbean revolutions over a decade ago, I came across Alasdair MacIntyre's small piece, "Ideology, Social Science and Revolution".[2] I was, at the time, impressed by his argument that stressed the necessity for theorists to reveal their own biography as a central and indispensable part of any scholarly exercise of social-theoretical engagement. MacIntyre contended, en passant, that whereas in the social sciences objectivity and absolute truth were always elusive targets, one could, at least, gain some mooring by understanding the history from which the writer derived. This insight is of even greater relevance today, as postmodernism – on which MacIntyre has had a profound influence – is beginning to wane in the academy, and the baby is therefore in danger of being thrown out with the bath water.

Everyone belongs to a tradition – indeed, to multiple traditions. While it is true that the act of deciding which of these traditions to emphasize and which to deny is itself a deeply subjective process of sifting, it is, at minimum, occurring at a second tier of thought, beyond the cruder construct of the omniscient, objective observer. It is possible to further deconstruct the voiced tradition and, beyond that, the deconstruction of the deconstruction, though the obvious and ultimate danger is the nihilist's paralysis of thought and action. So, with full recognition of the dangers, here is an open-ended biographical sketch.

I grew up in Jamaica and consider myself in spirit and essence Jamaican, though the actual history is more complex than this. My father is Jamaican and he met my Trinidadian mother while studying at McGill University in Montreal, Canada, where they were married and I was born. He became a dentist and has practised dentistry for most of his working, adult life. She, an island scholar from Trinidad, left to do medicine but, in a moment of revelation, threw her books into the snow one day and ended up doing a liberal arts degree. Thus, my background is decidedly middle class professional and goes back, in somewhat uncharacteristic fashion for the Caribbean, some three generations. A further critical Caribbean indicator relates to colour, in that both families are of mixed African and European descent – 'brown', in the Jamaican lexicon – with Chinese and Amerindian forbears thrown into the mix from the Trinidadian side.

These powerful markers of privilege have been somewhat leavened by my intellectual development in Jamaica and Trinidad in the late sixties and early seventies. At Jamaica College, in the aftermath of Walter Rodney's expulsion from the island in 1968, many of us were won over to a militant Black Power ideology, influenced and, in some cases, superseded by Rastafarianism. Later, at the University of the West Indies' (UWI) St Augustine campus, I learned about Marxism and radical, direct action in the effervescent politics that followed the street phase of the 1970 Black Power revolution.

Back in Jamaica, as a graduate student on the UWI Mona campus, I was influenced by and eventually joined the Workers' Liberation League, headed by Trevor Munroe, with its brand of pro-Soviet, orthodox Marxism. In 1976, I joined the staff of the Jamaica Broadcasting Corporation (JBC) as a current affairs producer. This provided an immense opportunity to travel throughout Jamaica and meet with hundreds of people from differing walks of life. Along with many other young persons who worked in news and current affairs at the JBC, I was a militant supporter of the increasingly radical policies of Michael Manley's democratic socialist People's National Party (PNP). When the PNP was defeated in the bloody 1980 general elections, I was among the first victims fired by the Seaga-led Jamaica Labour Party (JLP) government, along with the entire cadre from news and current affairs at the JBC.

Between 1981 and 1983 I travelled to Grenada, to work first at Radio Free Grenada and later as editor of the *Free West Indian,* the newspaper of the Grenada revolution. I left Grenada for Jamaica in September 1983, to begin my doctoral dissertation on the Grenada revolution, only to discover a few weeks after returning that, following Maurice Bishop's house arrest, the revolution was in crisis and about to self-destruct. My intellectual career since then has been largely an attempt to come to terms with the traumatic outcome of the Grenadian revolution and the collapse of the Caribbean Left. This career has included theoretical forays into the meaning of revolution, the causes of revolutionary upsurges, the reasons why 'revolutions' take particular courses and, more recently, the cultural and ideological determinants that accelerate and, in some instances, retard revolutionary movements.

My own ideological development has largely followed this sequential history, from a vague Black Power militancy to a Marxism tinged by Mao Tse Tung's thought, through a long period of pro-Soviet, pro-Cuban Marxism to the present moment, which is described elsewhere in this volume as 'Caribbean subaltern'. This emerging perspective is profoundly influenced by Marxian political economy, though it seeks to read politics from below, from the perspective of the ideational constructs of the people themselves, in order to avoid the almost inevitable danger of the vanguard, which assumes to act 'in the interests of ' the people. The chapters that follow reflect, naturally, the central thesis, as they are coloured by this peculiar personal trajectory.

The introduction, "Downtown Stirs", focuses on recent Jamaican politics and suggests that the country has moved in the last three decades from a period of popular upsurge (the seventies), to a period of quiescence (the eighties), to an early and embryonic renaissance (the nineties). This new period is chaotic and contradictory, and it has within it the potential to descend into anarchy as well as to initiate a phase of democratic renewal. All of this is happening at a fortuitous moment in world history, when the hold of the neoliberal paradigm – dominant for much of the past two decades – is weakening. At the intellectual level, however, while there is undoubtedly a revival in thought, the revival is lagging behind the pace of the national upsurge. The final section critically mentions some of the trends in this revival.

The remaining chapters are divided, somewhat informally, into two parts. The first three chapters continue the engagement with revolution and revolts, as well as the comparative juxtaposition of Trinidad and Jamaica. This is done in order to tease out the nature of hegemony and the forms of resistance that accompany it; to suggest the specific and differing ways in which resistance is manifested in the two instances; and, in the case of the third chapter, to explore the usefulness of the novel as a complementary avenue to the study of these phenomena. Chapters 4, 5 and 6 concentrate on the contemporary politics of Jamaica, by way of separate engagements with the work of Carl Stone, the life of Michael Manley and the ubiquitous problem of driving.

The first chapter, "The Henry Rebellion: Counter-Hegemony and Jamaican Democracy", excavates and explores the Henry Rebellion, an obscure, aborted guerrilla movement that occurred in Jamaica in the penultimate year of colonialism. Ronald Henry and a group of US-based revolutionaries had hoped to overthrow the Jamaican government, with local support coming from his father's growing Rastafarian church. While the movement, it is argued, had little chance of success, its existence and the persistent themes of resistance voiced by its cadres raise important issues in relation to the nature of law and obedience. The event is then used to explore Gramscian notions of hegemony alongside James Scott's hypotheses on domination and resistance. The conclusion is that the Henry Rebellion cannot be seen as just the socially disconnected act of revolutionary adventurers, but as having roots in a longer genealogy of popular resistance to domination.

The second chapter shifts emphasis from Jamaica to Trinidad and Tobago and is entitled "NUFF at the Cusp of an Idea: Grassroots Guerrillas in Trinidad and Tobago". Trinidadian politics is introduced here as an arena of conflict in its own right, as well as a comparative tool to further understand the Jamaican situation. Like the first chapter on the Henry Rebellion, it introduces an instance of failed, under-researched and effectively erased revolt in the Caribbean, in this case the National United Freedom Fighters (NUFF) of Trinidad and Tobago, which functioned in the wake of that country's Black Power movement in the early seventies. Some recent theorizing on the nature and causes of revolt are introduced as a prelude to three revealing interviews with surviving members of the NUFF movement. The broad conclusion is that in order to understand why people rebel, there is the need to grasp both the international conjuncture as well as the local confluence of political ideas at the level of community, peer group and family. Such an approach, recognizing 'historical trajectories', needs to be counterpoised to one that adopts a dangerous, determinist, 'arrow of history' perspective, in which the future is already certain, but for its execution.

Chapter 3, "The Harder Dragon: Resistance in Earl Lovelace's *Dragon Can't Dance* and Michael Thelwell's *Harder They Come*", sustains the comparative dialogue between Jamaican and Trinidadian politics but, in this case, by using literature as the vehicle. It attempts to address a sharp critique from the Guyanese novelist Wilson Harris that Caribbean 'historians' have contributed to the poverty of their discipline by omitting the entire field of the imagination from their research. The chapter seeks to address Wilson's critique, using two well-received novels – one based in Trinidad, the other Jamaica – that address the question of social revolt. The broad conclusion is that there is much to be generated in the form of working hypotheses, if the tools of comparative research are sensitively introduced into the literary sphere.

Chapter 4, "Carl Stone: Political Scientist as People's Tribune", is an early attempt to critique the political thought of the late Jamaican political scientist, Carl Stone. Inevitably, it also naturally addresses critical questions on the character of Jamaican politics. For two and a half decades before his untimely death in 1993, Stone was, undoubtedly, the leading political scientist from Jamaica and arguably, the entire anglophone Caribbean. Stone, however, did not restrict his work to formal academic writing but was a pioneering pollster, whose predictions were uncannily accurate, and a consistent newspaper columnist. In an attempt to capture the main features of Stone's work, the chapter also examines the critical phases in Jamaica's postindependence political history. The central argument is that his oeuvre, despite its positivism and outwardly atheoretical appearance, operated within the broad parameters of a certain radical Caribbean tradition. While openly critical of Marxism, Stone's instinctive respect and reliance on the views of the 'ordinary' people was a precursor to the Caribbean subaltern perspective introduced here. Stone's sometimes narrowly constructed empiricism, however, might be understood from his conscious recognition of the hierarchical and potentially repressive restrictions in Caribbean liberal democracy. In his diligent attention to detail, therefore, he sought to attain the empirical high ground and make his critique from the unassailable perspective of the 'intellectual tribune'.

Chapter 5, "Remembering Michael Manley: 1924–1997", is a brief reminiscence on the life and times of the late, former Jamaican prime minister, Michael Manley. It takes up the Jamaican narrative beyond the Henry Rebellion. Manley, in the 1970s, became famous (or notorious) as the leader who put Jamaica on the international stage. His strong advocacy of a new international economic order, opposition to apartheid in South Africa, and close association with Fidel Castro and revolutionary Cuba were accompanied by long-delayed social reforms at home, under the slogan of 'democratic socialism'. The popular upsurge that he led continued, if sometimes reluctantly, the themes of black redemption embedded in Ronald Henry's aborted movement. These, after a long period of relative slumber, are re-emerging again. Manley himself came from a privileged background, his father, Norman, serving as premier twice and posthumously being given the title of national hero. Ironically, it was the father's regime – generally considered as reformist – against which Henry's rebellion was directed. The chapter critically traces the important stages in Manley's political development ending with the massive, unprecedented outpouring of sympathy at his death. This final act, it is suggested in concluding, was not only a mark of respect for his attempts to change Jamaican society but a final curtain call for the era of charismatic politics.

The sixth chapter is entitled "Careening on the Edge of the Abyss: Driving, Hegemony and the Rule of Law in Jamaica". It uses the contemporary state of driving and traffic in Jamaica as a metaphor for the particular moment of 'hegemonic dissolution' in that country. Jamaica has one of the highest death rates for vehicular accidents in the world. This, it is argued, emerges from a particular history in which rapacious multinational corporations, political and bureaucratic incompetence, and misplaced neoliberal dogma have all contributed to bringing the urban transport system to the point of gridlock. In a context where a variety of organizational forms have all failed, the proposed solution, also metaphorical in its reach, is to replace the system of free market anarchy with more centralized organization, though with important features of popular control. While this may not be an altogether novel conclusion, it emerges as a sensible option out of the wreckage of the recent past.

The conclusion, "The Caribbean Left at Century's End", returns to the wider Caribbean palate and seeks, in a more exploratory sense, to draw broad lessons on the future of the Caribbean and, more specifically, the political Left from the experiences of the recent past. As the world moves towards the consolidation of megablocks, the small island states and contiguous mainland territories of the Caribbean appear more marginalized and isolated than ever in their modern history. If the Caribbean nations and peoples are to survive as viable entities into the next century, strategies of deepening regional unification are inevitable, but these will not succeed unless they are accompanied by policies of democratization that genuinely include the people. Drawing on Jorge Castaneda's important survey of the Latin American Left *Utopia Unarmed,* the conclusion suggests that there is a future for a reconstructed Caribbean Left as the only force capable of consistently implementing a radical strategy of deeper democratization, the forging of new, transnational relationships and sustaining an ongoing critique of the neoliberal paradigm.

Acknowledgments

Many persons contributed to the realization of this volume. At the institutional level, I wish to specially thank Bill Allen and Scott Whiteford at Michigan State University, Terry Lynn Karl at Stanford University and Barrington Chevannes and Kenneth Hall at the University of the West Indies, who, at various times provided either financial support, or a quiet place to think and write. Others helped immeasurably through the granting of interviews and assistance in acquiring rare material. I thank in Jamaica, Minister of Transport and Works Peter Phillips, Senior Superintendent of Police Keith Gardener, Elsa Binns, the late Huntley Munroe, QC, and Trevor Munroe. In Trinidad, I am especially grateful to my friend the late Thelma Henderson, Victoria Pasley, and Rhoda Reddock, along with former NUFF militants Malcolm "Jai" Kernahan, Clem Haynes and Terrence Thornhill.

Many other friends and colleagues gave valuable and critical comments and encouragement, whether in oral or written form, which have, in one way or another, influenced the final manuscript. Among them, I mention and thank Lorna Goodison, Rupert Lewis, Fred Cooper, Hilbourne Watson, David Scott, Selwyn Ryan, Percy Hintzen, Norman Girvan, Kari Levitt, Winston James, Obika Gray, Linden Lewis, Denis Benn, Cecil Gutzmore, C.Y. Thomas, Paget Henry, Tony Bogues, Clinton Hutton, Pat Mohammed, Folke Lindahl, Pedro Noguera, Gordon Rohlehr, Bobby Hill, Maurice St Pierre and my dear wife Patsy Lewis.

I wish, finally, to recognize Pansy Benn, Joanne Blake and Shivaun Hearne, and the professional team at the University of the West Indies Press and the two reviewers of the first draft of this manuscript, both of whom gave excellent and detailed comments. I sincerely thank them all and hasten to add that the responsibility for the flaws in the final product, despite all of their efforts, is ultimately mine.

Abbreviations

BET	British Electric Traction
BITU	Bustamante Industrial Trade Union
CARICOM	Caribbean Community
CIA	Central Intelligence Agency
IMF	International Monetary Fund
INS	Immigration and Naturalization Service
JAMAL	Jamaica Adult Literacy
JBC	Jamaica Broadcasting Corporation
JLP	Jamaica Labour Party
JOS	Jamaica Omnibus Service
NAFTA	North American Free Trade Agreement
NDM	National Democratic Movement
NGO	nongovernmental organization
NJAC	National Joint Action Committee
NJM	New Jewel Movement
NUFF	National United Freedom Fighters
NWU	National Workers' Union
OECD	Organization for Economic Cooperation and Development
OWTU	Oilfield Workers' Trade Union
PNM	People's National Movement
PNP	People's National Party
PPP	People's Progressive Party
PRA	People's Revolutionary Army
PRG	People's Revolutionary Government
PSOJ	Private Sector Organization of Jamaica

TUC	Trades Union Congress
UAWU	University and Allied Workers' Union
ULF	United Labour Front
UNIA	Universal Negro Improvement Association
UNDP	United Nations Development Programme
UWI	University of the West Indies
WLL	Workers' Liberation League
WOLF	Western United Liberation Front
WTO	World Trade Organization
WPA	Working People's Alliance
WPJ	Workers' Party Jamaica

Introduction

Downtown Stirs

Zeeks

On the morning of Wednesday 23 September 1998, the normally bustling and chaotic downtown commercial district of Kingston was even further disturbed by a sudden and dramatic escalation of activity. A wave of gunfire erupted; people were running everywhere; shopkeepers hurriedly pulled down their galvanized steel shutters; and commuters anxiously jostled to catch the few remaining taxis and buses for transport to the relative safety of other parts of the city. Earlier that morning, Donald 'Zeeks' Phipps – a slim-bodied, brown-skinned, somewhat inconsequential-looking, forty-one-year-old man – had been detained by the police for questioning in a case of kidnapping, attempted murder and wounding with intent allegedly committed in the city some two months earlier. But unlike the numerous raids and arrests that punctuate life in the impoverished urban 'ghettos' of Kingston, the reaction to this one was unanticipated and unprecedented. Thousands of people angrily poured into the streets, blocking the roads with tyres, the carcasses of old cars and other debris, which were then set on fire. Hundreds of angry demonstrators converged on the Central Police Station where Zeeks was held, displaying their hurriedly made placards proclaiming: "No Zeeks, No Peace"; "Without Zeeks, No Life in the West"; "No Zeeks, No Business for Us"; and "If No Zeeks, No School, No Bus and No Store Open".[1]

Then a remarkable thing happened. In the face of the rapidly growing and angry crowd – fearful from past experience that harm might be done to their champion – the police command decided to bring their lawfully detained prisoner out to the balcony of the station in order for him to appeal to his supporters for calm and reassure them that he was well. With this, the cutting edge of the protest was blunted, though it would take several hours before the demonstrators were dispersed and a full four days – following his release on bail – before a semblance of normality returned to the centre of the city. In the interim, four persons were killed, including two members of the security forces and the riots had spread from western to eastern Kingston, where numerous roadblocks were deployed, in what the police disingenuously described as "unrelated . . . protests".[2]

The 'Zeeks riots' were, to say the least, a wake-up call for the government and people of Jamaica. For Zeeks was, after all, in the clearly demarcated political geography of lower Kingston, a 'don' – or grassroots leader/enforcer – from the governing People's National Party (PNP) enclave of Matthews Lane. Thus, the cardinal rule of postwar Jamaican politics had been shattered, in that the supporters of a governing party – the clients of the overarching patron – had risen in revolt, biting, as it were, the hand that had fed them. But even more significant (and cause for much comment in the newspapers and among the talking heads in the following weeks) was the decision of the police to call on their prisoner to help defuse the riotous crowd. In that single action was illuminated a critical fissure in the Jamaican state. Despite the presumed overwhelming control of force and despite the constitutional right to rule of the state, it was the don's appearance and reassuring words that ultimately averted bloody riot. The genie was out of the bottle and, though none then knew, the consequences would be manifest in an even more profound fashion within half a year.

On Thursday 15 April 1999, Finance Minister Omar Davies announced an increase in taxes of J$4 billion to close the gap in an overall budget expenditure of some J$160 billion. The brunt of the increase was to be borne by motorists, who were asked to shoulder large increases in the average price of gasoline.[3] Although there were some sporadic protests the following day, the real roadblocks and riots did not begin until after the weekend. On Monday, in a pattern that had occurred twice before in the country's modern history,[4] dense, widespread, burning roadblocks appeared throughout the capital city, the rural townships and even the remote countryside. Everywhere, feeling against the government of Prime Minister P.J. Patterson ran high. An anonymous demonstrator on Mountain View Avenue in eastern Kingston expressed this common view: "If P.J. (Patterson) can't handle it, him have to go . . . We the people can manage."[5] And a taxi driver outside of Montego Bay expressed this widespread sentiment of solidarity: "Is all a we a suffer and is fi all a we, we a do this for, so them fi stop working."[6] The government was at first confident that the demonstrations would peak and peter out and stood firm on its policy, but on Tuesday and Wednesday, things intensified. In a new and uglier phase, buildings were burned and looted, some rioters used the opportunity to demand tolls from hapless motorists at various roadblocks,[7] and confrontations with the police worsened. Eventually, on Wednesday, Prime Minister Patterson, who had refrained from speaking publicly for the first two days of protest, conceded and announced that a committee composed of private citizens drawn from different sectors of the society would be established to re-examine the increased taxes.[8] By the following Wednesday – nine days after the riots had started and with nine people dead and billions of dollars in damage – Patterson announced, as a result of the suggestions of the Moses Committee, a 45 percent reduction in the new gasoline tax. The lost income was to be in part recouped by a 15 percent tax on the interest earned from commercial paper, to be taxed at source.[9]

A new political situation is emerging in Jamaica. It is cold comfort, but nonetheless true to say, that those who argued that the old order was crumbling,[10] that the country was close to an "all class crisis"[11] or that there was "hegemonic dissolution"[12] were probably right. Two features are evident in this ever-dynamic situation. First, the state, evident in the police decision to bring Zeeks onto the balcony and even more so in the decision to, in effect, concede the power to amend the budget to a private committee, is floundering and increasingly unable to rule in the old way.[13] Second, the people, or significant cross-sections of them, have declared their autonomy and, if they have yet to reach the stage of being unwilling to be ruled in the old way, they are fast approaching that notional point of ungovernability.

In the rich, if sporadic, debate on failed states,[14] quasi-states[15] and collapsed states[16] that emerged in the wake of the tragic experiences in Liberia, Sierra Leone, Somalia and Rwanda, Jamaica does not strictly conform to any of the proposed models. It does, however, borrow many causative and descriptive features. Thus the present impasse has arisen in part due to the collapse of the system of clientelism in the eighties,[17] the undermining of sovereignty that accompanied the assertion of International Monetary Fund (IMF) authority after 1976, and the growing political and economic marginalization of small states in the last two decades of the century. These have all contributed to the weakened, tentative character of the state, but it has not collapsed, in the Liberian sense, nor is it a quasi-state. The Jamaican state still possesses significant capacity for intervention – both in an economic sense and from a security perspective. There is also the substantive reality of a functioning, if flawed, liberal democratic, parliamentary electoral system, which has witnessed regular regime changes for the past forty-odd years. Yet it is the very fact of rapid transition from sometimes ideologically opposed governments – each proclaiming deliverance but, ultimately, none delivering – that has contributed significantly to the present moment of widespread alienation from parties and politics. Thus, the Jamaica Labour Party (JLP), still dominated by its venerable cold warrior Edward Seaga, is unable to escape from a not-unfounded authoritarian and elitist image. In the 1997 general elections, the JLP was only able to secure 38.5 percent of the national vote. Except for 1993, when it gained marginally less, this was the lowest percentage the party had secured since 1955.[18] The new National Democratic Movement (NDM), composed primarily of disenchanted JLP supporters and some from the PNP, appears unable to distance itself from the legacy of the past, despite a credible programme of political reform.[19] And the ruling PNP, still seeking to minimize the radical profile of the seventies, is increasingly associated in the popular mind with the harshest policies of structural adjustment along with bailouts for rich bankers. Its toleration in the present climate is no doubt facilitated by the perception that it is the lesser of two evils.[20]

If analytical priority, then, is to be given to movement, the direction is evident. The Jamaican state, while not yet to be described as a failure or as collapsed, might best be termed a 'tottering state'. However, even if there is no clearly identifiable alternative to the present (dis)order, and the primary feature of the present moment is a tendency toward anarchy, ironically, there is also an implicit, albeit now very secondary, element of renewal.[21] Both the Zeeks and April events demonstrate the re-emergence of the Jamaican poor and working people on the political stage after almost two decades of quiescence, retreat or absorption in the daily struggle of survival. This new political activity, directed against the state and its policies, has already yielded fruit. For what was the appearance of Zeeks on the balcony but a concession by the police that they must stand accountable for the health of those they detain? And what was the Moses Committee but the result of an assertion that the parliamentary system, as presently defined, is an insufficient instrument to mirror the democratic wishes of the majority and, simultaneously, an announcement that the policies of structural adjustment/neoliberalism must, at some point, be accountable to the wishes of the entire people? Without a new project of social renewal, a new vision of alternative futures for the poor, dispossessed and marginalized, however, such a potential is likely to dissipate, with the even greater certainty of frustration, disillusionment and anarchy.

This is a peculiarly Jamaican moment that cannot be generalized even within the narrow parameters of the insular Caribbean; yet it harbours within it resonances that both indicate the country's insertion into wider global currents and, perhaps, its potential example as an early indicator of future trajectories.

The End of Illusions

The global events of the last two years of the twentieth century suggest that at its moment of triumph, the neoliberal project is already in severe crisis. If Francis Fukuyama's *The End of History and the Last Man*[22] and Samuel Huntington's *The Third Wave*[23] epitomized the triumphant and triumphalist vision that followed the collapse of communism, then if any single work stands as a leitmotif for the end of century, it is John Gray's *False Dawn.*[24] Not only is the latter book a scathing attack on the freewheeling, neoliberalist agenda but it carries special weight, coming as it does from a former close advisor of Margaret Thatcher – the godmother, as it were, of neoliberalism.

Two momentous and repeatedly discussed events have served to underline the tenuous and fragile nature of existing global economic relations. The East Asian crisis of 1997–98 led to the collapse of the Indonesian economy and the overthrow of the Suharto regime. The South Korean, Thai and Malaysian economies, experiencing massive outflows of capital, were all suddenly highly indebted and crippled. While there is little debate as to the fact that, once it was clear that they were in trouble, open-market policies facilitated the rapid outflow of capital from these countries, there is also the less consensual conclusion that their adoption of the open-market policies of the 'Washington Consensus', as opposed to their internal high debt models, had led to crisis in the first place.[25] Even more significant is the fact that these economies now face denationalization on an unprecedented scale as devaluations and IMF-imposed deregulatory policies lead to a virtual fire sale of assets:

Whatever their degree of intentionality, and their method of concerting strategy, there is no doubt that Western and Japanese corporations are the big winners . . . The combination of massive devaluations, IMF-pushed financial liberalization, and IMF-facilitated recovery may even precipitate the biggest peacetime transfer of assets from domestic to foreign owners in the past fifty years anywhere in the world . . . One recalls the statement attributed to Andrew Mellon, "In a depression, assets return to their rightful owners."[26]

The East Asian collapse is even more poignant in small states such as Jamaica, because in the eighties, following the unsuccessful experiments with various 'socialist' models, the success of the Asian Tigers was used to drive home the view that in the new global economy all ships would float, once they were able to get the 'essentials' right. To those who were close observers, the irony was that even as the Tigers were held up as models of rectitude, the reality was that the struggle was already hotly engaged to open them up, due to their statist protections against Western financial incursion.

The other milestone, of course, was the collapse of the Russian rouble in the summer of 1998, described by *Newsweek* as "the most dangerous moment for the post Cold War period since Saddam Hussein invaded Kuwait".[27] While Russia's economy – not much larger than that of the Netherlands – is relatively insignificant in world terms, its collapse has both a knock-on effect, in that it sends the signal that so-called emerging markets are unstable, and an even more overwhelming symbolic effect. Russia is, after all, the core of the old Soviet Union and remains the second global nuclear power. If capitalism with a global face fails there then there is diminished reason as to why it should serve as a model for development elsewhere.[28]

These events, and what seemed in early 1999 to be the imminent collapse of the Brazilian economy in the wake of Russia, led to a revealing debate in the popular press on the state of Western capitalism. Robert Samuelson, in *Newsweek*, mooted the possibility of a global economic meltdown:

It is time to stop pretending that the 'economic crisis' is an 'Asian crisis' or a 'Japanese crisis' or a 'Russian crisis' or an 'emerging markets crisis'. Last week's selloff on world stock markets signals something bigger and much more threatening. Massive capital flight from poorer regions . . . is dragging them into depression and, as the downdraft gathers momentum, menacing the prosperity of Europe and the United States. With Japan already in its worst postwar recession, slumps in the United States and Europe – about 40 percent of the world economy – could lead to a global meltdown.[29]

Michael Elliott, quoting Marx and Engels, argued that the old Anglo-Saxon 'Washington Consensus' on the rules of the game – free markets, deregulation, the minimal state – was breaking down, with some of the most vociferous opponents coming from within the system:

What's plain is that the old order has changed; unregulated markets are not seen any longer as the only path to global prosperity and political freedom. "We're all casting around for new things," says the World Bank's John Williamson. "Plainly there are some areas in which governments need to play a more active role than people would have said 18 months ago."[30]

And, important for more than symbolic reasons, financier extraordinaire George Soros argued that distress at the 'periphery' could not be good for the 'centre', that IMF programmes did not seem to be working and if the crisis was allowed to continue, the global capitalist system itself might be swept away.[31] His solution, also ironic from the perspective of the neoliberal consensus, was for an international credit insurance corporation to regulate the movement of capital and supportive international political institutions – a world government, in embryo – led by the United States.

And, while it does not appear as a headline-grabbing event in its own right, the slow-burning growth in inequality between rich and poor nations, fuelled by deteriorating terms of trade as well as adverse movements of capital, has led to the resurgence of a close-to-radical militance in, among other places, the definitively centrist pages of the United Nations Development Programme (UNDP) *Human Development Report*:

Over the past 30 years the global growth in income has been spread very unequally – and the inequality is increasing. Consider the relative income shares of the richest and poorest 20% of the world's people. Between 1960 and 1991 the share of the richest 20% rose from 70% of global income to 85% – while that of the poorest declined from 2.3% to 1.4% . . . All but the richest quintile saw their income share fall, so that by 1991 more than 85% of the world's population received only 15% of its income . . . This imbalance can also be viewed in more personal terms. Today, the net worth of the 358 richest people, the dollar billionaires, is equal to the combined income of the poorest 45% of the world's population – 2.3 billion people.[32]

Michael Elliott's invocation of Marx and Engels, then, even if done as spectral warning, may not be wholly inappropriate. After a decade of lying dusty on the shelves, the basic predictions on the circuit of capital to be found in *The Communist Manifesto* are worth reading again.[33] For while pauperization in the centres of European capital may not have occurred in the way Marx foresaw,[34] if one is to take a global perspective the picture changes substantially. Global wealth has increased exponentially in the past century, but so too has global misery. Evidently, in its technology and financial resources, the global capitalist system has the wherewithal to end hunger, malnutrition, illiteracy and disease, and yet, among vast swathes of the world's population, these conditions are more entrenched than ever. If the end of the century, then, has not witnessed the collapse of the neoliberal paradigm, it has lost its gloss. The illusion has ended; the window is opening on the search for alternative futures. As Kari Levitt, from her long period of sojourn between the Caribbean and Canada, appropriately suggests:

The ideological hold of the neo-liberal paradigm is weakening. The agenda of accelerated 'globalization' is giving way to more cautious approaches. At the international level, there is talk of measures to slow the global movement of cross border funds and monitor the activities of private lenders and borrowers. At the regional level – including East Asia – global recessionary trends may give rise to new initiatives of regional trade and credit mechanisms, including balanced (barter) trade between member countries.[35]

The Lost Twenty Years

The electoral defeat of Michael Manley's democratic socialist PNP government in the bloody 1980 elections coincided with a 'regime change' in the macroeconomic policies followed by the Organization for Economic Cooperation and Development (OECD) countries, favouring creditors over debtors and capital over labour.[36] The result was a quantum increase in US interest rates in the early eighties, which contributed in no small measure to the Latin American debt crisis. The new pro-American Seaga regime that replaced Manley avoided the typical Latin American problem because Jamaica, due to its then left-leaning government, had been excluded from the heavy private investment of the seventies. Seaga – favoured by the Reagan presidency for his anticommunist policies – was bolstered by a generous infusion of loans, which left the country indebted to the sum of some US$4 billion dollars at the end of the decade. While there was some growth towards the end of his term, economic and social conditions for the majority of the people deteriorated. Migration levels in the 1980s surpassed those reached in the two previous decades.[37]

With almost the same popular fervour with which they had been thrown out in 1980, the PNP was returned to power in 1989. The expectation among wide sections of the population was that the re-ascendancy of Manley would see the resumption of the reformist policies of the seventies, but the irony is that the new regime, more effectively than its predecessor, pushed through the classic features of the neoliberal agenda. Financial and exchange rate liberalizations were initiated, leading to devaluation and a spiralling rate of inflation. A series of new banking and financial institutions emerged, which – in the absence of the appropriate regulatory mechanisms – engaged in spurious practices. Since the mid 1990s, new policies of credit restriction, with punishing interest rates, have controlled inflation but at the expense of manufacturing and construction, which have ground to a halt. In the latest phase, the financial bubble has burst, with the collapse of many of the new institutions and the decision by the government to bail them out – purportedly in the interest of the many thousands of small investors who would otherwise have lost their entire savings. This decision lay behind the drastic gasoline price increases of April's budget and the momentous events that followed.

Through all of this, the main losers have been the poor in Kingston and the other urban centres and in the countryside. While it is difficult to disaggregate the macro statistics (Jamaica's World Bank rating on the gini index of inequality is 41.1 percent[38] – only middling by any standard) there are, nonetheless, clear indicators to support this contention. Over two decades, there has been little or no growth in the economy. Growth rates, which averaged 2.0 percent in the decade 1980–90, were barely 0.8 percent in the period 1990–97;[39] and real earnings per employee have actually declined for two decades – in the period 1970–80 at the rate of 0.2 percent and in the period 1980–92 at the increased rate of 1.5 percent.[40] Although on the positive side, life expectancy has increased between 1960 and 1993 from 62.8 to 73.7 years,[41] in the period from 1970 to 1983, adult literacy has declined from 97 percent to 84 percent,[42] and in the decade 1980–90, gross enrolment in schools has declined from 67 percent to 61 percent.[43] Indeed, with official development assistance reduced to a trickle,[44] the manufacturing sector shrinking rapidly, construction stagnant and with only limited possibilities for jobs in the relatively successful hotel and tourism sector, the only real possibility for employment and upward mobility for the majority of the poor is to leave the island.[45] From this perspective, it might be appropriate to consider – from the perspective of the poor and in many respects, for the country as a whole – the period since the collapse of democratic socialism as the 'lost twenty years'.

The People

The popular response has evolved through two phases. The collapse of democratic socialism also signalled the end of patron clientelism and the tradition of dependency on the state. This was immediately evident to the defeated PNP supporters, but as the eighties wore on, it became apparent to the JLP faithful that the benefits of power were going to be equally scarce. The immediate result was an accelerated migration to the United States and Canada, through both legal and illegal channels.

This, too, was the era of the higgler. Poor families scraped together all of their available resources and sent one enterprising member forth to find new markets. Jamaican higglers scoured the region to become familiar presences in Panama, Curaçao, the Cayman Islands, Haiti and Miami. Everywhere they brought their boisterous aggressiveness, forged in the hard scrabble jungle of downtown Kingston. A few were successful, built gaudy mansions in Norbrook and Beverly Hills, and sent their children to the best schools, to the consternation of the traditional upper classes. Most barely made ends meet, as they trod the interminable circuit of searching for scarce foreign exchange, pleading with stern customs officials for mild duty assessments and bribing policemen to look the other way as they fought for a stall on the steaming sidewalks of the city.[46] Legal migrants to Brooklyn and the Bronx juggled three or four jobs as countless others had done before them in order to live, save and fill the barrel with goods for the children and family 'back a yard'. An entire new category of 'barrel children' – whose parents had left them with relatives and friends at home in order to work abroad – arose, with deleterious social consequences.

Other Jamaicans, unable to get the hallowed visa, took the illegal route into the United States by any means necessary. Among these were many young men who had been 'soldiers' for the two dominant political parties in the internecine warfare that had raged in the seventies. They brought specific and useful skills to their new environment, including knowledge of the use of light arms, basic urban guerrilla tactics and a certain ruthlessness, forged in the near civil war conditions that prevailed at home at the end of the decade.[47] Between these legals and illegals – many drawn from the poorest strata of the society – the entire structure of foreign exchange earnings was transformed. As recently as 1991, private remittances amounted to only US$153.3 million; by 1997 this had increased to US$606.3 million and was the third most important foreign exchange earner after merchandise trade and tourism.[48]

In the popular culture, this was the era when the dancehall emerged as the central space for performance and the gold-chained, jewel-encrusted deejay was king. The music of the 1970s, now commonly referred to as 'classical' reggae and dominated by Bob Marley, Peter Tosh, Burning Spear, the Abyssinians and others, took the aesthetic form and lyrical content of a movement for black solidarity and resistance. Its slow, almost mystical off-beat was both symptomatic of a personal 'dreadness' as it was of a gathering tidal wave of popular upheaval that was simultaneously national, diasporic and international. The new form was, particularly to those who grew to maturity on the steady, millenarian and revolutionary traditions of the seventies, to say the least, enigmatic. It praised personal, as opposed to collective wealth and power. It glorified the all-conquering, phallic male – a theme that was never absent, but certainly muted, in the more political focus of classic reggae. Instead of the dreadlocked, counter-hegemonic pose of a Marley or Tosh, there was the caricature of the wealthy in the gold-chained, gold-toothed Shabba Ranks, to whom 'girls' gravitated – not just because of his alleged sexual potency – but his ample stash of dollars. It is, however, also possible to argue that embedded in the gaudy, reactionary and defeatist garb of 1980s dancehall were also important elements of recovery and consolidation.

Classic reggae looked out to the world, a world in which there were welcoming supports among left wing intellectuals in Jamaica, countercultural adherents in the United States and Europe and far-flung constituents of the African diaspora. Thus Marley, Bunny Wailer, Tosh and most of the other leading exponents reached outward in the universally understood language of Jamaican English, with only a secondary use of the more difficult to penetrate, 'pure' Jamaican. With the new decade, all these pillars of the struggle seemed to vanish and the Jamaican poor retreated into themselves for protection, succour and interpretation of the new, disturbing conjuncture. The dancehall was, in this sense, then, with its secret language, an impenetrable retreat in which the poor spoke to the poor without the interpolation of the traditional Left, or any outside source with their preconfigured, structured and linear view of progress.[49] At first, this new, contradictory, dialogue from below toyed with the baubles of neoliberalism as, indeed, the wider population explored the promised manna of individual success. The decisive and rapid failure of the neoliberal model to deliver, however, soon led to a sea change among the people and in their dancehalls.

The second phase, then, is one in which the limits for individual exploration of the economic and social spaces purportedly offered under globalization are rapidly being exhausted. This is most evident in the immigration trends where, under pressure from the US Congress and the Immigration and Naturalization Service (INS), the numbers of legal migrants have gradually decreased over the past decade. In 1993 there were 21,991 legal immigrants into the United States, a figure that had diminished to some 12,157 in 1997.[50] This is matched at the illegal level, where, largely as a result of the US policy to deport illegal migrants entangled in the criminal justice system, some 1,699 Jamaicans were repatriated in 1997.[51] This latter development has had multiple effects. Many of these persons – called, appropriately, in the popular domain 'deportees' – are posse members who arrive home accustomed to operating at the highest levels of criminality in the United States and enjoying the accompanying wealthy lifestyles. They return to communities in which the political parties, without the resources for patronage of the seventies, have made critical concessions to the dons – their former, now independent operatives. Whereas in the past the dons were paid out of the contracts for road works, public works and construction, they now earn their own keep from the drug trade, the trade in guns and protection money from those businesses that continue to operate in the inner city. The dons are now perceived by many citizens not as selfish, self-interested drug lords but as protectors of the community. Faced with an overloaded and inefficient justice system, in which, as Munroe posits, the average number of cases for a resident magistrate increased from 3,462 per year in 1989 to 6,792 in 1996,[52] the people seek justice from the dons. It was, purportedly, such an instance of street justice that led to the arrest of Zeeks last year and triggered the enraged response from the people. The gradual usurpation of the powers of the state has reached a critical point. Numbers of ordinary citizens consider Zeeks and others like him surer, swifter and, perhaps, more just sources of retribution than anything the formal state has to offer. This moment of disconnection with the state and formal politics, and new adherence to an alternative system of justice, is vividly captured in two sets of statistics. Popular participation in general elections is rapidly declining, from a high of 86.1 percent in 1976 to 66.7 percent in 1993 and 65.22 percent in 1997[53] while, simultaneously, the tactic of communities mounting illegal roadblocks to draw attention to myriad social and economic problems has mushroomed from 23 per annum in 1986, to 207 in 1997.[54] Dual power may not yet exist but, in the semiautonomous communities of lower Kingston and St Andrew where the dons rule, it is fast approaching that point.

At the cultural level, if that distinction might be sustained, a similar process of disconnection is ripening. Gold-bedecked, individualist deejay music is giving way again to themes of collective resistance. Buju Banton's transition from 'loving his browning', in which, reflective of the old, colonial colour hierarchies, he expresses preference for a light-skinned 'browning' girl, is typical of the earlier period: "Mi love mi car, mi love mi bike, mi love mi money an ting / But most of all mi love mi browning."[55] While, only a year later in his landmark album *'Til Shiloh*, there is an evident sea change. In "'Til I'm Laid to Rest", Banton evokes themes of resistance, racial pride and national struggle not expressed so powerfully since the high point of the seventies:

Organize and centralize come as one
Our seeds shall be so many more than sand
Some new and replenish pure and clean heart
For too long we've been under this bond
Some a save a bag a riches
Yet they die empty hand
Go on saying I'm stupid and laugh all you can
Easier for a camel to go through a needle eye
Than a rich man to enter Zion
Take it from I man.[56]

Other examples include Anthony B, Capleton and Sizzla,[57] who all operate within a militant, Rastafarian tradition. Capleton's performance at the 1999 Reggae Sumfest show – perhaps the single most important showcase of reggae music – epitomized the new trend:

Capleton had little to do, for the horde was seemingly gratified with just his presence. The place erupted with loud applause and deafening firecracker blasts when the compere announced him, but it was when the deejay rushed onto the stage dousing the platform with bottled water that the crowd went wild.

Accompanied by two flag-waiving sidekicks on either side, he paced frantically across the platform, muttering only lines from his hits as the audience's roars drowned out his vocals.

He lambasted everything from fast food to cable television and touched on the Bill Clinton sex scandal.

"Put a fire pon Burger King and Kentucky," he commanded. "Put a fire pon de cable . . . cable a mash up de world," he declared.[58]

Sizzla, too, is particularly significant because not only is he a deejay but he has made the transition from 'art' into 'life', as the leading figure in a particularly militant Rastafarian sect in August Town. From this younger generation, then, Rastafarianism – sometimes to the consternation of elders in the movement – has been excavated and reinvented. It is a more militant stream than before, overtly nationalist and obedient to scripture, and its icon from the old school is more Peter Tosh, with his uncompromising lyrics, than Marley or anyone else. While embedded within it is a not insignificant Luddite strain, there is, too, a healthy unwillingness to be bowled over by the commercial excesses of late capitalism. It is not surprising, then, that in the uprisings of April the slogan went up from more than one source that "We want a Rasta government".

In the autonomous spaces that opened up after 1980, a new politics is emerging. It is still immature and unformed, but it is based on the lived experiences of the poor, on their reading of and resistance to a hostile world, and their forging of an alternative identity out of the transnational experiences of late globalization.

The Scholars

For the most part, the intellectuals, both those in Jamaica and in the wider Jamaican and Caribbean diaspora, have lagged behind these new events. After the collapse of democratic socialism and, even more so, the tragic implosion of the Grenada revolution, radical intellectuals retreated into a deep somnolence. The high point of the intellectual engagement with the Manley regime was undoubtedly the period following the 1976 electoral victory when, for a moment, it seemed as though the government might have sought an alternative, self-reliant path to the typical IMF prescription.[59] When Manley decided to travel the IMF route, however, persons such as George Beckford, Louis Lindsay and Michael Witter felt a keen sense of betrayal. The demoralization that set in – compounded by the economic marginalization of the entire middle class from which these persons were but a subset – severely affected the output and critical edge of the New World/Plantation School, which had advanced the most important radical critique of Caribbean society in the previous decade.[60]

The other significant trend was Marxist-Leninist and centred on Trevor Munroe and the Workers' Party of Jamaica (WPJ). In the postelection atmosphere of the early eighties, when hostility to the Seaga regime still raged among the radicalized poor, the WPJ's political stocks at first seemed to rise and then came crashing to the ground following the Grenada events. Grenada signalled a profound, paralysing defeat because it was not only military but also political and ideological. The bitter, homicidal struggle between rival elements in the New Jewel Movement (NJM) in September, leading to the murder of the prime minister and some of his closest associates, fulfilled all the anticommunist predictions as to the nature of Marxism and Marxist parties. The subsequent popular reception of the invading American troops and utter hostility to the surviving members of the NJM drove the nail into the coffin of its closest regional allies, among them the WPJ and its version of Marxism. The party would hobble on for the remainder of the decade, but its subsequent complete dispersal was predetermined in 1983. Grenada also severely undermined the political credibility of the left wing within the PNP, who were, in the popular imagination, associated with the 'Coardite' wing of the NJM, which was held responsible for the death of Maurice Bishop. The eclipse of that once powerful trend, too, was evident by the mid eighties. Beyond the revealing and interesting debates that preceded the break-up of the WPJ, little of theoretical interest emerged from the Marxist left for this entire decade.[61] The only voice in the wilderness was that of Carl Stone, the prolific political scientist and pollster, who many on the Left regarded, at best, as a renegade. Stone, however, as is developed elsewhere in this volume, had his own agenda. In his own eccentric way, he sought to develop an alternative approach of reading politics from below, with careful attention to the mood and lived experiences of the people.

A real revival in social and political thought did not begin until the political abertura that came after the return to power of the PNP under Manley in 1989. Certain events and publications mark the growth and gathering momentum of a new and rich discourse on the state of Caribbean thought and society, of which some of the most outstanding are: the 1991 conference at Wellesley on the life and work of C.L.R. James; the 1991 publication of *Rethinking Development*[62] at the University of the West Indies' (UWI) Mona campus; the publication in 1992 of the collection *Intellectuals in the Twentieth Century Caribbean,* edited by Alistair Hennessy;[63] the special issue, "New Currents in Caribbean Thought", of the journal *Social and Economic Studies* published in September 1994;[64] the conference in honour of Rex Nettleford at UWI Mona in 1995; the commencement of publication of the journal *Small Axe,* edited by David Scott, in 1996; the conference, New Currents in Caribbean Thought: Looking Towards the Twenty-first Century, at Michigan State University in April 1997; the April 1998 African Diaspora Studies conference at the University of California, Berkeley; the August 1998 conference, Jamaica in the Seventies, at UWI Mona; and the annual Caribbean Studies Association conference that, since at least 1990, has increasingly become a forum for critical social debate.

It would not be premature to suggest that out of this heightened, if still tender, conversation on the nature(s) and future(s) of the Caribbean, clear trends are emerging. In the closing section, an attempt will be made to identify some of these trends, though serious critical engagement is somewhat beyond the purposes of this introduction. Five nascent trends are emerging, including:

1. Political reform
2. Postcolonial discourse
3. Orthodox Marxism
4. Renascent New World
5. Caribbean subaltern

Political Reform

The trend of political reform would certainly include the two former leaders of the WPJ, Don Robotham and Trevor Munroe. It is best characterized by a search for alternative, unconventional solutions to the crisis of Jamaican politics and society while acceding to the terms of reference of the global economy as given and predetermined. Robotham's perspective is the more disappointing of the two. In his at times insightful booklet *Vision and Voluntarism: Reviving Voluntarism in Jamaica,* he accurately identifies the state of social crisis in Jamaica and proposes the revival of the spirit of "voluntarism" as a means of reuniting the population and restarting a stalled national project. Robotham argues that the critical problem retarding national unity is a misplaced racial and colour chauvinism, directed at the lighter-skinned minorities by the black majority. This must be shed, he contends, and instead, the "common Jamaicanness" of the entire people must be emphasized.[65] His position, however, fails to appreciate the contested histories of racial and colour antagonisms in Jamaica, as is suggested elsewhere in this volume.[66] Asking the black majority to disarm itself of critical ideological defences in the interest of an as yet to be defined national project, without an appropriate quid pro quo, is unlikely to yield the desired result.[67]

Munroe's recent book, *Renewing Democracy into the Millennium: The Jamaican Experience in Perspective,* is also insightful in recognizing not only the existence of crisis, but, as supported here, the possibility of renewal in the current upsurge of popular engagement. His specific and detailed suggestions as to the ways to deepen political participation, reduce conflict between contesting political parties, strengthen civil society, address corruption, and skew government policy in the direction of the poor and dispossessed are both thorough and compelling.[68] The paradox in Munroe's study, though, is that while there is much to agree with in the project of strengthening and deepening democracy, these arguments are advanced with little reference to global political economy. What are the real constraints on advancing an agenda of radical reform in a world increasingly dominated by global, capitalist institutions? If such a reality is recognized – never absolutely clear in Munroe's framework – what tactical approach might a radically reforming government engage in to avoid the typical routine culminating in economic and political disaster? What are the political strategies to be employed to sensitize and mobilize the populace to the fact that powerful forces may actually be hostile to a country with a radically 'deepened' democracy? None of these questions – closely tied to any project of radical reform and learned by hard experience in the seventies – are rigorously explored in Munroe's analysis, seriously weakening its theoretical usefulness.

Postcolonial Discourse

David Scott is the most prominent writer in a trend that, for want of a better title, can be identified as 'postcolonial discourse'. Scott returned to Jamaica from the University of Chicago in 1996 and his views were immediately a cause for consternation among the more traditional empiricists on the Mona campus. Operating within Foucauldian and neo-Foucauldian terms of reference, Scott's novel readings of Caribbean freedom, of revolution and other themes in Caribbean politics were a breath of fresh air in an atmosphere dominated by narrow positivism and widespread surrender to the neoliberal paradigm.[69] His most significant achievement has unquestionably been the initiation of the quality journal *Small Axe*. The inclusion in each volume of a major interview featuring prominent Caribbean or Caribbeanist intellectuals, including Stuart Hall, Richard Hart and Ken Post, has, in a short time, added immeasurably to the oral history of the radical Left in the region. More significantly, he has interviewed the aforementioned Jamaican dub poet/deejay Anthony B, one of the leading spokespersons of the new Rastafarian upsurge. This willingness to connect with the actual movement 'on the ground' is a refreshing dimension, which distances him from some of the more esoteric thinkers within the postmodern and postcolonial traditions.

There remain, however, troubling features in Scott's work. This writer ran afoul of Scott, who criticized my earlier study entitled *Caribbean Revolutions and Revolutionary Theory: An Assessment of Cuba, Nicaragua and Grenada*.[70] That book sought to explore social science theories as to what revolutions are and how they are made, as the basis for a comparative exploration of the revolutionary experiences in the three named states. Scott's basic criticism was that the concept of revolution had not itself been historicized:

Meeks in short, does not historicize his conceptual objects . . . I should like to suggest that what is crucial is not such questions as what really causes revolutions (or how much economic crisis and how much state and how much intellectual will and how much ideology go into the making of them) or what causes them to go bad and what might induce them to do so and so on . . . what is crucial, to me, is whether the cognitive political world in which we live continues to make revolution plausible to think and think with – as criticism.[71]

My objections to this are twofold. The first is straightforward, in that there is and must be a place for causal explanation in social analysis.[72] While Scott's willingness to interrogate 'meaning' is useful, indeed, indispensable to the social theoretician, there is a point at which real phenomena have to be explored. It is undoubtedly true that the concept of revolution is a moving target, that the Cuban, Nicaraguan and Grenadian 'events' are, in their formation and evolution, quite distinct phenomena. However, a comparative explanation of causes and outcomes is one of the few fertile avenues available to precisely explore the differences and similarities and to formulate (or dismiss) a 'theory' of revolution. By denying or sidelining the centrality of causal explanation, Scott is paralysing the social theorist; carried to its logical conclusion, one might forever forestall the object of examination because its actual meaning is inherently elusive. The only feasible answer in such a closed circle is the somewhat unsatisfactory one of abandoning altogether the exercise of social investigation.

The second objection is a more fundamental disagreement with Scott's central thesis that the era of revolution is somehow passé, that the binaries of Left/Right, reactionary/progressive, revolutionary/conservative are products of a certain style of reasoning to be associated with modernity and have somehow been transcended by the experience of contemporary life.[73] This assertion, which comes close in its essence to Fukuyama's 'end of history' thesis, is contradicted by the very cognitive political world that he invokes in defence of the argument. If the events of the last two years, introduced at the beginning of this chapter, are to be used as evidence, then what appears to be evolving is the classic crisis of capital, with localized resistance developing on its own historical foundations and with its own logic and trajectory. Rather than an ending of history and a dissolution of binaries, what seems to be emerging is a reformulation of the terms of engagement within and across national boundaries. Scott's criticism, then, is distinctly a mid decade one, in which the old forms of resistance had collapsed and the new ones were still embryonic, in which in the absence of visible organized social forces in opposition to domination, history *appeared* to have ended. The picture from the end of century is strikingly different.

Orthodox Marxism

It is striking that in searching for individuals to fill the category of orthodox Marxism that there were no obvious candidates from Jamaica. This can perhaps be understood as arising out of the historical experience surrounding the folding of the WPJ and the nature of the collapse of the Grenadian revolution. Distance from these cockpits of action has, in the instance of the US-based Barbadian political scientist Hilbourne Watson, been both a strength and a weakness. Watson's careful and detailed work on the nature of evolving global capitalism has, in contrast to the other writers so far mentioned, kept the flag of political economy flying.[74] Watson's close focus on the technical character of modern productive processes, borrowing from, but not dominated by, Wallersteinian theory, is useful as a counterpoint to liberal and discourse-led approaches that deny or elide the reality of a capitalist world economy with clear historical tendencies.

It is when he moves from the general to the particular, however, that problems arise. The example is, again, an instance of long polemical engagement with this writer. Watson severely criticized my article "Re-reading *The Black Jacobins*: James the Dialectic and the Revolutionary Conjuncture"[75] as a signal of my break with Marxism and entrance into an unspecified postmodernism.[76] That article had sought to probe a nagging problem in C.L.R. James' brilliant study of the Haitian Revolution. The problem, which James himself identified but, it is argued, never adequately explored, was how to fit a 'materialist', that is, Marxist, analysis into an explanation of the making of the Haitian Revolution, in which the individual Toussaint L'Ouverture played such a seminal, central role. My conclusion, which I still adhere to, was not to deny James' brilliant explanation for the underlying 'political economy' causes for the insurrection but to find a mode of analysis that would give full flight to the equally important role of the agent. Watson, in what I still think was a complete misreading of the thrust of the critique, saw this as a retreat into liberalism and the introduction of 'negative freedom' and the autonomous individual.[77]

Yet there is a lesson to be rescued here, for hidden in Watson's vehement critique and defence of the orthodoxy is the old methodology and approach that led to the collapse of Caribbean Marxism in the mid eighties. Watson, like the Marxists in the WPJ and the NJM, relies too much on the 'certainty' of the doctrine. This position came precisely from a reading of Marxism that lays emphasis on its technological and scientific 'truth' and not on its usefulness as a broad, methodological guide to action. While the wheels of contemporary capitalism will grind on, bringing the inevitable booms and crises, it is only in the area of popular movements, of cultural change, of the emergence of new ideas and leaders, that the system will ultimately be transcended or, occasionally, modified to protect itself. A thorough re-examination of this terrain – Marxism's Achilles' heel – is a necessity if the theory is to remain a useful tool for antisystemic movements. Watson's invocation of the orthodoxy in this context is, in style and content, a form of damning closure on critical inquiry, the opposite of what is appropriate to the self-critical debate necessary in any radical renewal.

Renascent New World

While it is true to say that members of the 'Plantation School' never ceased critical engagement,[78] there has been a resurgence in recent years, which is important both historically and theoretically. Among the more important milestones are: the conference in memory of George Beckford at UWI, Mona, and the subsequent edited collection of papers by Kari Levitt and Michael Witter;[79] the conference on plantation economics at UWI St Augustine; the publication of the special issue of *Marronage* on plantation economics;[80] and, though not a single event, the continued publication of the remarkable journal/newspaper the *Trinidad and Tobago Review* by Lloyd Best.

New World, in its original form, as the foremost critical journal from the anglophone Caribbean in the sixties, never represented a monolithic perspective, and that is even more the situation among its former members today. Lloyd Best, in particular, has always maintained a critical distance from Marxisms of various stripes, as, to a lesser extent, did George Beckford and his peasant-oriented notion of national development. Yet the same cannot be said of Best's early collaborator Kari Levitt, whose work has always incorporated a healthy regard for Marxist political economy, or C.Y. Thomas' varied oeuvre, which operates, though with great sensitivity to Caribbean realities, within Marxist categories. However, common themes can be suggested as predominating amidst the differing perspectives, including a concern for specific, national and local analyses to qualify broader, global generalization; a sensitivity to the specific manifestations of race and ethnicity as qualifiers to purely 'class' analysis; a concern for sovereignty, both on national and regional foundations; and, closely related to this, a focus on independent economic development – so-called self-reliance – as opposed to foreign investment driven, 'dependency'.[81] These core elements remain today, though with significant attempts to adapt to the exigencies of the nineties. Thus Girvan, for example, has sought to incorporate a redefined, wider Caribbean in any new project of 'sovereign' development and has made an important call for broader consultation in the rethinking of Jamaican politics;[82] Thomas has sought to introduce issues such as the household economy, social capital and engendered economics alongside the traditional question of small size;[83] and Levitt has attempted to locate Caribbean economies within the specific movement of the global system.[84]

If there is any criticism to be made of a trend with which this writer has many points of agreement, it is that renascent New World has failed to connect its analysis to real social and political movements and therefore remains somewhat abstract and tentative. Thus, reading Girvan and Levitt in particular, it is never quite clear whether their critical comments on the direction of government policy emanate from the hat of the technocrat, whose job is to dispassionately inform the government of the day as to the feasible options, or, as was more evidently the case in the sixties, from the radical, often oppositionist academic, whose job was to fundamentally criticize an unequal and inherently unjust system.

This dilemma – not unique, however, to persons within this school – is inevitable in a situation where there appear to be no options but attempting to nudge the status quo in this or that more favourable direction.

Caribbean Subaltern

The final trend, again for want of a more appropriate title, and to which this writer undoubtedly belongs, might be called Caribbean subaltern. Its roots can be located in the collapse of the Marxist Left in the eighties and the subsequent analysis that a critical part of the reason for the collapse of the Grenada revolution and of the failure of the other Marxist trends throughout the region to gain serious credibility lay in their wholesale adaptation of a determinist and mechanistic Marxism-Leninism. Some sought, in the wake of the Grenada debacle, to abandon radical politics altogether. Others, perhaps facilitated by the absence of the ideological policing, which parties such as the WPJ inevitably imposed, began to read eclectically across the range of postmodern, postcolonial, feminist and 'post-Marxist' literature, as well as within and around the streams of Afrocentric literature that were consolidating, particularly in the United States.

A relatively small group of influential thinkers, however, would probably be at the top of most short lists within this tendency, including C.L.R. James, whose work on Caribbean culture and its relationship to politics in *Beyond a Boundary*,[85] radical reading of the role of the 'ordinary' people in the making of the Haitian Revolution and general disdain for the role of intellectuals, leaders and parties in revolutionary processes, had been elided from the mainstream Left in the seventies; Walter Rodney, who attained the status of an icon in Jamaican radical politics only to be disregarded intellectually. His *History of the Guyanese Working People*[86] suggested an alternative way to write history from below, in the tradition of E.P. Thompson; Antonio Gramsci, whose pioneering work on hegemony was virtually unknown in the anglophone Caribbean until after the collapse of the Grenada revolution; Stuart Hall, the British-based, Jamaican pioneer of cultural studies, whose work, in thinking beyond Gramsci, provides powerful insights into the role of language, symbol and sign in hegemonic projects; James Scott, who in *Domination and the Arts of Resistance, Weapons of the Weak* and elsewhere,[87] has sought to question some of Gramsci's conclusions, opening further the space for a politics from below; and the Indian subaltern school,[88] who, working through various disciplines on the subcontinent, have probably done the most to elaborate alternative approaches to writing history, placing the people and their projects first.

Caribbean subalternism, then, is a still-embryonic attempt to rethink the approach to understanding history and to comprehending society. It is sensitive to the role of hegemony – of ideological and cultural determinants in political formations – but not to the exclusion of a clear appreciation of the role of deep-seated economic, social and political conditions.[89] It is keenly aware that the intellectual and political error of the Left in the seventies was to consider 'the people' a blank page on which the intellectuals would write their own glorious history. This is being replaced by an approach that recognizes that people construct their own forms of resistance to adversity including their own philosophical universe, through which they interpret and work through this resistance. The understanding of this simple, yet profound, assertion is the beginning of a different relationship between the 'scholars' and the people, and a radically different kind of social movement, in which parties and leaders no longer play the role of overarching hero.

If one were to search for a genealogy of this tendency, it would have to include Barry Chevannes' study on Rastafari;[90] Horace Campbell's *Rasta and Resistance*;[91] Rupert Lewis' dense reading of the sociopolitical situation in Jamaica in the sixties, which lay the basis for Jamaican Black Power and the Rodney events of October 1968;[92] the ongoing work by Pat Mohammed, Rhoda Reddock, Linden Lewis and others to rethink the role of gender in Caribbean politics;[93] Obika Gray's work on the social power of the Jamaican poor;[94] and Tony Bogues continuing work that is trying to rethink the meaning of freedom as it was interpreted and developed by new world Africans.[95] The profound weakness of this new tendency is that it is very much at the preliminary stage of thinking through methodological approaches and re-searching and rereading historical narratives, while the popular movement – chaotic, contradictory, but very much alive – is gaining momentum.[96]

It may be that the emerging movement will proceed on its own, without the input and (potentially retarding) effect of an intellectual intervention. But if there is a role to be played by the scholars, at the level of historical explanation and the proposal of alternative futures, then the gap between the two needs necessarily to be narrowed. This volume is, hopefully, a modest contribution to that effort.

1

The Henry Rebellion, Counter-Hegemony and Jamaican Democracy

The End[1]

It is 2:40 a.m. on Monday 27 June 1960, and Assistant Superintendent William Samuel Howard and his team of police and West India Regiment soldiers are tired. They have been camping in the hills around Sligoville in east central Jamaica for five days, searching without success for five – Or is it four? No one is quite clear – armed fugitives, the remnants of what appears to be a recently discovered guerrilla base camp. But Howard's luck, and that of the thousand-odd British and Jamaican military engaged in the "biggest manhunt in Jamaica's history",[2] is about to change. One Septimus Higgins, a shopkeeper of Orange Grove, St Catherine, emerges from the gloom and informs the assistant superintendent that four heavily armed men are sleeping in his shop. They arrived the night before, Higgins explains, cleaned themselves of ticks and other parasites, requested food, which he cooked and served, and fell immediately into a deep sleep.

Moving quickly, Howard and his party arrive at the nearby shop attached to Higgins' modest house and cordon it off at 3:30 a.m. At daybreak, 5:00 a.m., Sergeant Hibbert smashes one of the shop windows and, covered by other members of the party, orders the four men within who are just awakening, to raise their hands above their heads and march out. One is a short "brown" man. Two are described as tall with "fair" or "cool" complexions; the fourth is black. On the way to the door, the short brown man, the apparent leader of the group, one Ronald Henry, reaches for his .30 calibre US carbine, but he is anticipated by a soldier who clubs him to the ground. Another, Howard Rollins, also called Quasim Abdullah, tries to draw a concealed revolver, but he too is anticipated, shot and wounded. He is rushed to hospital, while the others are driven under heavy guard to the Central Police Station in Kingston, some twenty miles distant.

Thus ended, before it had truly begun, one of the most significant threats to the Jamaican state in the postwar era,[3] though the sequence of events that would hold up for close scrutiny the apparent calm and consensual nature of Jamaican society had actually started three months before, in early April.

The Beginning

On 7 April, a *Daily Gleaner* front page headline reported:

Weapons Seized in Raid on Church Headquarters

A police raiding party in an early morning raid yesterday seized over 2,500 electrical detonators, 1,800 ordinary detonators, a shot gun, a .32 calibre revolver, a large quantity of machetes sharpened both sides like swords, placed in sheaths, cartridges, several sticks of dynamite and other articles at the headquarters of the African Reform Church, 78 Rosalie Avenue.[4]

Among the ten people held and charged under the Firearms Law, Gunpowder and Explosives Law and soon to be charged for treason felony was Claudius Henry, the head of the church and the aforementioned Ronald's father. The *Gleaner* also noted that "The Rev. Henry was the leader of the recent 'Back to Africa' movement during which hundreds of persons attended meetings at Rosalie Avenue for nearly a week, in the hope that they would be taken back to Africa on October 5 last year, but the trip did not materialise."[5]

Claudius Henry was born in Manchester, Central Jamaica, in 1903 and grew up in the Anglican church. He was given to 'visionary experiences', however, and questioned the Anglican authorities and soon abandoned them. Soon thereafter he became an independent preacher, and in his short career in this capacity he attracted a small following while giving himself the grandiose title "Repairer of the Breach".[6] In 1944 he migrated to the United States with his family where he stayed for the next thirteen years. What apparently prompted his return to Jamaica was a vision in which he was commanded to return to his homeland where God wanted him to play a role in leading his children back to the promised land.

Henry's movement was not unique among the many Rastafarian-oriented sects that blossomed in the late fifties,[7] but it was outstanding in the rapidity of its growth and its relatively high level of organization. With urban Kingston and its teeming thousands of black, unemployed persons as its main recruiting centre, though with a significant base also on the Vere Plains of Clarendon, Henry was, by the middle of 1959, the leader of hundreds of true believers who worshipped him as a prophet.

On the anniversary of Emancipation Day, 1 August 1959, Henry announced that he was declaring 5 October of that year as the day of the "Miraculous Repatriation Back Home to Africa". No one was clear how this feat was going to be accomplished, but large numbers – estimated at a minimum of five hundred – gathered at the church on Rosalie Avenue, with Henry's "Blue Card" – his substitute for a passport – in hand. When 5 October came and went without deliverance, many fell away from the movement, though as Chevannes suggests, the true believers grew stronger in their faith.[8] But even as this outwardly bizarre, millenarian incident faded into the past, subsequent events would show that at the leadership of Henry's movement a far more secular, tactical reorientation was already in progress.

Chevannes notes that Henry said he had made a trip to Ethiopia to visit Emperor Haile Selassie the previous September and Selassie had told him that Jamaica was a country built by black men and women and was therefore a part of Africa and should not be abandoned by them.[9] Whether this was factual or not, evidence found by police on the 6 April raid points to the Jamaican-centred revolutionary direction the organization had taken. A letter to Fidel Castro signed by seven members of the church, including Claudius himself, said, in part:

We now desire to return home in peace, to live under our own vine and fig tree, otherwise a government like yours that give justice to the poor. All our efforts to have a peaceful repatriation has proven a total failure.

The greater nations that occupies Africa is bitterly against our returning home. Hence we must fight a war for what is ours by right. Therefore we want to assure you Sir, and your Government, that Jamaica and the rest of the British West Indies will be turned over to you and your Government, after this war we are preparing to start for Africa's freedom is completed; and we her scattered children are restored. We are getting ready for an invasion on the Jamaican Govt. therefore we need your help and personal advice.

We have the necessary men for the job. Since you cannot know Sir without our information, the Black people of Jamaica are with you and your govt one hundred per cent and desire to see Jamaica get into your hands before we leave for Africa.[10]

If Claudius Henry's 5 October fiasco could have been considered an instance of delusional fantasy, the same could not be said of his new thrust toward popular revolt. In December 1959, Ronald Henry and members of his Bronx-based First Africa Corps visited Jamaica and spoke to the faithful at Rosalie Avenue. Adolphus Christie, also known as "Dolly", a faithful member of the church, was there:

[Ronald] spoke at Rosalie Avenue saying he understood that some of us wanted to go to Africa but a next portion that don't want to go and it might cause some disturbance on the two sides, so for that reason we will have to prepare to meet anything that come across as they may be fight between those who want to go and those who do not. For that reason we will have [to] prepare ourselves . . . He used the word 'trained' but I don't remember how it was used.[11]

Ronald's particular usage of the word 'trained', which Christie seemed to have conveniently forgotten, referred to the fact that the younger Henry was building a team of dedicated revolutionists among young Jamaicans and African Americans in New York City. Eldred Morgan, also known as "Eldrie" and "Rex", a twenty-two-year-old Montego Bay-born welder and electrician with strong black nationalist views, had been approached by Ronald in New York in the summer of 1959 and asked if he would like to help in the liberation of a 'colony'. Later, in his interview with the staff of the corps, he was told that they were going to Jamaica in order to train five hundred Rastafarians to liberate this colony.[12] Titus Damons, a twenty-nine-year-old African American spot welder from South Carolina and living in Harlem, also got involved in the organization because it was going to liberate a "certain colony" in Africa. He was told that one David Ambrister, otherwise known as "Kenyatta", was its head. Ron Henry was the chief organizer and commander.[13] Donald Harper, also known as "Leroy Malachi", was an African American from Brooklyn. He met Ronald through a branch of the United Sons of Africa Movement and became an active member of the First Africa Corps only in late 1959. Henry told him they were going to Africa to do some guerrilla fighting and he, with his self-described "strong racial feeling",[14] willingly agreed.

Ronald's Letters

Gradually, over the summer and fall of 1959, the corps grew and consolidated. In early 1960, Al Thomas and Howard Rollins (Quasim Abdullah) robbed a "white man" of $6,000 at the corner of Fifteenth Street and Seventh Avenue. The proceeds of this and other robberies went into the purchase of arms and equipment. Shortly after a visit to New York by his father in early 1960, Ronald purchased eighteen rifles and twenty pistols.[15] The visit from Claudius was evidently the upshot of an ongoing correspondence between himself and Ronald concerning their revolutionary plans. Three incriminating letters from the son to the father were found after the Rosalie Avenue raid. The first, obviously written in the early stages of planning, outlined what appears to be the main objective:

I have started [the] First Africa Corps and doing fine so far with Agard and several other fellows. It is very time consuming and leaves me with no time for school or social activities that I don't mind a bit as long as it is for the cause of our race.

The plan is this. To gather a force of about 600 and leave secretly and land on the shore of a certain Colony, take the capital and proceed to occupy the place and round up all the Europeans and either kill or ship the hell to their ice box Europe.

I only wish I could name the colony but that wouldn't be wise by mail.

There is about 35 of us now. I have also found a place that we can get all the machine guns and carbines we want, but it is expensive, however, we shall do our best, recruiting is slow as it is by word of mouth but about 75% of the ones we have seem to be dedicated.

This colony can be taken. I know it can, if I can only keep these so-called negroes together long enough to reach the entire amount and cost off.[16]

And somewhat later, with growing confidence in his little organization, he again writes:

We have a growing little corps here and expect to leave by late 1961 fully armed to take this colony lock, stock and but plate . . . If they don't jail me for gun running and whipping unfaithful niggers I hope to see you in Oct.

We have been collecting money to purchase arms and will have shipment coming to us the 16 of this month, all M.G.

I now have only about 55 men but I hope to get 300–400 which will be enough to take the capital and part of the country we have it figured out as best we can.[17]

Reading between the lines of Ronald's letters and the letter to Castro, a tentative conclusion can be reached as to the shared plans of the father's church and the son's corps. Ronald's group of trained Americans and Jamaicans – some, as the evidence would suggest, having had stints in the US armed forces,[18] but numbering no more than fifty initially – would be infiltrated into Jamaica along with the requisite weapons and equipment. In Jamaica, they would train an army of Rastafarians who would take power locally, perhaps with the assistance of the neighbouring Castro government, but certainly modelling their tactics from the experience of the successful Cuban guerrilla movement. This, however, was only to be the first stage in a longer-term strategy that would involve repatriation and the liberation of Africa.

Throughout the letters from Ronald and the cautioned statements of his thwarted comrades, references to a "certain colony" – presumably in Africa – keep recurring. However, there is no evidence of any concrete, logistical arrangements to move to Africa, much less to 'take' an African colony, with the vastly greater resources such an adventure would require. Until other evidence appears, it would seem that the plan was to overthrow the Jamaican government with Africa as a future strategic goal in order to hold the interest of Rastafarians and black nationalist Americans, who variously considered Jamaica part of the corrupt West, or too insignificant a target to be worth the risk of insurrection.

Ronald's plans were to build the resources and tactical capacity of his elite corps gradually in the Bronx while simultaneously infiltrating trusted members into Jamaica to begin the training of the guerrilla army; but his father's relatively open, popularly based church was, at least from a security perspective, a very weak link. Even as the first of the guerrilla trainers – Eldred Morgan – had left Idlewild airport on 5 April for Jamaica, local intelligence officers had already received notice of subversive activities at Rosalie Avenue and had planned their raid for the following morning.

The discovery of the letter to Fidel Castro along with notes from Ronald to his father threw the organization into a tailspin. With Claudius in jail and facing a variety of charges, including treason felony, the First Africa Corps had the option of either postponing its plans indefinitely or making a bold and desperate attempt at early insurrection. Obviously confident in his carefully worked out plans, but fatally misjudging the political mood in Jamaica and the new reality that the security forces were now on the alert for any subversion bearing the name Henry, Ronald and his comrades took the fateful decision to move. This wilfulness and boldness, which appear to be dominant features in his personality, quite evidently made Ronald a strong leader of men but not one who brooked opposition, as would very soon be demonstrated. With barely concealed contempt for the Jamaican and British forces, Ronald was determined to move even without the critical element of surprise. Morgan, as noted, had arrived on the eve of the raid; on 16 April Howard (Quasim) Rollins landed at Palisadoes Airport near Kingston, to be followed on 26 April by Titus Damons. On 8 May Larry Reichburg, undercover as one Joseph Lee Williams, arrived at Montego Bay Airport, followed by William Jeter and Al Thomas on 26 May. Finally, on 12 June Ronald Henry, calling himself "Adolphus Holmes", and Donald Harper (Leroy Malachi) landed.

In the Field

In an era before airborne terrorism, all the men had arrived with one or more guns strapped to their bodies and ammunition, short wave radios and binoculars in their luggage. The plan, in its detail, reflected not only Ronald's organizational abilities but also the islandwide reach of his father's movement. There were two holding areas: in Montego Bay, arriving cadres went to a house in Salt Springs, two miles outside the town, before travelling cross country to Kingston; those who landed at Palisadoes Airport made their way to 33 Fairbourne Road in east Kingston where they waited before being transported to the guerrilla base camp in Red Hills. While they waited, at least one shipment of guns and equipment (accompanied, significantly, by two photographs of Marcus Garvey) arrived and was cleared from the port of Kingston, concealed in a used refrigerator.

The Red Hills camp had been established by one Claudius "Thunder" Beckford, Claudius Henry's number two man in the church and, since the 6 April raid, at large and wanted by the security forces on treason felony charges. Deep rifts existed between the Beckford view of revolution and that which Ronald and his American-based compatriots entertained. Donald Harper discovered this in speaking with Thunder soon after his arrival at the base camp:

Unknown to me Beckford was not really interested in going to Africa as we all from the United States had anticipated. His plans was to take Jamaica. When I found out this I told Beckford this was not what Ronald wants. Our original plan was to train men to go to Africa and to help liberate this colony. Beckford laughed at me and said "Africa is too big a proposition to handle." After knowing this I kinda lost interest in the thing because he began to lecture me about racial issues, especially the small minority groups who were living in Jamaica. He said he wanted to liquidate them. I asked him who would help him do it and he said he and his men. All he is asking of us is to help him train his men. I told him that this was not what Ronald and himself spoke about for our objective was Africa and Jamaica is only a island and Africa is a continent and it is much better to fight for a continent than an island. I also said to him, "Come to think of it your idea of this island is absurd when you say you want to liquidate the small minority group because there is no nation in this world that is built up with one kind of people." He began to ridicule me and asked me if I loved the Chinese men in this country who are only opportunists. I told him I don't hate them I admire them for they are a progressive people and that is the way we should be. On one occasion he said something which made me sick to my very bone when he said he was in the process of obtaining some deadly poison to poison the reservoir and people private water supplies. I told him that it would be a barbarous act for murdering innocent people for no obvious reasons. He laughed and said my heart was too soft to be here.[19]

Two elements dominated in Beckford's perspective. First it is evident that his own hatred of the white, Chinese and fair-skinned Jamaican elites overrode any orthodox notion of warfare in which civilians are excluded from the struggle between combatants. Thunder, with the weight of history heavy on his shoulders, sought to wipe the slate clean, once and for all. Simultaneously, and perhaps logically, he was also crystal clear on his limited, though conceivably more achievable objectives. For him, it was the known quantity of the Jamaican state that had to be overthrown and not some starry-eyed pan-Africanist notion of continental revolution. Beckford's ruthlessness and evident thirst for blood frightened the young American and Jamaican returnees, and this, together with his cold 'Jamaican' calculus, alienated him from them. The hostility was quickly reciprocated and began to crystallize into a foreigner versus local split, with Beckford calling on his closest supporters not to associate with the Americans because they were pork eaters and therefore, in the Rastafarian belief, unclean. This growing schism was, however, not to last for long.

Ronald arrived in Red Hills on 12 June. On 15 June, a drumhead trial was held for Thunder Beckford and his closest comrades in arms. Albert Gabbidon, a twenty-eight-year-old delivery man of Cockburn Gardens, was commanded by Henry to execute Thunder and his allies:

Henry told the men to lay on their bellies. At this time Jeter had already brought a .25 Automatic which Henry had sent him for. He said "Gabby go and shot them five men in their head. If you don't you will be shot." I looked round and saw the Americans had their guns trained on me. I took the gun and shot the first three as I feared that if I had not done it I would be shot also. After shooting the three men, Scott, Beckford and McDonald I went back to Henry and said "Sir, I beg for the lives of these two". Henry said, "Gabby, are you sure these two men [meaning Taylor and Irving] can be trusted?". I said, "Yes". Thunder and McDonald was not quite dead and Henry took the gun from me and handed it to Taylor and told him to shoot Beckford. This Taylor did and he made Taylor hand the gun to Irving and told him to shoot McDonald which he did. Henry ordered Taylor and Irving back to the camp as he did not want them to know where the men were buried.[20]

The commander was now in full control of his camp, but with the entire leadership of his father's church in jail and with a national atmosphere bordering on hysteria towards Rastas, it would have been miraculous if information about the camp in Red Hills had not reached the ears of the security forces. On 21 June, six days after Thunder's death, a force of British Hampshire Regiment, West India Regiment soldiers and Jamaican police, surrounded the Red Hills camp in search of arms. Subsequent information would suggest that while they had received information of possible arms caches, they were not prepared for active resistance from well armed men.[21]

At the time of the raid, there were some thirty people at the camp. Adolphus "Dolly" Christie, whose testimony has already been introduced, was a member of the movement who lived close to the camp. Before daybreak he rushed into the camp to inform Henry that they were being surrounded. Most of the men, taken completely by surprise and at a stage when they were yet to be fully prepared for defending their camp, scattered into the surrounding bushes. Ronald, however, showing tremendous cool, rallied those closest to him, ordered them to collect the automatic weapons and called on Quasim, Al Thomas and Jeter – his trusted Bronx-based lieutenants – to go with him to "look for the British soldiers".

Moving through the brush, they outmanoeuvred and disarmed two members of the Hampshire Regiment and, while walking with these two single-file through the undergrowth, they encountered another pair of British soldiers. This time, guns were fired. Four British soldiers were shot. One died on the spot, another succumbed in the operating theatre, the other two were to survive their wounds. Breaking through the dense vegetation, Ronald and his three men evaded the now alerted armed forces and headed down the slope of the hill toward Washington Boulevard, the western corridor leading into Kingston.

There they hijacked a white Ford van and broke through a police checkpoint near the Ferry River, forcing a police car off the road under a hail of bullets.

For the next six days, the four men were at large in the Sligoville district to the north of Spanish Town. Sleeping in the bush, avoiding police checkpoints and aerial reconnaissance, demanding food from the occasional household or shopkeeper, Henry and his lieutenants still had a plan: if only they could get to Vere in Clarendon or Annotto Bay on the North Coast, where significant numbers of 'movement' people lived, then they would be able to gain shelter and slip out of the government dragnet. But then, their fatal flaw: hungry, exhausted and suffering from exposure, they committed the disastrous error of sleeping in Higgins' shop on the night of 26 June.

How might we try to explain this remarkable event that has been virtually written out of the history of contemporary Jamaica? Was it the ultimate extension of a millenarian fiasco, the first stage of which had been cast on 5 October 1959? Or was it an anomalous case of criminal banditry by foreign 'troublemakers', as the *Daily Gleaner,* government ministers and other 'official' spokesmen sought to assert as the events unfolded?[22] Was it an ill-conceived case of primitive rebellion that failed because the material and organizational prerequisites for success were absent? Or, closely related to this proposal, was it an early and portentous attempt to copy the Fidelista model of the guerrilla *foco*, a harbinger, perhaps, of other debacles, such as that suffered by Che Guevara in Bolivia seven years later? There is some usefulness in all of these proposals, yet none of them fully capture the significance and meaning of the "Henry Rebellion".

Henry's rebellion was an early, if ill-conceived, instance of a long, consolidating grass-roots radicalism. It was the ideological product of an alternative universe of resistance whose markers were the assertion of Africa, blackness and revolution. In his immediate tasks, Henry failed, but in his broader, ideational goals, subsequent history would suggest that he was far more successful. In order for us to further plumb these depths, however, it might be useful to detour for a moment to some recent thinking on the question of revolution.

New and Old Paths in the Study of Revolt

Recent scholarship on revolutions and revolt has moved in very different directions. If there has been an underlying theme, however, it is for the greater recognition of cultural and ideological factors as critical variables in social determination. Thus, while both Timothy Wickham-Crowley and Jeff Goodwin, in their respective studies of Latin American and 'Third World' revolutions follow in Theda Skocpol's macrosociological tradition, both, especially Goodwin, recognize the role of ideology and culture in contributing to the revolutionary situation and outcome.[23] This is also a central argument in Foran and Goodwin's comparative study of Iran and Nicaragua after the revolution,[24] as it definitely is the critical issue in Farideh Farhi's more substantial book on the same two countries.[25] And Skocpol herself, in her latest book on the subject, while defending her own state structuralist position against Marxist and rational choice critiques, calls for comparative analysts to "probe the patterns of interrelation among cultural idioms, political ideologies and the politics of revolutionary transformation".[26] Indeed, beyond the Skocpolian school, if it might be defined as such, other theorists have been running with cultural and ideological themes in new and sometimes interesting directions. For example, Forrest Colburn, in his reflections on what he considers as the causes for the striking similarities in the wave of revolutions that took place in the Third World in the seventies, concludes that revolution was a 'vogue' that caught the imagination of Third World intellectuals, based on the flawed belief that Marxist-Leninist revolution would solve the developmental problems of their countries. The "vogue of revolution", then, even though its time has now passed, had a powerful role of its own in determining the direction of history: "Explaining revolutionary elites' ideas is crucial, because in a revolution ideas are more than a kind of intervening variable that mediates interests and outcomes. Ideas transform perceptions of interests, sometimes wildly so. They shape actors' perceptions of possibilities as well as their understanding of their interests."[27] In a quite different vein, though with similar conclusions to Colburn, Bernard Yack identifies the "longing for total revolution" as a sort of false consciousness forged out of the Enlightenment, in which traditional faith, instead of being transcended by scientific logic is, rather, secularized into revolutionary zealotry.[28]

The striking similarity between the approaches of Colburn and Yack is not only their critical emphasis on ideology but the extent to which they focus on the ideas of the intellectual elites, who, admittedly, have played leading and crucial roles in virtually all modern revolutions. These attempts to locate revolutionary consciousness and, critically, the very notion of revolution as a construct with its own intellectual and historical trajectory are important. Not only might they help to explain, as Colburn suggests, why revolutionary movements of the mid to late twentieth century, with few exceptions, seemed to adopt a common platform based on various interpretations of Marxism-Leninism but also why, at the end of the century, the entire project of revolution lies prostrate, abandoned en masse by these very elites. They say less, however, on whether similar conclusions apply or, indeed, if it is necessary to identify a different set of impulses that motivated the popular support base, the 'cast of thousands' of peasants, workers and unemployed persons, without whom none of these potential intellectual leaders could have risen to national fame.

Approaches to Hegemony

Of course, the intellectual effort to understand the ideas that motivate people to revolt and to disaggregate the faceless crowd is nothing new. Particularly since Gramsci, thinkers in the Marxist tradition have sought to grasp the extent to which ideology and cultural traditions contributed to the maintenance of order and under what conditions that order might ultimately be undermined.

Gramsci, in the *Prison Notebooks,* differentiates between two types of ideology that the subordinate classes might possess: that which he calls "historically organic", arising out of a given socioeconomic structure, and that which is "arbitrary, rationalistic or willed".

To the extent that ideologies are historically necessary, they have a validity that is 'psychological'; they 'organise' human masses, and create the terrain on which men move, acquire consciousness of their position, struggle, etc. To the extent that they are arbitrary, they only create individual 'movements', polemics and so on.[29]

Within the Marxist tradition, Gramsci's main advance seems to be his break with the Leninist-inspired notion of consciousness versus false-consciousness. According to this approach, by themselves, working people are only able to achieve limited, 'trade union' consciousness. Genuine revolutionary consciousness can only come from without, from the vanguard party. Gramsci's "willed" or "arbitrary" ideology, which he occasionally refers to as "contradictory consciousness", cannot simply be equated with the Leninist notion of false consciousness, rather, in contrast to 'false' consciousness, which is usually understood as awaiting the intervention from without and above of (socialist) intellectuals with their 'ideas', Gramsci's contention is that within contradictory consciousness there exists the potential – indeed bases – for class consciousness, the role of the socialist intellectual being in this case that of developing (socialist) consciousness in a dialectical relation-ship with the working class.[30]

George Rudé, in further refining Gramsci's approach, differentiates between what he calls "inherent" ideology, "a sort of 'mother's milk' ideology, based on direct experience, oral tradition or false memory"[31] and "derived ideology", a more structured system borrowed from outside, such as "the Rights of Man, popular sovereignty, socialism, or Marxism-Leninism".[32] There is no "Wall of Babylon" separating the two, Rudé insists, but in order for successful revolt, the balance must tilt toward the formal, derived, forward-looking ideology and away from the inherent.

Writing in the Caribbean tradition, Abigail Bakan has sought to combine Gramsci's approach and Rudé's modifications:

Both inherent and derived ideas could loosely be considered to fall within Gramsci's concept of 'willed' ideology, as they are not historically time bound. Further, Gramsci's notion of 'organic' ideas can, for our purposes, be more narrowly defined than he had intended. We can consider certain ideas concerning available means of practical resistance that are immediately and historically specific to the organisation of produc-tion to be 'organic'.[33]

In a rich and nuanced study of three Jamaican rebellions – the 1831 uprising against slavery; the 1865 Morant Bay Rebellion; and the 1938 labour rebellion – Bakan seeks to illustrate how inherent, derived and organic ideologies interacted to facilitate these three rebellions and, after 1938, to inhibit further uprising from below. While the study reveals many important insights into Jamaican society, her conclusions are particularly important for this argument. Bakan concludes that Jamaica has had a rebellious traditional culture and a tradition of courageous militancy, but this is better understood as one of militant reformism and not revolutionism. Rebels have invariably sought, she contends, allies in the church and the state in order to legitimate their protest "even when the dictates of church and state were the very targets of protest".[34] Thus, even with Bakan's careful attention to the details of the beliefs of ordinary people, the unavoidable conclusion is that some intervention from without is necessary to carry through the revolt to its conclusion.

In 1831 and 1865 the objective basis for a fundamental transformation of society did not fully exist. In 1938 the strategic power of the working class was far greater, and the impact of the rebellion of that year was far more profound than in the previous rebellions. There was not however, a sufficiently self conscious and organised political force, a mass revolutionary party, capable of achieving a revolutionary transformation.[35]

Without arriving too precipitously to judgement, it would seem that common to the Leninist false consciousness approach, Gramsci's intervention, Rudé's modification and Bakan's combined application is an underlying assumption that the people by themselves are incapable of moving beyond the stage of militant reformism to revolutionism without intellectual input, whether it be Gramsci's "dialectical interaction", Rudé's "shift to the derived" or, overtly, Bakan's "revolutionary party". Any notion that so-called militant reformism may indeed be a tactic in recognition of an adverse political situation is muted or absent from these perspectives.

Scott's Intervention

This assumption is not made in James Scott's remarkable study *Domination and the Arts of Resistance*. In a study that, if not paradigm shattering certainly breaks new ground, Scott interrogates the entire notion of hegemony and the politics of subordinate classes in hierarchically organized societies.[36] To try to summarize his complex arguments, he proposes that both from the Right (Parsonian sociology) and the Left (Gramscian neo-Marxists) it is assumed that in "stable" societies subordinate groups have internalized the dominant norms:

In the structural-functional world of Parsonian sociology, subordinate groups came naturally to an acceptance of the normative principles behind the social order without which no society could endure. In the neo-Marxist critique, it is also assumed that subordinate groups have internalised the dominant norms, but now these norms are seen to be a false view of their objective interests. In each instance, ideological incorporation produces social stability; in the former case, the stability is laudable, while in the latter case it is a stability that permits the continuation of class-based exploitation.[37]

First, Scott carefully examines the component arguments to be found in the notion of hegemony. He differentiates between what he considers as a 'thick' theory of hegemony, in which people are literally brainwashed into believing that the repressive state actually functions in their own interest, and a 'thin', presumably more realistic, theory, in which subordinate classes are not convinced but see no feasible alternative and therefore submit to rule. Neither, he argues, can explain the historical reality in which under feudalism, modern slavery and other oppressive, hierarchical systems, recorded rebellions have been numerous and persistent. If either thick or thin theories are true, he proposes, then so much rebelliousness should not take place. Focusing on the thin theory, Scott is persuasive when he suggests that the assumption that "there are no alternatives" is a false one, because even to uneducated peasants, there is always the option of "turning things upside down", or negating what exists. Finally, and convincingly, Scott questions the further assumption underlying hegemony that belief in a system necessarily brings more rather than less peace. Belief may create more unrest when the contradictions between the belief and the oppressive reality become apparent.[38]

Scott's central thesis, then, is to question the notion of ideological incorporation. Yes, he admits, there is an "official transcript" in which subordinate peoples praise the king and support the status quo. However, this is only tactical and is performed precisely because of the perceived and evident weaknesses of those below. No serf would be in his right mind to say "Down with the king" in front of the royal entourage when that would mean certain death. Beyond this official transcript, though, Scott asserts that there is a "hidden transcript" of ridicule, subversive acts, pilfering, poaching, tax evasion and shabby work, which is developed as a means of resistance to the dominant.[39] This hidden transcript, expressed equally in carnival as it might be in religious ritual and praedial larceny, is not, he contends, a safety valve which releases steam and postpones the moment of open revolt. Rather,

far from being a relief-valve taking the place of actual resistance, the discursive practices offstage sustain resistance in the same way in which the informal peer pressure of factory workers discourages any individual worker from exceeding work norms and becoming a rate buster . . . it would be more accurate in short, to think of the hidden transcript as a condition of practical resistance rather than a substitute for it.[40]

Thus, and in conclusion, there is constant resistance to the official transcript and belief in it is the exception rather than the rule. There is a constant testing of the boundaries of domination and what may outwardly appear to be a series of 'petty' acts may seem inconsequential, but poaching and squatting on a large scale can restructure the control of property. Peasant tax evasion on a large scale has brought about crises of appropriation that threaten the state. Massive desertion by serf or peasant conscripts has helped bring down more than one ancien regime. Under the appropriate conditions, the accumulation of petty acts can, rather like snow flakes on a steep mountainside, set off an avalanche.[41]

Scouting Scott

There seem to be at least four significant issues to consider if we were for the moment to conclude that Scott's approach is a more useful way to look at hegemony, ideology and popular resistance. The first has serious consequences for the role of the vanguard or intellectual elite. While a particular technical vision of future social and political transformation can only realistically come from an elite cadre trained in political economy, the view that *revolutionary consciousness*, the conceiving of the possibility of fundamental change, is the privileged sphere of such an elite is severely undermined by Scott. If, following Scott's argument, what Lenin perceived as 'trade union consciousness' is not false consciousness but a purely tactical transcript trotted out for official purposes while, all along, there is another hidden transcript of resistance and revolt awaiting the appropriate moment to take the public form, then the 'truly' conscious intellectual becomes redundant or, worse yet, an impediment in the popular movement of tactical resistance. Simply put, Scott tips the balance decisively in favour of the people and away from the hitherto indispensable vanguard in revolutionary situations as, indeed, in ordinary politics.

The second implication would seem to apply to the state, because if hegemony is no longer to be understood as willed consent,[42] then the begged question is, How do states retain power? Evidently, force re-enters the picture, perhaps with emphases on exemplary instances of punishment, parades demonstrating the overwhelming might of the army, and the like. But it would seem that a rethinking of how force is manifest needs to be approached if Scott is not to fall into the trap of conflating all regimes as being based on naked force and concluding that all subordinate classes are equally involved in revolutionary resistance.

The third issue relates to another conflation evident in Scott's framework, in that he insufficiently, if at all, explores the applicability of his theory to spatially and temporally distinct social systems. This omission leaves the impression that his theory is equally effective in explaining forms of resistance which occur under slavery and feudalism as well as more modern and less overtly oppressive forms. While the notion of a hidden transcript seems eminently defensible in highly undemocratic and repressive contexts, with slavery being the obvious paradigm, it begins to fray at the edges when applied to other instances, such as one where there may be a great deal of hierarchy and repression but these exist alongside representative forms of democracy. In such cases, the core of Scott's argument might have to be rescued from its peripheral elements. In cases of partial or flawed democracy, while the text could hardly be described as hidden, it might be still appropriate to speak of a subterranean, veiled, "transcript from below" that emerges and provides an alternative world view, explaining the harsh realities of life and nurturing resistance across the gamut of possible strategies and tactics. The critical thing rescued from Scott is the notion that in such contexts, belief or acquiescence to the world view of the dominant remains minimal. The text, however, far from being hidden, is spoken in public every day. Inverting Scott's own phrase, we can call this a "paper thin theory of the hidden text".[43]

The fourth implication is methodological, for if there is substance in Scott's conclusions then the entire approach to studying social revolutions needs to be rethought. Instead of sketching sharp dichotomies between societies (or the same society at different times) in consensus or rebellion, the researcher now has to focus on the much more difficult to perceive instances of foot dragging, dissimulation, parody and larceny. The researcher must locate the social spaces in which the discourse of the transcript from below is fleshed out and identify how this operates in guerrilla fashion on the fringes of the official transcript. Without this undertaking, it is impossible to fully understand the conditions under which the transcript from below is spoken out loud and the people rise up in open resistance against their dominators.

Back to Henry

After having taken this somewhat winding detour into theory, we can return to the assertion made earlier in this chapter. With sensitivity to Scott's perspective, the Henry Rebellion might be understood as not simply the quixotic act of some millenarian prophet or the desperate deed of isolated bandits, hopelessly disconnected from the society in which they hoped to make revolution.[44] Rather, the rebellion can be viewed as a rare, but not unprecedented, testing of the boundaries of dominance, from persons operating within a subordinate ideology scripted over centuries of resistance. It failed due to technical reasons associated with the 'art' of insurrection, but its very failure, and the exemplary demonstration of state violence that accompanied it, shifted the transcript from below into new strategies that largely avoided the frontal assault. Thus Henry's hanging for treason presaged and helped determine the political struggle for democratic socialism in the seventies and, with that tactical failure, the wide-ranging battle for cultural hegemony that continues to rage beyond the nineties.

The Technique of Insurrection and the Transcript from Below

In lieu of 'proof' for this proposal, this final section of the chapter seeks to explore two dimensions of the proposition: first, the reasons for the technical failure of the Henry Rebellion, and second, the character of the transcript from below, as spoken by the erstwhile revolutionaries as they retreated for the first and last time. For it is in this moment of absolute freedom, when the military threshold has been breached, when turning back is nigh impossible, that the underlying ideological premisses that inform subordinate peoples reveal themselves in clearest perspective.

The Technical

Friedrich Engels' famous statement on insurrection being an art is as good a point as any to start in an examination of the technical failure of Henry's movement. Engels proposes at least five necessary conditions for the success of the insurrection once it has begun. These begin with a general warning that insurrection is to be taken seriously, as the stakes are, inevitably, life and death. He then proposes that the insurrectionary forces can never afford to go on the defensive, for they face the superior might, organization and traditions of the state's army, and if that army is allowed to consolidate after the initial offensive, the weaker forces of the revolutionaries will never be able to defeat it. Third, Engels submits, in what is now conventional wisdom for modern guerrilla armies, that the insurrectionists, wherever they engage the state, must bring superior forces to bear against their opponents at the point of engagement. Fourth, he asserts that the element of surprise must always be used to keep the enemy off guard; and finally, the insurgents must win a continual stream of victories, however small, in order to retain the advantage of their morale over the official armed forces.[45]

Claudius Henry's movement, of course, was defeated even before it got off the ground. It is still useful, nonetheless, to examine what he did 'right' and what he did 'wrong'. Let us approach the question by imagining what would have happened had Ronald not decided, precipitously, to come to Jamaica even as details of their plan had been revealed to the security forces after the Rosalie Avenue raid. What if he had bided his time, infiltrated his guerrilla trainers in over the ensuing months when the hysteria had calmed down and systematically begun, with the appropriate security cover, to train his six hundred or so Rastas in basic military tactics and guerrilla warfare? What if his efforts at 'raising' funds in New York had continued to be successful and he was able to purchase and ship, without exposure, sufficient weapons to equip his army? Given the loose security measures in his father's church, it is highly improbable, though not impossible, that such an alternative scenario could have taken place. With six hundred armed personnel, strategic bases of support in the slums of Kingston and at other points throughout the island, such a force, with a few tactical victories and the right atmosphere of national hysteria, could have created tremendous dislocation and seriously strained the social pact that had developed between the two dominant parties, the trade unions and the business sector in pre-independence Jamaica.

But Claudius Henry could not have taken power in 1960. Despite the letter to Fidel Castro, it is evident that the only 'international' contact the movement had was its own New York connection. This worked as an adequate source for limited funds and light weapons, but short of significant diplomatic break-throughs, which Henry's millenarian philosophy and enigmatic character would certainly militate against, without important regional allies, the move-ment would soon be isolated and outmanoeuvred.[46] It is highly unlikely that Castro himself, with his regime in its earliest and most difficult phase, would have risked further international censure to support a marginal, charismatic Jamaican preacher. More critically, Jamaica was still a British colony and neither Britain nor the United States would have easily tolerated radical revolt ninety miles away from Cuba, as was certainly the case with the elected Jagan regime in British Guiana in 1953 and would soon be again in 1963.

This, of course, is conjecture. Henry failed because he lacked the element of surprise; because the vast majority of people were unaware of the existence of a revolutionary movement, much less supportive of its programme and platform; and further, despite the real economic and social hardships faced by tens of thousands of black Jamaicans in the late fifties, the availability of avenues of migration to Britain, which were still open, the existence of a parliamentary democratic system, which had been functioning effectively for fifteen years, and real improvements in social services in the postwar period all discouraged the development of anything resembling a revolutionary situation which would have been a necessary condition for his success.

The Transcript from Below

This is not to say, however, that Henry operated outside the social realities of Jamaican society. In 1960, although Norman Manley's nominally socialist PNP was in power, its left wing had been expelled some nine years earlier and the urban, radical constituency, as it was, could no longer be said to be firmly within the PNP. Despite the growing tactical differences as to whether Jamaica should seek independence singly or as part of a West Indian federation, the two parties, in their adoption of industrialization by invitation and state-led development, were as programmatically close as they have ever been (apart from the most contemporary period). It is true that the PNP was still considered by many as the party of reform and change, but it presided over a sharply divided society. The growing pauperization of the peasantry and the drift from the countryside to the slums of Kingston and from there to the United Kingdom, were the experiences of many Jamaicans. The official transcript of this society was one of national inclusiveness and racial harmony, moving together towards greater self-government and independence. But close to the surface was another reality, not just of economic privation but of caste, language and colour hierarchy and daily social slights, captured eloquently in this report of a party in a wealthy private home after a cricket match:

The men wore blazers and white flannels, and the women wore white skirts. They were carrying tennis racquets. On the lawn they leaped about, striking at the balls, and the garden boy, who served for every purpose and had been dressed in white for the occasion, ran up and down in the hedge looking for lost balls . . . "Jolly well played, Aston," said one of the young men. He was a clerk in my father's office. He was fat and brown, and spoke with a Jamaican accent . . . now he was calling my father by his Christian name, and my father smiled and didn't seem to mind . . . [W]hen it grew dark . . . everyone went inside. Mother put a record on the Victrola, and the young people danced . . . The fat brown clerk from my father's office stood at the side of the drawing room smiling at everyone . . . "Oh jolly well danced", he said loudly. My father came by. "This isn't the tennis court, Henriques," he said. The clerk was silent and I felt sorry for him . . .

The next day the lawn was littered with cigarette butts, tinfoil and empty packets. There were glasses under the hedge. The garden boy was cleaning the lawn. He picked up all the cigarette butts and put them in a can. He smoked them for weeks, taking a butt out of the can after he had eaten lunch. "Players are best," he said with the air of a connoisseur, "But Four Aces are also good." From time to time as he went about his duties in the yard he would stop and make striking motions with an imaginary tennis racquet. Then he'd say, "Jolly well played." And sometimes, "Oh, hard luck." Then he'd shake his head, and go back to pushing the lawnmower.[47]

This sense of marginalization of the black majority in a context of extreme hierarchy, as well as the concomitant alienation and rage that it generates behind the everyday mask of apparent acceptance, is a leitmotif of Jamaican society.[48] It is the foundation out of which Paul Bogle, leader of the Morant Bay Rebellion, called on his followers to remember their colour and "cleave to the black";[49] it is the basis on which Bedward, the leader of the turn of the century millenarian movement, prophesied that there was a white wall and a black wall and that the black wall was going to rise up and oppress the white wall that had been oppressing it for years;[50] and it was the foundation on which the Garveyite movement grew after the deportation of Marcus Garvey from the United States to Jamaica in 1927.[51] Indeed, the Rastafarian movement can be considered as the river that grew from these tributaries and that, by the mid to late fifties, had consolidated as an alternative approach to viewing the world. From this perspective, Henry's camp was only one (albeit of great importance) of many Rasta camps that were the social spaces in which the transcript of resistance was fleshed out in the late fifties.[52]

Aspects of this transcript are spoken as Henry and his men, on the run, hunted but having declared their resistance, sought food and shelter and searched in vain for an avenue of escape. Patrick Kerr, a farmer of Cedar's

Settlement in St Catherine, gave this statement about Ronald's brief visit to his house:

While the meal was being prepared Henry said if I hear anything about Henry they have in custody. They – the men – want the government to let him loose for Marcus Garvey prophesy that there should be bloodshed in Jamaica this said year 1960; and in that respect they are here to get all Chinese and whites out of this country and to bring Jamaica to be a new Jamaica. He then showed a picture which seemed to have been cut out of books. The pictures show about days of old – slavery – . . . He then said, "These pictures are to represent our fore-parents the white men steal away from Africa and take to Jamaica here. For instance if they should take a shipload, only half the amount reaches Jamaica. The white men forgery the black people and bring those coloured so in case of that your skin is red but you are still negro. And this is the reason they would like to see the Chinese and white sweep as they have the negro down." He says again, "The gates of the prison that they lock against Marcus Garvey when they take him in cannot be opened any more and the one he walk through still leave wide open." He said, "Swallowfield should be the battleground in this said year 1960, where blood should shed."[53]

The transcript from below as spoken by Henry had within it the following elements:

- A denial of any notion of racial harmony as the norm in Jamaica, but rather, a conception of the country as a place where black people are oppressed
- A limited, if at all existent, notion of Jamaican nationalism, transcended by a broader pan-African or "Black Atlantic" sensibility[54]
- A well-developed notion of revolution as a good thing and as a cleansing action, overturning the past and setting things right

In 1960, deeply alienated individuals, operating within the parameters of this transcript, tested the limits of power with open revolt and failed. But even as Henry and his co-conspirators faced trial, the Norman Manley government had made a significant concession by preparing the ground for a Back to Africa mission.[55] As Henry and his allies lay mouldering in their graves, the 1963 Coral Gardens incident, in which a personal vendetta carried out by some Rastafarians was interpreted as a new uprising,[56] illustrated the real fear and paranoia that Henry's movement had instilled in 'official' Jamaica. Twelve years later, as Ronald's memory faded into obscurity, his father, now released from prison, was to play an important role, manipulating Rastafarian symbols, in the election of Norman's son Michael to the highest office in the land;[57]

and thirty-six years later, when only the oldest and most loyal members of the movement and gnomish academics remember Ronald's deeds, a broad-based struggle is underway for Jamaica's cultural future, with the issues of Africa, colour and the complexion of Jamaican society at the forefront.[58] Ronald's mistaken tactics may have been forgotten, but the transcript from below lives on and is spoken openly today in Jamaica.

2

NUFF at the Cusp of an Idea:
Grassroots Guerrillas and the Politics of the Seventies in Trinidad and Tobago[1]

Remember Basil Davis and Guy Harewood and Brother Valentine
Beverly Jones, Brian Jeffers and the others whose lives went down on the line
I wonder if these people
Gave their lives for a hopeless cause
And for these deaths all those responsible
People the verdict is yours
                    – Brother Valentino, "The Roaring Seventies"

The Clash at Caura

Clem Haynes' story:

We reach Caura from Valencia after the raid: about four to five days? And when we reach we split up. Guy went to check the Maracas Police Station. One morning I remember waking Thornhill to do guard duty. We used to work it out from the night to six o' clock next morning. After I did mine, I woke up Thornhill, and after he was finished, he woke up Jennifer Jones. Just a few minutes after she went on the post, we heard this machine gun and Burroughs' voice saying "We coming in the bush now for all yuh!" (When we had gone to blow up the Textel plant in Blanchisseuse, we told the clerk to tell Burroughs that if he wanted us to come in the bush for us.) Then the shooting started. All the time we looking to see if Jennifer would come back up. When we didn't see her, we thought she was shot, so we decided to head to the top of the ridge. On top we saw a lot of boot prints, so we realized that soldiers were around. We continued up the ridge, but after a little while we stopped. Ahead was a clump of trees and we were getting a funny vibe, so we went back down the hill to walk across. But when we went a little way, we heard a voice saying, "Drop your guns!" and they opened fire. We survived that ambush, but then another exchange took place and Beverly [Jones] was wounded. She got shot in her face – you could see her teeth – and one in her leg. Another brother, Kenneth Tenia, was about to crawl over a log and got shot and died instantly.[2]

Terrence Thornhill's story:

They ambushed us in the camp. When we went up the hill, they had another ambush. It was a real scamper. We met this log going down the hill and, reading the books, Che Guevara et cetera, you remember to always keep your cool under fire. The log was a big one and had a space underneath, so I slid under. As I looked backward, there was Ken [Tenia] coming over the log and he got shot in his head. Beverly Jones got shot – her face was ripped out – and also in her knee. I had some medication and put it on her face and knee. We lay down in the bush with Alan [Harewood]. Everyone else was separated. I bounced up shooters four times that day. The third time is when Beverly was wounded. The fourth time is when she was killed. We laying in the bush and soldiers came right up to us. Then they see us and start to shoot. Me and Alan rolled down the hill, then we heard when they shot her. They said they found her trying to reload a shotgun, but she had no gun. So it was that kind of thing, where police were on our heels, people were selling us out and we just running from ambush to ambush.[3]

This was 13 September 1973, in the northern range of Trinidad, and the beginning of the end of the National United Freedom Fighters (NUFF) of Trinidad and Tobago. The origins of the second serious guerrilla movement in modern Anglo-Caribbean history and the only one to sustain prolonged military engagement in the field, can be precisely located some three years before these events.[4]

In February 1970, outwardly calm and peaceful Trinidad and Tobago erupted in a series of massive Black Power demonstrations in the wake of that year's carnival celebrations.[5] Tens of thousands of overwhelmingly young people marched daily in the streets of Port of Spain, San Fernando and other towns under slogans of black solidarity, African-Indian unity, and an end to white and foreign domination of the country's economy. The leading, though by no means only, organization in the demonstrations was the National Joint Action Committee (NJAC), an organization formed largely of university students the previous year as an expression of solidarity with the Caribbean students who had been arrested following a computer-smashing incident – the culmination of an antiracist demonstration – at Sir George Williams University in Montreal, Canada.

To the surprise of many, particularly the People's National Movement (PNM) government of Prime Minister Eric Williams, the demonstrations steadily gathered momentum, peaking with an estimated crowd in excess of one hundred thousand persons attending the funeral of Basil Davis, a young man who had been shot by policemen at one of the daily rallies and who became the first "martyr of the revolution".

The crisis came to a head on 21 April, following a rapid sequence of events. Earlier, Deputy Prime Minister A.N.R. Robinson had resigned, revealing glaring splits at the highest level of the government; then, days before, oil and sugar workers in south and central Trinidad had decided to strike, threatening to shut down the most critical sections of the economy. Such a development would have been disastrous for the regime of Williams. It would have signalled not only a new and potentially threatening alliance between the marching students and unemployed youth, now supported by the organized working class, but an even more frightening historical rapprochement between Afro-Creole Trinidad, concentrated in Port of Spain and the southern oil belt, and the Indian sugar workers from "Central", undermining the very political bloc from which the PNM had carved out its winning majority for fourteen years.[6]

Williams' response was to declare the state of emergency, order the arrest of the leaders of the movement, and call on the Trinidad and Tobago Regiment to leave its barracks in Chaguaramas on the western outskirts of the capital and enforce the law. But the revolutionary mood had run much deeper than Williams and his government had anticipated. Led by young lieutenants, a large contingent of the regiment mutinied. In an action interpreted in various ways, but that was ultimately defensive, the junior officers who led the mutiny refused to carry out the instructions of the government to enforce the decree. After a prolonged negotiation, doubtless spurred on, in part, by the imminent and visible threat of Venezuelan and US warships on the horizon, the rebels surrendered, the government re-established its authority and the active, offensive phase of the "February Revolution" appeared to have been broken.

Such a profound political sequence, however, thrusting tens of thousands of young people into active political discourse, could not simply end by proclamation. Even as the ink was drying on the soon to be ignored agreement between the senior officers and their subordinates, which ended the mutiny, other decisions were being taken a few miles away in working class districts in the western Port of Spain suburb of St James. Here, in a part of the community renamed by its young unemployed men as "Block Five", an organization, pre-dating the 1970 upsurge, called the Western United Liberation Front (WOLF), had been formed. It was a loose grouping, borrowing its themes from the Black Power slogans and styles that had become pervasive in the city and from longer traditions of intercommunity rivalry, centring on the infamous steelband clashes that often occurred at carnival time. Of particular significance was the fact that many of the members of WOLF were active soldiers who came from St James, though serving in the regiment at Chaguaramas.

It followed, then, that when the popular movement ballooned in February WOLF might prove to be a critical link between the militants in the streets and those who had simultaneously emerged in the barracks. According to Malcolm "Jai" Kernahan, founding and surviving member of NUFF,[7] who lived at least part-time in St James, some soldiers had already begun to prepare for insurrection long before the declaration of the state of emergency:

Malcolm "Jai" Kernahan: Well, we used to cooperate with Raffique [Shah] and Rex [LaSalle][8] through a fella named Jessop. He was a rootsman who used to come on the block and say that Raf and them saying so and so . . . As a matter of fact, in February there was a night when Raf and them was supposed to hand out guns on the different blocks. We were supposed to strike. We wanted a one-strike action because we didn't want no prolonged war, because Trinidad was too small for that. They were supposed to arm all the blocks and we were supposed to move that night. But we came out that night and nothing happened.

Brian Meeks: But did any of the men getting arms know how to use them?

MJK: Yes, a lot of men didn't know how to use them, but we got formal training from the soldiers. Jessop taught us how to shoot. How to operate a SMG [submachine gun], how to operate a SLR [self-loading rifle], plus there were other grass-roots soldiers who were members of our block. We had a block named Block Five in St James. Block Four and Block Five were two militant blocks. We had three soldiers between us and they taught men how to combat and strip them. A lot of soldiers were involved at the block level.[9]

Then, if Kernahan's testimony is to be given weight, when the state of emergency was declared and the soldiers mutinied, not all remained confined to the Chaguaramas peninsula. Others were actively preparing for a more prolonged and coordinated struggle:

This is April. The state of emergency is called and the soldiers rebel. What really happened is that Raf and them seized the ammunition bunker and started to hand out arms. Some of the soldiers took arms and crossed the hill. When the Coast Guard shelled the hill and blocked the road, Raf and them turned back. Some brothers now took arms and climbed over the hill and they were in St Barbs [Belmont] and Jeffers went up in St Barbs and joined them. And they were moving all up in Morvant and all those areas in the country to try and initiate guerrilla warfare. Among them were Lai Leung, Johnson . . . a lot of privates. And Jeffers and them got together and they were moving. They would come on the block and tell us what was going on, that we have to come up . . . we would carry food for them sometime. And then Jeffers came and said "those fellas gave up" and "we will have to go on", you know?[10]

This decision by the de facto leader of Block Five, Brian Jeffers, to 'go on', dating precisely from the moment it was known that the soldiers had surrendered, effectively marks the beginning of the guerrilla movement, though it had yet to take its eventual organizational form or name.

From the very start, however, the key figures in the movement were inspired by an extreme "*foquista*" vision of how to make revolution. The grass-roots brothers of Block Five had grown increasingly wary of the cultural nationalist, middle class leaders of NJAC, who interpreted the struggle as a "black thing". Jeffers, Kernahan and others were moving towards an outlook where they viewed the struggle as one of the poor and working classes against their exploiters. But they were equally suspicious of what they considered as traditional Marxist and Leninist notions of agitation and propaganda. The most effective means to communicate their views to the people, they felt, was the armed action, which in itself vividly illustrated the direction and objectives of the movement. Kernahan again explains:

The working class people in the organization, Brian Jeffers, Clem [Haynes], Madoo, me, related more to Che Guevara, War of the Flea, Regis Debray, the kind of guerrilla warfare, militant thing. Guy Harewood, John Beddoe, Jennifer [Jones] – not Thornhill, because he was on a kind of spiritual thing – Andrea Jacob, they related more to the Marxist classics – *Foundations of Leninism*. But I couldn't relate to that. John Beddoe was saying we have to cool it and build the flats organization to support the organization in the hills. We couldn't see that. We were saying we support Che Guevara. Peace has already been broken. When we raid a police station the people know that this is the revolution and that in itself is propaganda.[11]

Despite the warning from Beddoe and others to consolidate, however, it was this boldly aggressive and militaristic position that dominated in the councils of the movement for the entire time of its existence.

The Sequence of Events

The first act of the yet to be named guerrilla movement, was the shooting of the chief prosecutor in the court martial of the rebel soldiers, Theodore Guerra in 1971.[12] The second, also in early 1971, was the shooting of the Coast Guard commander David Bloom, one of the key figures in the defeat of the rebel initiative in 1970, at his suburban home in Federation Park. The choice of these targets not only illustrated the close link that had existed between the Block Five militants and the soldiers but also the absolute commitment to life or death struggle that prevailed from the very beginning. For them, this was certainly not the traditional carnival masquerade but a no-holds-barred fight for the future of Trinidad and Tobago.

While neither action proved fatal, knowledge as to the perpetrators soon circulated among the militants of Port of Spain and strengthened the credibility of the St James grouping as serious and militant brothers. This caught the attention of a number of NJAC members who had grown dissatisfied with that organization's virtual collapse after the state of emergency and with its increasingly "cultural nationalist" positions. Guy Harewood, who was a leader of the NJAC area committee in Woodbrook, left that organization and joined with Block Five. One Ambrose, then NJAC's "defence minister", in what was evidently a serious case of defection, also joined up, as did the chairman of the NJAC Diego Martin Committee. Ambrose also served to connect the St James group to another cell of disenchanted NJAC members in San Juan. Clearly, as the Block Five leaders began to surmise, the slogan, popular in 1970, that "armed revolution was the only solution" had not only taken root in St James but was now a definite current in the 'movement', certainly in the urban north and perhaps even in the south.

And it was in the south that the first truly coordinated action took place. In late 1971 Jai Kernahan was unhappy with what he considered as the adventurism of the St James militants, where youths would 'lime' on the streets, weapons in hand, in full view of passers-by. He made a tactical retreat to his original home in the southern oil belt in Fyzabad. Here he found in the 'countryside', with its long traditions of trade union militancy, a warm reception for the 'guerrilla line'. A new unit with nine members was soon organized and a camp established in the Fyzabad forest. The first raid by the newly named NUFF was on the Estate Police Station at the Texaco compound in Fyzabad. Six guns and over a thousand rounds of ammunition were taken, and Trinidad woke up on 31 May 1972 to the possibility that there was an active guerrilla movement on its soil. From then until October 1973, the movement engaged in a series of offensives and encounters with the armed forces of the state. Only some of the most significant of these offensives can be highlighted here:

- 1 June 1972: Armed NUFF members rob the Barclays' Bank at UWI St Augustine of some $40,000.[13]
- 1 July 1972: Armed guerrillas, returning in a van from the northern range to the city, encounter a police blockade near Arima. In the first serious battle with the police, Hillary Valentine is killed and three policemen shot. Valentine is later given a large, enthusiastic, martyr's funeral in Black Power–style, with the four thousand-odd mourners dressed in red.[14]
- 22 February 1973: The Barclays' Bank on Tragerete Road in Port of Spain is robbed of some TT$127,000. Later that day, on a tip-off, police ambush and kill three NUFF members – John Beddoe, Mervyn Belgrave and Ulric Gransaul – in a safe house in Trou Macaque, Laventille.[15] Beddoe's death, in particular, is a major blow to the movement as he is one of the people with genuine organizational capability and the leading advocate of the line for greater propaganda, education and consolidation.
- 1 June 1973: The TT$2.2 million Textel Earth Station on the north coast, linking Trinidad and Tobago's telecommunication facilities with the world is attacked by NUFF militants and four policemen shot.[16]
- 6 August 1973: In what is the high point of the movement from a tactical perspective, both the southern and northern units of NUFF are able to coordinate and execute operations within days of each other. The first is a successful attack on the police station at the Trinidad-Tesoro Oil Company in the south and the second is the highly successful attack on 9 August on the Matelot Police Station on the north coast, where the police had to flee into the night.[17] After this raid, the northern contingent, though still only equipped with shotguns and revolvers, had twice as many weapons as men to carry them.

- 13 September 1973: This is the date of the Caura encounter, recalled in the narratives at the beginning of this chapter. Earlier on 11 August, the prime minister, alarmed at the new level of coordination among the guerrillas, had recalled a number of ministers who had been on missions overseas and instructed the regiment to formally join the police force in the manhunt. By then, the rewards on the heads of the leading and known guerrillas, including Guy Harewood, Brian Jeffers and Andrea Jacob, is $50,000, a princely sum at the time. This carrot, together with the increasingly repressive measures undertaken by the police to force suspects to reveal information, was beginning to yield results. The first portent of a new situation occurred on 28 August when the northern group was completely surprised at its camp in Valencia. One policeman is shot and all the guerrillas managed to escape with only minor injuries, but it is an indication that Superintendent Randolph Burroughs and his special squad have made important intelligence breakthroughs. This is confirmed in the 13 September raid when Beverly Jones and Kenneth Tenia are killed. It signals the beginning of the end. Prior to this, despite the regular attrition rate of militants in various clashes with the police, NUFF, for the most part, still had the initiative. After Caura, even with the occasional robbery or reprisal against informers, the organization is largely on the defensive, hunted and harried.

The last of the leading militants, Clem Haynes, would not be held until November 1974, as he tried to escape by jumping from the upstairs window of a house in Laventille; but the movement is effectively broken after Guy Harewood, its political chief, is killed on 17 October 1973. Terrence Thornhill, Harewood's friend from childhood, describes his last moments:

We stayed in this house in Riverside Road (Curepe) and made arrangements for someone to pick us up that night with the foodstuff. The foodstuff came and we were still waiting for that person to come with the car but no one came. On the third day waiting, I saw a white VW van making a round. My gun was under the mattress. There were two men in the house together with Guy and myself. One was the owner and one a friend. I saw the friend put his hand up in the doorway and look with surprise. Then someone shouted "Don't move!" Guy ran for his gun; I went through the window. Guns started to bark. Someone said, "Look! One dey!" I jumped in the river, shots all around me, water splashing, bullets. God just didn't have them to hit me. Then someone said: "Look a next one!" Guy dived in the river. I went north, he went south. I came up on the other side in some thick undergrowth. Then I heard when they killed Guy. I heard the two shots go through the body. I heard when they started to rejoice. I heard when they said, "We get one! Is Guy Harewood!" They knew the names. They knew the two guns. Burroughs said, "What gun does he have?" So after that soldiers came right in front where I was and secure the whole place.[18]

The NUFF is a novel and important development in modern, anglophone Caribbean politics. In the wake of the Grenadian revolution and its subsequent debacle, of the rise and fall of democratic socialism in Jamaica, of the collapse of Cuba's economy (and, therefore, its questionable viability as a model of socialist development), few recall that, in the early seventies, guerrillas sought to overthrow the state and transform Trinidad and Tobago in the interest, purportedly, of the poor and dispossessed. The focus of this chapter is not to present that history in its fullest detail, though that necessarily needs to be done, nor is it fundamentally to pass judgement on the efficacy or, indeed, justification for a guerrilla movement in nominally democratic Trinidad and Tobago one decade after independence. Indeed, one trend of thought, impatient of focusing on marginal movements when the great affairs of state require attention, might wish to dismiss this, in Madisonian fashion, as one of the inevitable factions which emerge in small states with great danger to the survival of democracy.[19]

I disagree with such a position from the perspective that an understanding of what motivated the cadres of NUFF to engage in guerrilla warfare might throw some light on the flawed character of Trinidadian, and Anglo-Caribbean 'democracy'. One of my motivating questions, then, is: What would make a cross-section of fairly ordinary Trinidadians, invariably caricatured in the literature as a "fun-loving" or "eudaemonious",[20] seek to sacrifice family, normality, limb and, ultimately, life for a cause that was, at best, ill defined and for a goal that was always uncertain?

The truth is that the story of NUFF is very much the story of my generation's coming of age. In my case, I am the son of a Jamaican father and Trinidadian mother who grew up in Jamaica, but did my undergraduate work at the UWI in Trinidad precisely in those three years, 1970–73 when NUFF was on the move. For me, studying in Trinidad was both a homecoming and the source of a more fundamental education than the UWI could ever give. People whom I knew and 'limed' with on the St Augustine campus, such as Carl Peters who worked in the cafeteria, disappeared from sight, only for it to be rumoured that they were fighting 'up in the hills'. This was a time of heightened political debate and great tension. My closest friends, such as Russell "Slim" Andalcio who had been detained in 1970, David Abdullah and Gerry Kangalee who both went on to become senior officials in the powerful Oilfield Workers' Trade Union (OWTU), were all moving from a vague Black Power position to a Marxism strongly influenced by Mao Tse Tung's thought. I remember taking part in a march organized by UWI students in support of "our black soldiers" – those who had just been declared guilty in the military's court martial. Three months later, a student friend who had 'contacts' in the police force showed me a picture of myself in the demonstration with an arrow pointing at me and a serial number underneath. He said, "Be careful. They have your name." I was not yet eighteen years old. When Guy Harewood was killed, I had just graduated and returned to Jamaica. I wrote a poem, "To a Guy I Knew, but Didn't Meet", which saw Guy's death as mirroring the "Bleached bones of our beached dreams" and echoing the profound sadness and sense of personal loss that I and many others felt at his death. He and the other NUFF militants had chosen a path from which there were few come-backs, and they had paid the supreme price. For the ideal of a better world for the poor and oppressed, Harewood, in particular, had given up a life of relative comfort – his father was a respected academic and his mother an artist – for a life of privation and, finally, death. This inquiry, then, is also a profoundly selfish attempt to interrogate 'our' generation and to ask the question Valentino asks at the beginning of this chapter as to whether Guy, Beverly, Brian Jeffers and the others died for a "hopeless cause".

The second motivation for writing stems from a somewhat obscure but heated debate between myself and a Barbadian colleague, Hilbourne Watson, over methodological issues in Marxism and the question of agency. I had written a critique of C.L.R. James' seminal study of the Haitian Revolution, *The Black Jacobins*,[21] in which it was argued that, while James was sensitive to the great importance of Toussaint L'Ouverture's personality in the making of the Haitian Revolution, there were still unresolved problems in his analysis. Although James had made a brilliant, materialist case for the conditions that brought the French colony of St Domingue to the brink of revolution, his recognition of Toussaint's overarching role in the military and diplomatic victories of the revolting slaves, raised psychosocial issues that did not fit neatly with the earlier analysis.

Watson took this critique as an announcement of my "break with Marxism and . . . a transition into what seems like an unspecified postmodernism".[22] In a sustained broadside, he argued, *inter alia,* that my "genuflection to a postmodernist bias" reinforced "bourgeois modernism as hegemony" and was "a closure and conservative attack on the future".[23] Needless to say, this was not my own conclusion as to the purpose of the essay. The conscious aim was to interrogate what was thought to be a mechanical approach to Marxism that prevailed in much of the anglophone Caribbean in the 1970s and that I think contributed, in no small part, to the tragic collapse of the Grenada revolution in 1983.[24] James' *Black Jacobins* – the polar opposite in theoretical spirit to the dominant approaches of that era – was used in order to best illustrate the problem. For even James, it is argued, had not fully confronted the tension between agency and conjuncture in his insightful study. Far from abandoning the critical analytical tools forged in classical Marxism, the essay sought to find an approach to historical analysis that would only abandon the smug certainty of a *particular* Marxism.[25]

The purpose of this chapter, then, at least in part, is to continue that search – spurred on by Watson's somewhat strident comments – for a style and approach to historical analysis sensitive to both materialist conjuncture and human intervention and, also, the extent to which the two artificial categories fold into each other.

Narratives of Commitment and the Question of Capacity

In any attempt to depart from a politics of certainty towards an approach based on historical trajectories, the question of 'capacity', or the ability of social forces to take advantage of conjunctural windows, seems to be central. The problem can be stated as this: assume that the contradictions between the forces and relations of production have ripened, the economy is stagnating and people are being laid off; it is evident to many that capitalism is bankrupt and there is even a growing conventional wisdom that revolt will change things for the better. The relevant question here is whether, even in these optimal conditions for revolution, men and women will rebel. According to a debate popularized by Jon Elster and other "Rational Choice Marxists", if people are, as they claim, "rational egoists", there is a strong case that they will not revolt:

Clearly, whatever anyone else does, it is in my interest to abstain. If all others engage in collective action, I can get the freerider benefit by abstaining, and if everyone else abstains I can avoid the loss from unilateralism by abstaining too. Since the reasoning applies to each agent . . . all will decide to abstain and no collective action will be forthcoming.[26]

But evidently, and quite often, people do rebel and often in circumstances in which very few benefits for our "egoistic rational maximizers" are apparent. The first explanation for this, then, can be taken by an approach that searches for hidden factors to explain revolt while retaining fealty to the central construct that individuals are, indeed, rational egoists. The second tack – more 'traditionally' Marxist – would oppose the notion of egoism as being some universal state of mind and recognize it as a historic construct of the liberal bourgeoisie. The act of revolt, then, with its evident risk-taking, can be seen as a harbinger of the new 'social personality' that will consolidate once new social relations are in place.

Rather than engage in a philosophical debate between these two counter-poised positions, it might be useful in the closing part of this chapter to utilize the experience of NUFF more to open up the debate in the form of an agenda of topics for further research on this limited, though significant, dimension of capacity than to arrive at conclusions. A number of thinkers have explored, through different disciplines and for different projects, the question as to what leads people to revolt. Scanning the literature in a cursory and highly selective manner, we might suggest five not necessarily exclusive approaches:

1. *Hegemony and its Offshoots:* Starting with Gramsci,[27] this approach argues that people derive the capacity to revolt through a process of ideological transformation in which classes possessing 'contradictory consciousness' (as opposed to *false* consciousness) are eventually won over to a position of 'class consciousness'. From this new perspective, they become aware of their interests as an exploited class in opposition to their exploiters and this prepares them for rebellion. Implicit in this approach is the requirement of some shift in awareness or understanding that is, at least in part, derived from without, because the class by itself is incapable of making the critical transition to genuine class consciousness.

2. *Inherent Resistance:* At least one effective, if itself flawed, critique of hegemony is presented by James Scott,[28] who suggests a persistent, subversive resistance to domination in the hearts and minds of the dominated,

transcending historical epochs. Thus, from such a perspective, people know who their 'dominators' are and in the course of daily life constantly resist them. That resistance may take the form of revolt, when the appropriate conditions emerge, but the need for 'consciousness bearers' from without is not only unnecessary but perhaps even damaging to the hidden agenda of the 'dominated'. The somewhat ahistorical character of Scott's framework, with its failure to explore the real differences, say, between slavery and the contemporary period, is one of its weaknesses. Equally, its tendency to see revolt in every act, and therefore to lose analytical focus on the real, substantial differences between periods of calm and periods of rebellion, is another failure in a perspective which nonetheless sheds new light on the inherent necessity of intellectual hierarchies in revolutionary movements.

3. *Tactical Power:* From a different angle, and with different emphases, the notion of 'tactical power' is advanced by a school of thought beginning with Barrington Moore in *Social Origins of Dictatorship and Democracy* and Eric Wolf in *Peasant Wars of the Twentieth Century.*[29] The argument, based on empirical assessments of peasant rebellions, focuses not so much on the ideas people possess – as it assumes that people are already deeply disgruntled – as it does on the material capability to resist. The poorest peasants should, by virtue of their abject poverty, have the most to gain from rebellion, the argument goes. However, revolt usually comes from the middle peasant who possesses 'tactical power' or the effective material base and autonomy to resist. This is an interesting dimension, in that it might be considered complementary to either hegemony or Scott's notion of a hidden text of resistance. People may be dissatisfied, they may be conscious of their 'true' interests and even aware as to how to attain them, but one needs to consider the dimension of the available resources and their confidence that these resources are capable of sustaining them in the attenuated struggle to dislodge those 'above'. Of course, Moore and others restrict this argument to the peasantry, but it can be laterally applied to other classes engaged in rebellion with equal effect.

4. *The Perceived Weakness of the State:* This is an argument fine tuned by Theda Skocpol, Timothy Wickham-Crowley and others, though its origins are probably to be found in the work of Charles Tilley.[30] Essentially, the weakening of the state – through war, the rapacious activities of

"mafiacracies",[31] and the like – gives encouragement to social alliances who already have their own agenda of revolt generated by a previous history of oppression. Therefore, part of the reason why people rebel is to be located in the availability of a window of opportunity that gives them, de facto, greater capacity than they possessed before. This also is not an alternative to the hegemony/hidden resistance duo but can be seen as an incremental and important explanatory factor.

5. *Revolt as Only Rational Option:* This approach, operating within a broad 'rational choice' framework, argues that what appears to be irrational in the context, say, of the 'freerider' proposal may ultimately be explained within the notion of individuals as 'rational egoists'. Looking at what he considers instances of "persistent insurgencies" in Latin America, Jeff Goodwin argues effectively that, despite the tremendous privation and sacrifice involved in committing oneself to rebellions that continue for years without any sign of victory, people join them and stay with them because the military closes off avenues for a peaceful life.[32] Thus state terror is a fact of life and the chances of survival become greater if one is a combatant rather than a disinterested civilian. Without necessarily caving in to the obvious philosophical implications, it is evident that Goodwin's argument provides a powerful tool for comparative analysis, which may complement at times, but also contradict, ideological and 'material capacity' attempts to explain this phenomenon.

While there are substantial differences in the respective frames, surprisingly, there are also recurring themes that may contribute to a general hypothetical framework. Among them, we can suggest, first, that apparent calm, the absence of overt rebellion, does not mean for all persons an acceptance of the status quo. Undoubtedly, this may be the case for some, but for others it may simply be a tactical approach, biding the time when open insurrection becomes a feasible option. Second, revolt is in part determined by the perceived weakness of the powers that be. The latter phrase is used to distinguish it from the state – a local phenomenon – and to include the strength and availability of external repressive forces in the equation. Third, revolt gathers momentum to the extent that the powers that be shut down the options for peaceful alternatives through widespread acts of repression against the entire class and not just the immediate, recalcitrant offenders. Fourth, revolt is facilitated to the extent that there is an intersection of factors, both local and international. Economic stasis is accompanied by a rising world view justifying and explaining why revolt is necessary; individuals are reinforced and given strength by their peers; local groups hear their own sentiments echoed in far flung communities, and what is at first only radical fringe opinion becomes gospel; ultimately, the tributaries join forces and there is a deluge.

Through the narratives of three former members of NUFF, focusing on their backgrounds and the routes that led them to an insurrectionary form of politics, some of these themes can be explored and other potentially fruitful areas for further research proposed.

Malcolm "Jai" Kernahan's Story

Brian Meeks: Tell me a little bit about yourself. Where are you from? How would you describe yourself?

Malcolm "Jai" Kernahan: Well, my father was an oil worker, production department. We used to live in company quarters . . . near to Fyzabad. In 1953 when I was about four to five years old, he got blind and the company throw we out the house. Well, from that we become dirt poor, you know, because he had spent some money to buy some land and then he come and got blind. While working, some steel thing damage the eye and he lost his sight. He couldn't work again; they didn't need his service, so they told him to leave the house in a month's time. Well, we just become poor after that, you know. He went to one and two obeah man to try and get back his sight – you know the masses.

BM: How many of you were in the family?

MJK: Three boys. Yeah, well, then we started to live by family. We had to go by an uncle and live a little time. But one of the agreements we had come to with the oil company is that when we reach of age, the children would get work in the oilfield. So we all knew that when we were of age we would get work in the oilfield. But my father was a really militant oil worker. I remember when I was a little fella they used to tell me how they used to beat people who used to break the strike – scabs, no? – So I never got work in the oilfields.

BM: So, what did they tell you?

MJK: Well, they just pushed me around, you know? "Come back so and so, come back so and so . . ." I get to hate the oil company and the white people and t'ing in them times, you know, so it was easy for me to fall into the Black Power movement when that time came around. In 1967 . . . they had a consciousness movement was building . . . a lot of progressive literature started to find its way in Trinidad. Eldridge Cleaver's *Soul on Ice,* Walter Rodney's *Groundings With my Brothers,* a lot of progressive literature, and I started to read books. As a matter of fact, I have been in the struggle since '67.

BM: What happened in '67?

MJK: Well, I always used to look at the Oilfield Workers' Trade Union as a kind of militant organization. I admired George Weekes. Well, they had a fella by the name of Clive . . . who went to Cuba and he came back and said, "the only solution was armed revolution". I found that the concept was nice and romantic and I get to like it, you know? . . . Well, my mother was from St James. Her family was involved in the gang warfare, the rioting business, and my cousins and them were gang warfare people.

BM: Were you ever involved in gang warfare?

MJK: No. I was never involved. All my cousins, my brother, were involved. As a matter of fact, where we used to call home in St James – my grandmother's house – everybody used to riot except me. I didn't have the belly for it and I couldn't understand it, so I never get involved in the gang warfare.

BM: In those days the riots involved mainly cutlasses, not guns?

MJK: No, not gun, cutlass. One and two people made home-made bombs, but it was cutlass and razor; razor in the dancehall and you slash a man, and iron bolt. But I didn't get involved in that. And then '69 came around and St James had an organization named WOLF – Western United Liberation Front – that was some soldiers . . . during this time too a dance troupe . . . came from Uganda and they had their hair in an Afro with a part, and from that everyone used to wear dashikis and part their hair in a certain style. And a kind a consciousness started to come along, a kinda blackness; and then we came and got involved with NJAC, but I was never a member of NJAC.

BM: Why?

MJK: I thought they were middle class. Talking about the dashiki and sandal . . . culturally, I couldn't deal with them.

BM: But didn't a lot of grass-roots youths get involved with NJAC?

MJK: As far as the "block man" was concerned, NJAC was middle class. Them fellas wasn't ready. They were only talking . . . But we still supported the movement. We marched with them, you know? And then from 1969 to 1970 we started to get *Peking Review* on the block and Errol Balfour he came around and started to talk about Marxism, and suddenly we started to see the struggle in terms of class. We still used to attend all NJAC demonstrations, but we saw the struggle in that early period in terms of class. Brian Jeffers who was a friend from St James – we used to play pan together in Tripoli – he became active in WOLF with the soldiers. He wasn't a big theoretician; he didn't like to read; he was mixed – African, Spanish and Indian. He said he didn't like the Black Power programme, he was fighting for a humanitarian cause. He influenced me a lot in the struggle because he was a very brave, daring fella. By 1970 he had become involved with the soldiers. When they mutinied in '70, he was with them.

BM: Let me reverse a bit. Eric Williams: What was your attitude to "The Doctor"? How did it develop?

MJK: Well, Williams as an individual? I never really hated Williams. I grew up in a PNM family. My mother was PNM. My grandmother was PNM.

BM: But how did you come to terms with this new reality? The demonstrations in the streets are for Black Power, but they are also against Williams.

MJK: Well, there was a perception, and I figure I shared that view too, that a part of Eric Williams was kind of progressive, but the rest of him was a waste of time and if he was siding with them, then you would have to get rid of him too. But the real animosity wasn't in me because of that PNM upbringing.

BM: So this is 1970, you expect weapons to be delivered on the block, but none arrive. But during those months (February–April) what was happening on your block in St James?

MJK: The St James Block attacked the police station with Molotov cocktails. I think about half of it got scorched and they shot behind us and we had to retreat.

BM: This was before or after Basil Davis' death?

MJK: This was after the funeral, after things intensified. The police used to look for sympathizers of the movement. Once you had an Afro, a dungaree jeans and a black jersey, you would get licks. They would beat you, trim you and kick you up. So the pressure was very intense.

BM: Was there any element in the police force which was sympathetic, or did it appear that the entire police force was opposed to the youths on the block?

MJK: They were united against the youth. And they had a special squad, you know, a political squad. Burroughs had a squad of men who used to raid the block.

BM: I want to come back to what was going on in your mind. That transition is a serious one, to decide to take up arms and fight the government. How easy was that decision?

MJK: . . . My life was hard, real tough. So I say that I would rather die than live under the system. I don't want to live under the system anymore. Because you getting turned back anywhere you go to look for jobs; your name not recognized; you is nobody; you ain't living nowhere; you poor. So I say is better you dead for something. So I make up my mind to fight. If death come, no big thing. And I think Brian Jeffers had that same kind of thinking too.

BM: So it wasn't a hard decision?

MJK: No, it wasn't a hard decision at all. As a matter of fact, I feel I was waiting for that. I was living and only waiting for that.

BM: Looking back more than twenty years later, do you think that what you did was wrong?

MJK: To be honest, based on the vibes we had taken at that time, we couldn't do anything else. I believe that if I hadn't picked up a gun and gone to armed struggle I would be a mad man or a vagrant. I couldn't fit into nothing in the society . . . I think that the 1970 Revolution saved me.[33]

Terrence Thornhill's Story

Brian Meeks: Tell me a little bit about yourself.

Terrence Thornhill: I was born July 27, 1949 in Glencoe. It was a residential area in a middle class setting . . . My father was one of the first black men to get degrees at universities in England along with Eric Williams. His was in English at Cambridge. Both parents were teachers. My father was a head teacher and my mother a common-entrance teacher. It was a middle class family. As far as I can remember, we always had a car, the house had hot and cold water. I went to Tranquility Primary School and later to Queen's Royal College.

BM: How did you become involved with the 'Movement'?

TT: I did track and field in school and went to the US in 1969 on a track scholarship to study at the Catholic University in Washington, DC. While there, seeing the way how black people were treated, I went through some changes in my life. When I left here, I wasn't into black consciousness, just parties, track and field and football. But then I started to see the sufferings of black people and identified with them. One day I had a conversation with the (black) captain of the track team. We started to talk about the Lord, Jesus Christ, how he was real and what they did to him; how he went about trying to help and the suffering he experienced. And I was able to link His suffering to that of black people and see where the system always oppresses those who are good. That was November 23, 1970 and that day it came to me very strongly that my life wouldn't be just to continue in school like this, but to search for that truth which Jesus brought to mankind and help somebody in the way of life . . . By May 1971, my teachers were asking me if I was still in their class. But I did scrape through to complete two years of university. After that, a roommate and myself decided to go to India to find the truth.

I worked in the States for a month, saved all my money, came back to Trinidad and worked for a few months. At the end of 1971, we left on a trip to the Himalayas. We had a vision of going to the Himalayas, meeting a guru and coming back with long, grey beards, full of wisdom to give mankind.

When I returned to Trinidad in June 1971, it was under a state of emergency. Guy Harewood was my good friend from primary school days. When I came back, he was fully involved with NJAC. In those days, we had Mao's *Little Red Book.* One of his sayings was that "the political man is the real man". So as far as Guy and a few others were concerned, NJAC was only talking, theorizing, but not willing to put their life on the line for the cause in the way that we thought it should be, in terms of guerrilla warfare. So Guy and them were now branching off from NJAC, and just a little group talking among themselves. So I came back and met that. I started to go around with them. I had access to cars and so I used to go and purchase weapons with them, because the cars that I had would be 'cool'. So I got involved, though I used to tell them, this set of revolution thing is not me, because I am for Jesus, which is peace. But then I listened to them, noted their sincerity and I was on a search for truth also. And there were slogans on the walls, like "armed revolution is the only solution" and "the voice of the people is the voice of God", and it was slowly coming to me that maybe armed revolution is the way. I went back to the Bible because my whole experience is Bible oriented and every time I opened it I would read where Moses saw the Egyptians advantaging the Hebrews and he took a sword and killed an Egyptian. So my interpretation was that maybe we should take up the gun, because the people are being advantaged.

So that was between June 1971 and October. In late October, I left for my trip and the war in Bangladesh was on. We got the motorcycles in Germany, went through Germany, Austria, Yugoslavia, going down to the border with Turkey, me and my roommate (he was white American). At the Turkish border we were told that it was impossible to go through. There was turbulence in Turkey and they told us that if two strangers attempted to ride through with two BMW bikes they would kill us and take the bikes. So we decided to turn back.

When I left Trinidad, Guy had taken me to the airport. When I came back in December 1971, he was wanted by the police. He was my best friend. Here he was wanted and I got to realize that a small group of men were in the hills. I went to see them, talked to them and then I lent myself fully to the cause. I was what you could call a "cool man". I wasn't wanted, wasn't known by the authorities, so I could do anything, get medication, foodstuff, whatever.[34]

Clem Haynes' Story

Brian Meeks: Tell me a little bit about yourself.

Clem Haynes: I was born in East Dry River, Laventille, Port of Spain, in 1952. I came from a working class family. My father died when I was one. My mom is still alive, but not too well for the last couple days. She used to do odds and ends. She worked for sometime in the grapefruit factory, Citrus Growers' Association, and sometimes ironed for people, to raise five of us, three boys and two girls. It was tough seeing what she had to go through. I went to the John Donaldson Technical Institute and did a course in welding. I didn't finish secondary school. And then I started working at SPCK [Society for Promoting Christian Knowledge] (Christian) Bookshop, some time in 1969. I remember in that year, 1969, they had the bus strike where a lot of workers were beaten and arrested. That was something that triggered my consciousness as to how workers making just demands, peaceful demonstrations . . . were met with this action by the state.

BM: Were you involved?

CH: No. Then, in 1970, I wasn't even active, although I went to a couple of the demonstrations. I remember my brother Clyde, he used to come home with a couple of the pamphlets from NJAC and read it to us. At that time I was living with my aunt and eleven cousins in Sea Lots. Because of the difficult time my mom was going through, she sent me there to help ease the burden. So he used to read the literature and I started thinking more in a militant way.

BM: What was Clyde doing?

CH: At that time he was a moulder, making aluminium pots and coal pots. It was a small company in Sea Lots that exported to Grenada and St Vincent . . . I didn't see the killing of Basil Davis, but hearing about it, it raised my emotion as to how come is only one set of people facing this kind of thing? It was a kind of gradual build up. I would say it started from very small, watching my mom toil.

BM: So, the state of emergency is declared in April. What is happening to you?

CH: I was just around, not active. I was sympathetic with the rebel soldiers, because I saw it as an act in favour of the people, because they didn't want to come to Port of Spain to carry out the state's orders.

BM: How did you come to join NUFF?

CH: In 1972, I remember observing my brother's movements. I saw a couple people checking him and I decided he was in some kind of underground movement, some militant thing . . . One day, a Friday afternoon, he came from work. I was doing my practical course at John Donaldson . . . so that Friday he was sitting by himself reading a paper and I said, "Clyde, I want to join you all." He said, "You know what it is about?" I said, "I have a good idea, but as time go on I might get to know better." So he saw my interest and started telling me. I had been hearing of men in the hills, but something about it, I was telling myself is not bandits. I knew these men were some kind of militants or revolutionaries . . . The first person he introduced me to was John Beddoe, he was on the run, though the name NUFF wasn't given to the organization yet. He had been shot in the eye. He came down to get medication. There was a doctor who was sympathetic to the cause and we used to check him.

BM: You are a young man going to John Donaldson. Your career and future look open. This thing has the possibility of death, injury and jail. Did it ever cross your mind not to become involved?

CH: No, not really. When I made the decision to become part of it, I knew what was involved in and that I might end up going to prison and getting killed. But I think that once a person has a conviction, once they know what they are about, the idea of death comes easy. You just look towards that day of final victory.

BM: After you were captured and convicted, you spent eight years in prison. Do you have any regrets?

CH: No. My only regret is that we didn't succeed. To struggle against injustice and oppression is a right. It is a duty of the oppressed people. And it is just that I have known that the people in order for the struggle to succeed must be actively involved. I am still anti-imperialist and I think more so now than ever. I still hold my revolutionary views, which I hope to pass on to my daughter who is nine. So, in reflecting, I think I have strengthened my mind and conviction. But I would not get involved without the support of the masses.[35]

Kernahan's deep alienation from a society that rejected his father and repeatedly rejected him, leading to his almost seamless transition to guerrilla fighter against that system; Thornhill's fantastic odyssey of thought and movement from the United States to Trinidad, his aborted rendezvous with a guru in the Himalayas, and his eventual commitment to the cause, through friendship and an intellectualization of the Bible; and Haynes' almost accidental, pedestrian transition from skilled worker in training to guerrilla cadre, at least partly through admiration of his brother: Can these very distinct, individual narratives be woven together in a credible manner? The following conclusions, drawing liberally on the five broad schools of analysis mentioned above, can be advanced.

On the 'blocks' of Port of Spain and in other working class communities, such as Fyzabad in the south, tightly knit groups of young male 'limers' – usually casually employed or without work – had elaborated a politics of resistance to society and its status quo long before the 1970 Revolution. This subculture[36] of violence and territorial warfare, directed horizontally against rival communities, is captured eloquently in Earl Lovelace's classic novel about life in the Port of Spain working class community of Laventille, *The Dragon Can't Dance*. Philo the calypsonian has finally made it in his profession, moves into the middle class community of Diego Martin, but he wishes to keep his contacts with his friends on the hill. Fisheye, the leader of the limers, is adamantly opposed to Philo coming in to the community to 'show off' his new found wealth. The dilemma lies with Aldrick, who is Philo's friend but whose loyalty is torn between this friendship and the deeper fraternity that exists on the corner:

Indeed, Aldrick understood Fisheye's position. At the corner, power lay not so much in the might of the small company as in their steadfast pose of rebellion, in their rejection of the ordinary world, its rewards and promises. How could Philo with his flashy clothes and his car and his women, all gained in the service of that other world against which they were rebelling, be their friend? Yet, Philo was a friend. Aldrick thought to try to explain it, to defend Philo as a friend should, but he didn't know how to explain it. He didn't know. And so he began even then to console himself with the thought that Philo had chosen his success . . . If it were a burden now, Aldrick felt that Philo now was the one to bear it for himself.

"I don't want him on this Hill," Fisheye said.[37]

Prior to 1970, this transcript of resistance remained fragmentary and contradictory. At the political level, this was most evident, as captured in Kernahan's narrative, in the favourable attitude towards Eric Williams as opposed to that which existed towards other members of his government and 'important' people in the society. Thus Valentino, among the most overtly political calypsonians and keenly attuned to the popular movement, was still singing his "No Revolution" as late as 1971 to "The Doctor", with an apologetic criticism of his policies and an assertion that the 'movement' in intent, was not revolutionary:

Well when I heard you address the nation
I knew what was your intention
But some of the powers you exercise
Unfortunately I must criticise
We don't want them trigger happy police
We only wanted to demonstrate in peace
Yet my people was held and charged for sedition
We was marching for equality, Black unity and Black dignity
Dr Williams no, we didn't want no revolution.[38]

But two years later, as Williams' credibility plunged in many of his former strongholds, as police repression of the radical movement increased and as NUFF's activity approached its apogee, Valentino, tracking a certain mood, had shifted to this uncompromising refrain in "Liberation":

Now I quite agree that right now in this country
That my life eh worth 50 cents
Because some SLR bullet could catch me
And put me clean out of existence
You have authority to use your trigger
And you're getting away with murder
But like you're blind Mr Policeman
This is a family affair as if you don't know
Check out your mind try and understand
Is your own Black people you treating so
But if I see the man, I'll do the best I can
To make him understand for Afro-Indian
Be he Coast Guard, Regiment or Policeman
I'll die for my people's liberation.[39]

In this context, the mass movement of 1970 did a number of things simultaneously. First, it broke the belief in Williams as popular hero and thus removed the last integument that had prevented rebellion from taking a vertical course. Second, in massive demonstrations, such as that for Basil Davis' funeral, it gave the young, radicalized marchers a sense of their own collective strength and a feeling of invincibility that could not exist so long as different 'blocks' were isolated and hostile. Third, the brutality of the police against the mobilized population served, in a manner not dissimilar to that suggested by Goodwin, to radicalize the inner-city young people who faced the brunt of the violence, although this phenomenon was not nationwide. Fourth, the state of emergency, even as it laid bare the tactical and organizational weaknesses of the movement, which had virtually folded in the days following its announcement, also revealed, in the army rebellion, the weakness and fragility of the state. The integrity of the military had been breached and belief in its monolithic and invincible character could not easily be restored. Fifth, these factors were underwritten by what has elsewhere been referred to as a "cumulative and available ideological context",[40] but which can perhaps also be called the Trinidadian interpretation of the revolutionary spirit of 1968.[41] In summary, this perspective emerged out of a series of intersecting events, including the continued and effective resistance of the Vietnamese to the US forces, exemplified in the 1968 Tet Offensive and the concomitant acceleration of the peace movement in the United States; the intensification of the national liberation struggle in the Portuguese colonies; the 'consolidation' of the Cuban

Revolution in a period of stable world prices for sugar; and most critically, the upsurge in the Black Power movement in the United States. In a sense, these factors came together to 'overdetermine' a specifically Trinidadian context in which revolution moved from being an obscure pipe dream to a tangible reality.

The revolution also took the form of what can be coined a 'generational imperative' in which being a part of the movement, in however peripheral a sense, began to carry with it a certain élan and acted like a vortex, sucking in the uncommitted, as with Clem Haynes and his brother Clyde, drawing in middle class youngsters with comfortable futures laid out before them, and leading even religious idealists such as Thornhill to rethink and reinterpret their beliefs in light of the new imperatives. NUFF, from this perspective, was very much a product of those times and yet apart from them. It was a vanguard organization, and it adopted wholesale some of the most elitist notions of the role of the revolutionary leadership sifted through Guevarist and Debrayist concepts of the *foco*. NUFF adopted all the features of a certain Marxism of the mid to late twentieth century, in which the prevailing notion was that revolution was imminent and only required the intervention of brave men guiding the arrow of history to its target. And it was this abstraction and disconnectedness from the real mood of the society that contributed significantly to the isolation and rapid decimation of the organization.

At the same time, NUFF was also profoundly different. Far more than NJAC, with its university beginnings, it was an organization of the grass roots. People such as Harewood, Thornhill and Beddoe, although they played important roles, were not the heart and soul of the movement. The real motivations of NUFF lay in the absolute alienation and disconnection from 'official' society, which Kernahan describes in sketching his own life, which Jeffers, in his military boldness and fearlessness, represented. This duality needs to be understood if NUFF is to be appreciated as not simply a fringe element but a representation of the deep hostilities that dwell beneath the surface of Trinidad.

It is useful here to also compare and contrast NUFF with the Henry events of an earlier time and different place. The ideological profiles of both NUFF and the Henry movement possessed, at their core, critical readings of race and revolution. These emerged out of an intense process of grass-roots philosophizing; though it is true to say that NUFF's development, a decade later and in the specific moment in Trinidadian politics, was far more influenced by

Marxism. What they shared in common was a sense of direct action, an almost reflexive view of revolution as a purge. NUFF developed in a revolutionary conjuncture that was both national and international in scope. Henry's rebellion took place at a time when, despite the proximity to the Cuban Revolution, neither national nor international conditions existed for successful insurrection. Both failed, yet NUFF, in a favourable window and with the relative fluidity of the Trinidadian matrix, might have conceivably, with different tactics, succeeded.

All the reasons for its failure cannot be pursued in this chapter, though it is useful to recall that even if, somehow, adequate forces had accumulated and power taken, on the signal that the regiment had mutinied in Chaguaramas, both the US and Venezuelan navies set sail for Trinidad.[42] Nevertheless, while acknowledging this overarching geopolitical reality, it might still be useful to focus on the specifics of the Trinidadian moment and make the following proposals: there is a strong argument that can be advanced that the state of emergency did not break the momentum of the movement but simply radicalized it. The widespread resistance to the government's 1971 Public Order Bill, leading to its tactical withdrawal; the massive boycott of the 1971 elections where Williams, at the nadir of his popularity, offered his resignation; the growing radicalization among high school students and, far more importantly, the organized working class, which eventually took the form of the United Labour Front (ULF) and did not crest until 1975;[43] and last but not least, the very decision of hundreds to commit themselves to a radical guerrilla organization, these elements all suggest that popular resistance and the possibility of radical change was still on the national agenda for the first half of the decade. But this possibility was squandered in part by the failure of a credible, popular organization to emerge after the state of emergency with the prestige that NJAC had possessed before. It also failed due to an atmosphere of police rule and emergency law, which severely dampened the organizational capability of the entire radical movement. Such an atmosphere was, at least in part, precipitated by NUFF itself and contributed immensely to its ultimate decimation.

On the one hand, then, NUFF was the architect of its own demise, but the militants of NUFF could also argue, as Kernahan has done, that from the perspective of the 'brothers on the block', the police, in their relentless harassment and pursuit of Black Power supporters and activists, had already broken the peace, at least from the time of the death of Basil Davis, and for them, the only feasible alternative was to fight back.

Revolutions and revolts in the mid to late twentieth century cannot be explained without an attempt to understand the factors that motivated insurgent individuals to move from relative passivity to open resistance. Other complementary histories need to be written to explain how the conjunctural door is opened. But without a conscious decision to move, no one will walk through that door. In Trinidad and Tobago in the early seventies, young men and women chose to take up arms in a revolutionary opening and were crushed. The wonder, questioning commonly held notions of egoistic rationality, is that they chose to sacrifice their lives for an ill-defined cause with no ironclad guarantees of success.

3

The Harder Dragon:
Resistance in Earl Lovelace's *Dragon Can't Dance* and Michael Thelwell's *Harder They Come*

Some kind of new critical writing in
depth needs to emerge to bridge the
gap between history and art.
  – Wilson Harris

Crossing the Chasm

In a memorable sequence in his essay "History, Fable and Myth in the Caribbean and the Guianas", Wilson Harris discusses the novelty and specificity of the uniquely Caribbean limbo dance. Though it undoubtedly possessed African characteristics, the limbo – in its contracting motion, reminiscent of the cramped limbs of the Middle Passage – was, in form and message, demonstrative of a new and liberating Caribbean ethos:

The limbo dance therefore implies, I believe, a profound art of compensation which seeks to re-play a dismemberment of tribes . . . and to invoke at the same time a curious psychic re-assembly of the parts of the dead god or gods. And that re-assembly which issued from a state of cramp to articulate a new growth – and to point to the necessity of a new kind of drama, novel and poem – is a creative phenomenon of the first importance in the imagination of a people violated by economic fates.[1]

Harris highlights the limbo and, later on, Haitian vodun in order to initiate a devastating broadside against Caribbean historians and, by implication, social scientists. Beginning with J.J. Thomas' celebrated critique of Froude's nineteenth century observations on the region, Harris supports Thomas' trenchant attack on Froude's racially motivated conservatism. But, he contends, does Thomas' critique "overwhelm" Froude, as C.L.R. James suggests in his introduction to the volume? In the end, he proposes that both Froude, the apologist for slavery and colonialism, and Thomas, the opponent, were captives of the same positivist prison that excluded the entire universe of the imagination:

In this connection we must note that both Thomas and Froude shared a common suspicion of Haitian vodun and other primitive manifestations which signified for them a "relapse into obeahism, devil-worship and children-eating". Therefore they consolidated an intellectual censorship of significant vestiges of the subconscious imagination which they needed to explore if they were to begin to apprehend a figurative meaning beyond its real one.[2]

Highlighting Eric Williams and Elsa Goveia, but sparing none of the then new generation of Caribbean historians, he further argues that their emphasis on the devastating effects of imperialism, without a concurrent grasp of the creative potential inherent in the people, left a deeply pessimistic and paralysing image of a West Indies "utterly deprived" and "gutted by exploitation".[3] The answer, he concluded, for the creation of an empowering Caribbean sensibility and ethos, was to bridge the gap between history and art.

The responses to Harris' heartfelt plea – perhaps also in typical Caribbean fashion – have been few. Of significance, however, is Denis Benn's comment in the conclusion of his important study, *The Growth and Development of Political Ideas in the Caribbean: 1774–1983*. Benn recognizes the 'legitimacy' of an intellectual exercise to search for the inner meaning of Caribbean reality, but concludes that the sociopolitical problems of the Caribbean "cannot be resolved simply by an appeal to the artistic imagination".[4] In a revealing elaboration, Benn argues that Harris "overstates the potentialities of the artistic imagination and elevates it almost to the level of scientific principle".[5] He concludes strongly that the discovery of a submerged cultural heritage "may enable us to endow a *de facto* situation of economic dispossession with a figurative meaning, but it cannot alter the reality of that condition and the consequences deriving therefrom".[6]

Benn's spirited, positivist response seems flawed on three related counts, however. First, Harris never suggests a substitution of the creative imagination for the empirical work of the 'historian' but, rather, a convergence of the two. Thus Benn has created a straw man sufficiently and necessarily weak in order to be easily knocked down. Second, he seems to misread the essence of the appeal. Harris is not proposing the invention or excavation of new principles of scientific analysis, which is what is implied in Benn's somewhat Manichaean dichotomy. Rather, what he appeals for is a search for the underpinnings of a Caribbean civilization, the recognition of a self-generated creativity that will allow Caribbean intellectuals to use the tools of scientific inquiry more effectively. Third, Benn, in his knockout punch, therefore misses the potential at the heart of Harris' comments, and that is, posing it as a question, How might the creative imagination, operating, as it were, in a universe of its own, be harnessed to the greater intellectual purpose of understanding and transforming the Caribbean?

Modern Anglo-Caribbean social science has proceeded, over the past four decades, in either wilful opposition to or blissful ignorance of Harris' remarks. Caribbean political scientists, in particular, have operated in the mainstream Anglo-American empirical tradition, or, when they were occasionally on the Left, with a Marxism possessing strong overtones of economic determinism. One searches with some despair through the oeuvres of Carl Stone,[7] Trevor Munroe, Selwyn Ryan, Pat Emmanuel, Neville Duncan and other patriarchs of the discipline to find even the occasional, sustained reference to literature, music or popular culture. The exception, which proves the rule, is, of course, Rex Nettleford, whose work has always operated within an enviable and exemplary multidisciplinary framework.[8] And in more recent times, the atmosphere, certainly at the UWI, has become more receptive to the idea that the creative imagination must have a central place in social analysis. Thus, the Reggae Studies Unit at Mona, the Institute of Cricket at Cave Hill and the Carnival Studies Unit at St Augustine are all part of a welcomed, if belated, recognition of the central importance of the popular arts in society and social analysis. The Department of Government at Mona has introduced courses linking sports and music to Caribbean politics;[9] the new journal *Small Axe* has dedicated itself to an interdisciplinary critique of the Caribbean condition; and a recent issue of the more established and establishment journal *Social and Economic Studies* has been devoted entirely to reggae studies;[10] and, in the wider sphere of Caribbeanists, new studies that seek to read and understand the Caribbean condition through the lens of popular culture are appearing with increasing frequency.[11]

If Harris is to be taken seriously, if it is admitted that there is, indeed, benefit in closing the cleavage between 'history' and the arts, what, approaching the question from the perspective of someone steeped in the arcane disciplines of the empirical social sciences, does this imply? In other words, what can social scientists bring to the study of literature, music, dance, the theatre and plastic arts that is not already being done, with all the advantages of tradition and a certain thoroughness, by the literary and other critics themselves?

I suggest four sources as a process of working toward a methodological approach that can begin to answer this question. The first, somewhat ironically, comes from the quantitative methodologists. Stung by the criticism that mathematical modelling, while often elegantly constructed, serves more as a means of obscuring real social problems, many methodologists are battling with ways to incorporate textual reading and specific social histories alongside broader quantitative generalizations. The simple suggestion for a fusion of the two approaches is made, with great persuasiveness, in this typical quantitative methodology text for historians:

Many pragmatic historians have begun to realize that interesting voices from the past need to be located in larger reference groups in order to understand for whom they speak. Instead of falling for one extreme of numerical zealotry into another extreme of textual fanaticism, researchers would do better to combine these methods judiciously. Reconstructing the past requires imaginative empathy as well as numerical generalization.[12]

The second source lies in the field of literary criticism, where there is intense debate, though for somewhat different reasons. Much postwar criticism of literature from the 'developing countries' has conveniently been captured under the rubric of 'postcolonial studies'. While the term itself has been widely and rightfully criticized, two relevant interventions in those debates serve to focus the issues being tabled here. In a biting polemical essay, Aijaz Ahmad attacked Frederick Jameson and, by extension, the North American literary establishment for their ethnocentricity and cultural myopia. Jameson, whom Ahmad had considered until then his Marxist ideological fellow traveller, had written an essay in which he broadly generalized on the nature of Third World literature as being "necessarily" nationalist.[13] Ahmad argued that not only did such an approach obscure the complexities of the so-called Third World, but also it effectively denied human agency to the people living within it:

As we come to the substance of what Jameson 'describes', I find it significant that First and Second Worlds are defined in terms of their production systems (capitalism and socialism respectively), whereas the third category – the Third World – is defined purely in terms of an 'experience' of externally inserted phenomena. That which is constitutive of human history itself is present in the first two cases, absent in the third case. Ideologically, this classification divides the world between those who make history and those who are mere objects of it.[14]

And, in an equally scathing comment, Barbara Christian, herself West Indian in origin, questioned what she defines as "the race for theory" in the North American literary establishment:

The race for theory, with its linguistic jargon, its emphasis on quoting its prophets, its tendency towards 'Biblical' exegesis, its refusal to even mention specific works of creative writers, far less contemporary ones, its preoccupations with mechanical analyses of language, graphs, algebraic equations, its gross generalisations about culture, has silenced many of us to the extent that some of us feel we can no longer discuss our own literature, while others have developed intense writing blocks and are puzzled by the incomprehensibility of the language set adrift in literary circles.[15]

Literary criticism had, she argued, taken off on a tangent of its own, obscuring and mystifying the literature – itself largely about the real world – on which it was based. The purpose of the critic, Christian proposed, was couched in the question of "for whom are we doing what we are doing when we do literary criticism?"[16] Her answer was that literary criticism was a necessary means of promoting the tenuous, fragile literature of a people out of power. If there was no response to the literary output in the form of accessible and comprehensible criticism, then the writing could disappear, with equal damage to the community from which it derived. Both Ahmad's and Christian's comments point in the direction of a kind of critical analysis that is weary of sweeping, stultifying generalizations, hostile to obscurantism and partisan in favour of the disempowered and dispossessed.

The final source derives from the field of archaeology, in which Miller, Rowlands and Tilley have argued convincingly for an approach to archaeological studies that focuses on domination and resistance as opposed to 'complexity' or, more crudely, 'inequality'. Social complexity, in itself, has been a central feature of modernity. But complexity in the West has invariably meant heterogeneity, which in turn has implied inequality. Inequality, however, as a concept possesses no inherent dynamic:

Inequality, therefore, if perceived superficially as the conditions of rank or status ordering, or as the relative distribution of power in society, is too unsubtle a concept to encompass this diversity of heterogeneity in social forms that might need to be addressed as being 'complex'. For this reason, the more specific concepts of domination and resistance were selected to elaborate a comparative study of all forms of social complexity.[17]

In a useful survey of Marx, Weber, Althusser, Gramsci, Foucault and Bourdieu, among others, the broad conclusion is that real advances have been made towards an understanding of the mechanics of domination and the mechanisms through which the subordinate are occasionally able to overcome the hegemony of their dominators. It is worthwhile noting that Miller et al. – first published a year before James Scott's important text with a similar title – does not focus on a central issue raised by the latter. Scott, questioning the fundamental assumption of both the Weberians and some Gramscians that hegemony implies the acceptance of domination, argues that the subordinate only reveal their open resistance when it is tactically permissible. Resistance, however, is never dormant but takes the form of "hidden transcripts":

Thus, slaves and serfs ordinarily dare not contest the terms of their subordination openly. Behind the scenes though, they are likely to create and defend a social space in which offstage dissent to the official transcript may be voiced . . . the specific forms . . . this social space takes or the specific content of its dissent . . . are as unique as the particular culture and history of the actors in question require.[18]

By focusing on the notion that rebelliousness is an almost necessary concomitant of domination, that it is internally generated rather than derived from outside 'bearers of the truth', that apparent submissiveness, therefore, is a very pragmatic, tactical decision, Scott opens up the space for an exploration of the 'hidden transcripts' of resistance as part of a wider canvas leading to open revolt.[19]

Riffing freely, then, around the suggested triangulation points, a rigorous approach to taking art and literature seriously might benefit from a sensitive merger of the specific reading of texts with quantitative data and higher level generalizations; from a careful sifting of the specific differences between countries and within the same country over time; from a clear recognition of the nature of the audience for whom the critique is being written; and from a focus on the binary opposites of domination and resistance as a central, though not exclusive, motor in the historical process.

Deconstructed even further for the itinerant political scientist with an eye for categories, it is proposed that Harris' charge might be addressed in the form of three searches. First, the textual search for the specific and novel forms of domination and resistance. Second, the search for and identification of cultural practices, philosophical perspectives, world views, and alternative trajectories into modernity that, as in Harris' limbo allegory, explain the world differently and provide shelter in the storm. And third, the search for and location of those rare moments when normal resistance (the hidden transcript) is transcended by open rebellion; for it is at this critical moment of rupture that both the causes of revolt and the reasons for the previous phase of tacit compliance are better understood.[20]

The Harder Dragon

Two texts are used as a tentative experiment to utilize the suggested approach. They are Earl Lovelace's *The Dragon Can't Dance* and Michael Thelwell's *The Harder They Come.*[21] They have been chosen largely for selfish reasons.[22] Both document the trajectory of my generation, those who attained adulthood in the late sixties and early seventies, in the decade after colonialism had ended. Both narrate and document the experiences and struggles of the urban poor, thus providing a relatively easy basis for comparative analysis. Both focus, if sometimes implicitly, on the mundane questions of day-to-day survival and on the larger, if necessarily rarer, question of open rebellion. They also provide a useful counterpoint to each other. Set in Jamaica, with its largely African-descended population, long history of British colonialism and the plantation, and equally long history of resistance from the Maroons and the slaves, *Harder* reveals the Caribbean polar opposite of the cacophonous Trinidad of *Dragon*, with its melting pot of ethnicities, Franco-Hispanic background and short plantation experience. Though little formal research has been done comparing these two societies frontally, they provide fertile ground for comparative research on the Caribbean.[23]

Beyond the obvious similarities, however, the two novels are quite different. Lovelace, following a pattern most evident in Naipaul and Mittelholzer,[24] develops his narrative through a series of richly detailed character sketches in order to trace the lives of the inhabitants of a 'yard' in the imaginary Port of Spain slum of Calvary Hill. There is Miss Cleothilda, the fading, mulatto, former third-placed beauty queen, who uses her fair complexion and shop-keeper status to exercise a tenuous, contested hegemony over some of the yard's residents. There is Miss Olive, the long-suffering mother of seven, who invariably finds herself at the receiving end of Cleothilda's mercurial and manipulative mood swings. There is Fisheye, the "badjohn" from Moruga, who arrives in the city with only his prodigious strength. In a moment of epiphany he recognizes that it is only the poor who fight the poor and launches out on his own path of spatial consolidation and then open, if ignominiously defeated, rebellion. There is Pariag – perhaps the most sympathetic of the characters – the Indian from the country, running from the suffocating safety of his family, who arrives on the Hill searching for modernity and acceptance, neither of which ever come in full measure. Then there is Philo the calypsonian, who wastes his youth courting the unattainable Cleothilda only to surpass her narrowly constructed prestige on his way to success as a singer. On the way, however, despite his wishes, his new found prosperity drives a wedge, which he is never able to overcome, between him and the people of the Hill. And there is Sylvia, Miss Olive's eldest daughter, with all the promise of budding womanhood but with her only perceived resource being her sexuality. She eventually succumbs to the advances of the sleazy and much older landlord's agent, Mr Guy, though, in a twist, Guy becomes a successful politician and offers her his hand in marriage. In the end, there is ambiguity as to whether Sylvia's tactic has brought her success or whether the price has been too high. And finally, there is Aldrick, in many respects the soul of the yard. He is unemployed and, perhaps, unemployable, but each year he finds the wherewithal to make a spectacular dragon costume that rules the streets on carnival day. However, in the end, crippled by his lack of resources, the loss of Sylvia (whom he never had) to Guy and the recognition of the futility of the militant but impotent dragon mas', he joins Fisheye's doomed gesture of revolt.

It is around the theme of carnival that the novel is built, for it is at carnival time that the Hill comes alive, that poverty and oppression are forgotten, that the people break into a dance of freedom:

Dance! If the words mourn the death of a neighbour, the music insists that you dance; if it tells the truth of a brother, the music says dance. Dance to the hurt! Dance! If you catching hell, dance, and the government don't care, dance! Your woman take your money and run away with another man, dance. Dance! Dance! Dance! It is in dancing that you ward off evil. Dancing is a chant that cuts off the power from the devil. Dance! Dance! Dance! Carnival brings this dancing to every crevice on this hill.[25]

After one particular carnival, however, the masquerade continues. Fisheye and his gang, joined by Aldrick, ambush two policemen, seize their jeep and, in a madcap parody of revolution, drive into the city calling on the people through a megaphone system to rise up. The 'rebellion' is defeated without loss of life, the rebels are given prison terms of seven years or less, and life continues on Calvary Hill. There is an epilogue to *Dragon,* but this act of insurrection is undoubtedly its climax.

The Harder They Come develops with a quite different structure. Based on the award-winning Perry Henzel film of the same title, *Harder,* its author Thelwell claims, is not the typical instance of the commercial 'novelization' of a film. Rather, what he sought was to write "the novel from which the film might have been derived were the process reversed".[26] Thelwell succeeds in crafting a credible narrative, which creates a past for the leading characters that is only hinted at in the screen version. Comparisons are inevitable, however, and the timeless beauty of the film, with its early, powerful reggae score and grainy, flawed authenticity, captures a snapshot of a moment in Jamaica's history that the book simply cannot.[27]

The story is that of Ivanhoe (Rhygin) Martin, based loosely on the life of Rhygin, the first of the notorious modern Jamaican gunmen. It traces the life of Ivan from his early beginnings in the small rural fishing village of Blue Bay. Ivan, in typical fashion, is raised single-handedly by his grandmother Miss 'Mando, his mother having gone to seek her fortune in the city. The village of Blue Bay at first appears to be a timeless, traditional community, but it is not. To its very core, it is a product of modernity. Many of its residents have migrated to the far points of the globe. Some, such as the influential and iconic Maas' Nattie, have returned with new ways of looking at the world. Even the outwardly haphazard and eternal forest is not what it appears to be. The very trees were brought from all over the world to feed the labourers of a modern productive enterprise.

The young Ivan is a great source of worry for his grandmother. From very early, his friends give him the alias 'Rhygin' (raging), for his adventurous, risk-taking nature. Miss 'Mando has already lost all her natural children to the world. Some have died. None have returned. And now her grandson, from an early age, is captivated by the lights and music coming from the "sporting lady",

Miss Ida's café. Her fears are justified. As soon as she is dead, Ivan does not wait a day to head to the city of Kingston, where he hopes to fulfil his ambition of being a "recording artiste".

The rest of the narrative is a catalogue of Ivan's disappointments as he experiences the harsh reality of life in 'Babylon'. As soon as he disembarks from the country bus, he is robbed of all his worldly belongings by a "samfie-man" (con man). He wends his way to his mother's house only to find a sick and broken woman living in a one-room shack. He is befriended by man-about-town Jose, who volunteers to show him the city but instead relieves him of his few remaining dollars. For days after, he wanders hungry and destitute in the gutters of Kingston until, at last, he remembers the card his dying mother had given him with the address of her church written on it.

Ivan is given a room at the Reverend Cyrus Ramsey's Tabernacle of the Faithful in exchange for doing odd jobs around the yard. There he meets the luckless Elsa, the reverend's ward, and the surly Longah, a former badman and now (supposedly reformed) jack-of-all-trades. In the course of his time at the reverend's church, Ivan makes his own bike from an old frame, takes up with a gang of young, itinerant workers from the area, and falls for Elsa. It is this last act that is his undoing, for 'Preacher' has other sexual plans for the young woman. Both Ivan and Elsa are kicked out of the yard, but not before he has made a critical step toward fulfilling his dream. Preacher has musical instruments for the tabernacle's choir and Ivan, with Elsa's help, surreptitiously practises his reggae composition, "The Harder They Come". Ivan secures a date to record at music mogul Hilton's studio, but when he returns to Preacher's house to secure his bike, he is told by Longah that it was always Preacher's property and now it had reverted to him. There is a knife fight, Longah is slashed repeatedly in the face by Ivan, who is later arrested and taken to court. The judge decrees that Ivan is to be whipped and there is a scene – particularly poignant on the screen – when he is beaten and reduced to urinating like an infant.

Ivan appears to recover from these successive blows, gets his day in the studio and records his song, which, from the opinion of all those listening, is destined to be a hit. But then, he is confronted with another reality of power as Mr Hilton offers him a pittance for it, with no future hope of royalties. Ivan proudly refuses and, living now with Elsa, is once again destitute and desperate. He meets Jose, of his first night in Kingston, who offers him a job, which turns out to be that of a runner in the ganja trade. Ivan willingly accepts and life becomes better for him, Elsa, and their new found associate, a proud Rastafarian named Ras Pedro and his sickly son, Prince Man-I.

But the same personality who refused to accept the injustice of Longah's seizure of his bike, who refused to accede to Hilton's exploitative offer, is unhappy with the meagre living being made by the runners in the ganja trade when others are obviously making a great deal of money. Ivan complains to Jose, but little does he know that Jose is but the middleman in an operation run by an ambitious police officer, Superintendent Ray Jones. Jones' strategy is to control the ganja industry by allowing it a limited freedom to exist in exchange for information on more dangerous criminal activity. Ivan's rebellious questioning of the terms of the trade cannot therefore be tolerated. As Ivan returns from one of his trips to the countryside, his bike laden with ganja, instead of being waved on by the familiar motorcycle policeman, he is suddenly pursued. With memory of the whipping fresh in his mind, Ivan – now the proud owner of a pair of revolvers – aims and shoots the cop.

The rest of the story is of the inevitable pursuit and death of Ivan. At first, the ganja traders give him support, but Jones puts the squeeze on them by threatening to close down the industry completely. Desperate, he tries to board a ship to go to Cuba from the small adjoining island of Lime Cay, but he fails and ends up desolate and exhausted on the sand spit. In the meantime, Elsa, in exchange for financial help for Ras Pedro's dying son, has betrayed Ivan's whereabouts. Soldiers arrive on the island and surround him. He comes out with guns blazing and is shot down.

The Field of Difference

1. Calvary Hill is poor; but in Kingston there is grinding poverty.

The poverty and hopelessness of life on Calvary Hill is evident in this sharp, vivid portrayal, so typical of Lovelace's stylish novel:

This is the Hill, Calvary Hill, where the sun set on starvation and rise on potholed roads, thrones for stray dogs that you could play banjo on their rib bones, holding garbage piled high like a cathedral spire, sparkling with flies buzzing like torpedoes; and if you want to pass from your yard to the road you have to be a high-jumper to jump over the gutter, full up with dirty water. Is noise whole day. Laughter is not laughter; it is a groan coming from the bosom of these houses – no – not houses, shacks that leap out of the red dirt and stone, thin like smoke, fragile like kite paper, balancing on their rickety pillars as broomsticks on the edge of a juggler's nose.[28]

However, nowhere in *Dragon* is to be found this image of utter Sisyphean destitution that confronts Ivan in his first days in the city:

He glanced idly up the street and into one of those moments when time seemed frozen. Poised almost motionless on the slope was a huge, unpainted handcart piled high with bottles. Behind and above the cart, he saw in that instance a man's straining torso, and gaunt darkly bearded face, tense with effort. The dreadlocks' eyes were bloodshot and bulging, his face furrowed by anguished lines. He and the cart were frozen in a desperate tension as the man strained against the weight of the load and the pull of the slope and the cart edged gradually out of control. His torso glistened in the sun muscles corded, veins swelled n the thin neck and shoulders. His eyes – filled with a baffled, defeated rage mixed with hopeless appeal – met Ivan's.[29]

Ivan helps the man – graphically portrayed, with torn, tyre-soled sandals and feet squishing in hot asphalt – saves the bottles and discovers the reason for his strain and rage. If he had been unable to save the bottles, his six children would not have eaten that night. The man, with Ivan's help, pushes the cart to the bottle factory, where, after all the sweat and toil, the imperious clerk summarily rejects many of the bottles. In a sudden motion, the now enraged dreadlocks raises a rock and crashes it down into the large pile of reject bottles.[30]

2.   Calvary Hill is poverty-stricken, but, unlike Kingston, everywhere there are signs of social movement.

If there is anyone equivalent to Ivan in *Dragon,* then it is Fisheye, from the village of Moruga. Yet Fisheye, through his fame as a fighter and member of the Calvary Hill panside, is able to establish a relationship with Yvonne, who went to high school and came "from a good family too".[31] Of more than passing interest is the fact that it is Yvonne who introduces Fisheye to the idea that the enemy should be the government and not the competing steelbands. And, in case it is imagined that Yvonne had somehow fallen irrecoverably in having established a relationship with the lower class Fisheye, she leaves him after being beaten and begins living with an upwardly mobile politician.

   This social porosity is also evident in Philo the calypsonian's onward progress. His success in the tents leads to his eventual purchase of a house in the quintessential Trinidad middle class neighbourhood of Diego Martin. Philo is never really comfortable with his more established middle class neighbours but, like a true suburbanite, he becomes preoccupied with maintaining his pristine lawn.[32] Social movement comes with a price, however. Philo is effectively banned from visiting the Hill by Fisheye and his gang and estranged from his friend Aldrick, whose loyalty proves to be more firmly tied to the Hill than to his calypsonian friend.[33] Most notably, Pariag, the last to arrive and the least recognized, is able, with his rural Indian work ethic intact, to trade and sell, save his money and eventually establish his own shop on the Hill. Even this, however, does not afford him the respect that he still craves up to the very end.

One searches *Harder* in vain for this evident fluidity. There is movement and it has been going on for a long time, but it is outward. All of Miss 'Mando's children have moved, to Kingston, Cuba, Britain and the United States, to fight and die in wars and to suffer quietly in tiny rooms, but Mando remains in her poor, if respectable, mode of rural subsistence. Maas' Nattie had travelled abroad, done well and owned land, but in the final analysis he had not transcended (nor, in his own deep Garveyite sensibilities, did he wish to transcend) his place in the poor rural community. There is ambition, as with Ivan and Elsa and all the members of the Salt Lake City Gang, but this is held in check by a different social reality. Nowhere in *Dragon* is there the definite sense of entrenched social oppression, policed at each rung of the ladder, that breathes on every page of *Harder*. Thus, there is this exchange with the foreman at the construction site when Ivan, in desperation, tries to get a job:

Ivan stepped up to the foreman.
"What party you follow?" the henchman asked.
"None sah," Ivan uttered truthfully.
"Well choose one," the man said. "You mus' follow one."
"What kind of work you do?" the foreman asked.
"I can do anyt'ing, y'know sah," Ivan answered, trying to smile.
"Anyt'ing? What name anyt'ing? You can pour concrete? You is a mason? You do carpenter work? Eh? Eh?"
"Ah never do it before you know, sah, but –"
"You can lay brick?"
"Ah can do anyt'ing sah, jus' gi' me a break!"
"How you mean give you a break?" There was anger in the man's voice that Ivan didn't quite understand. "Leave de place man."[34]

Such anger and hostility is evident, too, when Ivan, down and out, dares to wander onto the lawns of the middle class woman and ask, in his most polite country accent, for work. Her full response, only vented when he has left, is instructive:

She watches him walk away with a certain defiant deliberateness. "Who left the gate open?" She shrieks at the servants in the house. "Those people really getting bold though eh? Imagine how the boy look at me, like 'im want to beat me if I don't give him work! You know the gate must be locked at all times!" she shouts. "Next thing you know someone break in and kill us in our sleep!"[35]

Anger and hostility, however, are not the only markers of a more consolidated and confident ruling class. There is Hilton, with his vulgar, contemptuous but savvy understanding of the popular mood, walking with a gun in his waist and his finger on the pulse of popular culture. And there is Ray Jones, with his chess-playing approach to the art of policing and a sense for identifying and exploiting the economic Achilles' heel of the poor, ghetto dwellers.

3. The consolidated ruling class in *Harder* is mirrored in a consolidated state, capable of dealing effectively with a variety of threats to its existence.

This sense of confidence is pervasive in *Harder*. Thus, when a group of messianic Rastas tries to take over the centre of the city, they are quickly and methodically dispersed.[36] By comparison, when Fisheye, Aldrick and their gang make their move and try to take over Port of Spain, there is vacillation. They are allowed to leave the city centre and go back up the Hill to sleep the night in peace; then they are given the space to return and incite revolt the next morning! The debate rages in the city as to why this was allowed. The defence attorney's argument that the "authorities trusted these men to fail"[37] is a lawyer's argument, but not convincing. The more consolidated Jamaican state is far more confident and sure in its response. There is, for example, the formalized, set-piece humiliation of Ivan when he is given the whipping sentence. Most pointedly, Ivan the fugitive is hunted down until brought in dead, whereas Aldrick and Fisheye, whose rebellious gesture, with its general appeal for an uprising, has more potential to become widespread and damaging, live to tell the tale, are given short sentences and eventually set free.[38]

In such a setting, potential rebels in Trinidad might risk rebellion because they suspect that their fate might only be that of Aldrick and Fisheye and not that of Ivan. Trinidadian writer Wayne Brown, commenting on the recent islandwide gas price demonstrations in Jamaica,[39] seems to be on target in recognizing this peculiarity of revolt in Trinidad to go the full distance but always to fall short in Jamaica:

In Trinidad, smallish, egalitarian, and habituated to the contemptuous intimacies of the weekly press – the politicians feel familiar, dis-respectable. In Jamaica, imbued with the distances a class system bestows, they feel out of reach to the masses . . . In spirit, the political parties here are feudal structures. Protest is protest; but in such a situation, 'civil unrest' cannot go beyond a certain point.[40]

In Jamaica, he concludes, this peculiarity of the class structure refracts protest; it is always "the fire next time".

The Field of the Similar

4. In both novels, everywhere there is the common intrusion of magnetic modernity.

Beyond the evident differences in the Trinidadian and Jamaican social formations as captured in the two novels, there are many underlying similarities. Modernity/the market/capitalism asserts itself over everything and not only, nor even primarily, in the form of an economic imperative. Thus it is the baleful glitter of the city that attracts Ivan from the far reaches of Blue Bay. As a young boy, he is considered a 'bungo'[41] by his friend Dudus for not knowing what was implied when the gaudy owner of the café, Miss Ida, is referred to as a "sporting lady". And Ida herself, with flashing gold and painted lips, is the embodiment of a powerful and different kind of life beyond the confines of the rural village:

And the café filled with music. Or rather, to Ivan, the café filled with Miss Ida around whom throbbing, heady, erotically insistent rhythms swirled and played. The big lady was light on her feet; the carnal exuberance of her breasts and hips seemed to engulf him . . . Ivan's senses were assaulted in a new way. This was city music, café music, the music of pleasure and fleshly delight, and Miss Ida was its incarnation.[42]

This powerful attraction is equally evident in *Dragon,* as Lovelace describes the personal transformation of recent migrants from the countryside:

They come with country all over their face, their shoulders broad from cutlassing cocoa and felling mora trees, with caps on, cheap silver chains around their necks, their socks peeping out bold below the fold of their trousers, walking in a kind of slow, rolling crawl, trying to look like town men; and a few months later, cap gone, slim, cool, matchstick in mouth, they coasting in the swing of the city, asking a man for cigarette, shouting full-lunged to a friend across the street, moving up Calvary Hill as if they own it.[43]

Pariag, in particular, from the confining embrace of his Indian family, is both pulled and pushed:

It seemed to Pariag that he had been too long in all this: too long in the village, too long in the sugarcane, too long meek and silent before his uncle, and while he had nothing against his success, indeed, was proud of it . . . he longed to go beyond the cows and grass and cane, out beyond the droning chant of the pundit, into a world where people could see him, and he could be somebody in their eyes, for this Trinidad was itself a new land, and he had not seen it yet, nor had it seen him.[44]

In similar vein, Ivan is confident that he will one day, by virtue of escaping the claustrophobia of the hillside, become famous: "Dem think say man a go pen up yah 'pon mountainside like goat-kid all 'im life? Cho, dem wrong dereso. Definite! Why, dem can't even understand that it for dem too, mostly for dem in fack, that ah going turn meself famous."[45]

5.   The glitter of modernity turns out to be 'down-pression' and darkness.

The arrival in the city is a crushing disappointment. From childhood, Miss 'Mando, Maas' Nattie and others had reinforced in Ivan the fact that he was 'somebody';[46] Fisheye had come from a proud line of postslavery African migrants, and had come to the city as a champion stickfighter to "show Port of Spain what Moruga could do".[47] But there are no laurels for proud country boys or stickfighters in the city, only disrespect, hunger and alienation. Ivan's own sense of self-respect hits rock-bottom when, homeless and starving, he seeks shelter in a tree only to discover, to his dismay, that a vagrant already occupies it:

Ah could slip up into the tree, Ivan thought. Aiee, me – Ivanhoe Martin fe go asleep a tree like fowl! He was about to do so when the old man scampered past him, tossed his bundles into the lowest crotch of the tree and climbed like a monkey after them. Ivan stood with his mouth open, unable to choose between crying, laughing or cursing.[48]

In response to these tests to the human character, to its very existence, young, hopeful migrants, who have severed their ties with the past, struggle to define new strategies to reassert their humanity and to survive.

Forms of Resistance[49]

6. At the centre of the process of resistance is the forging of an alternative social universe.

There is no real escape from the world of work, from the imperative to earn a living in a postcolonial capitalist society. Or is there? Faced with a hostile world, where simply holding a steady job is a major indicator of success, the subaltern forge alternative strategies, redefining the markers of success away from those traditionally accepted in 'Babylon'. Thus, the denizens of Calvary Hill hold their poverty as though it were a 'possession';[50] laziness is elevated to an art form, as a means of avoiding the slavery that is wage labour;[51] those who seek to impress through signs of upward mobility are isolated, like the unsuspecting Indian, Pariag, in his purchase of the new bicycle;[52] and those who 'make it', like the unfortunate Philo, are excommunicated and cannot return:

Indeed, Aldrick understood Fisheye's position. At the corner, power lay not so much in the might of the small company as in their steadfast pose of rebellion, in their rejection of the ordinary world, its rewards and promises. How could Philo, with his flashy clothes and his car and his women, all gained in the service of that other world against which they were rebelling, be their friend? . . . Aldrick thought to try to explain it, to defend Philo as a friend should, but he didn't know how to explain it . . . And so he began even then to console himself with the thought that Philo had chosen his success, had, at least, called it forth, worked for it. If it were a burden now, Aldrick felt that Philo was the one to bear it for himself.[53]

Ivan and his new found *paseros* in the Salt Lake City Gang invent an alternative, 'real' world by night to negate the drudgery of their daytime jobs:

They sold newspapers, polished cars, did 'day work' or when necessary begged or stole in the streets. Some were by day garden 'boys' in the mansions in the foothills, which Ivan remembered as a place of insult and fear.

But by night when the employers huddled behind iron gates and high walls, their garden boys in the little rooms out behind the servant's quarters dressed in their night finery. They pocketed their *okapis*, answered only to their war names, and headed for the ranches in search of companionship, adventure and reputation.[54]

7. This critical space is not only a point of retreat, but of discourse, of the creation and recreation of an alternative world, defined by its own style.

Style is central in the forging of an alternative universe of resistance. As Hebdige suggests, for style to catch on, it must "say the right things in the right way at the right time. It must anticipate or encapsulate, a mood, a moment. It must embody a sensibility."[55]

In both *Dragon* and *Harder,* the sensibility is that of asserting power and control in a world of powerlessness and uncertainty. For Ivan, power is encapsulated in the dress and pose of the cowboy, with his quick and ever-accurate gun – hence the Western imagery in the name of the gang and the names given to individual members – but there is the overarching imagery of the 'star-bwai'. For in the end, individual cowboys only live within a particular film, but star-bwais attain a certain immortality, surviving and starring from film to film. The sense of power in the simple ability to purchase the star-bwai garb and the cool detached pose that complements the dress represent critical steps in Ivan's recovery from alienation:

He filled his lungs with the new smell; it was hard to accept that they were finally his. So sharp. He looked at the clothes hanging on the wall and wished he had a mirror so he could see himself in the complete outfit. But that wasn't really necessary; he knew how he would look. The day he had been waiting on for ten weeks had finally come. The saving had been worth it. Many times over. He lay back on his cot and looked at the new clothes and grinned and grinned. The slim jeans and western-cut shirt with billowy sleeves, the incandescent socks and the boots, all in shades of blue . . . He couldn't stop grinning.

"Star-bwai," he whispered, "star-bwai to raas."[56]

And Aldrick's dragon costume – built from scraps to become the beautiful but terrible devourer of society on carnival day – fulfils the same role, albeit concentrated in two days of intense bacchanalia, as a symbolic assertion of power and control:

For two full days Aldrick was a dragon in Port of Spain, moving through the loud, hot streets, dancing the bad-devil dance, dancing the stickman dance, dancing Sylvia and Inez and Basil and the fellars by the Corner, leaning against the wall, waiting for the police to raid them. He was Manzanilla, Calvary Hill, Congo, Dahomey, Ghana. He was Africa, the ancestral Masker, affirming the power of the warrior, prancing and bowing, breathing out fire, lunging against his chains, threatening with his claws, saying to the city: "I is a dragon. I have fire in my belly and claws on my hands; watch me! Note me well, for I am ready to burn down your city. I am ready to tear you apart, limb by limb."[57]

8. Resistance is forged at the margins of the real and the imaginary.

There is no significant carnival in the Jamaica of *Harder,* but there is the cinema every night, which is the stage for a similar and constant interplay of reality and role playing. Life at the margins imitates art as does art imitate life, or, as in Tony McNeil's aptly titled poem, this is a "reel from the life movie".[58] Thus when Ivan is confronted by Bogart, the leader of the Salt Lake City Gang, the latter collapses in a coughing fit. In an instance of revelation, Ivan exclaims "Oowee . . . Doc Holliday to raas!"[59] His recognition of Bogart's resemblance to the tuberculosis-wracked lead in *Gunfight at the OK Corral* is enough to induct him immediately into the gang. Similarly, when Fisheye, struggling to establish his 'badjohn' reputation in Port of Spain, refuses to pay the shop-keeper for his bread and shark he ends up in a fight with the police and, with many officers rushing towards him, he suddenly imagines himself as the hero of the Western *Guns Across the River,*[60] and when Aldrick, Fisheye and their team have driven into the square, calling on the people to rise up and take power, Fisheye glances back at his friend: "This is action, eh," Fisheye said to Aldrick. He was in his glee."[61] Most poignant of all is Rhygin's final shootout with the police on the beach at Lime Cay. Instead of advancing on him, the police at first take cover in the grass. It dawns on Ivan that perhaps they are afraid; maybe the star-bwai as in the movies will win out in the end, or at least survive until the last reel:

"Me one an' dem 'fraid me . . . Show doan over a rass! Star-bwai can' dead after all . . . " He rose to his feet shouting and staggering in the loose sand. "Cho – done de army business!" he challenged, laughing. "Who is de bad-man unnu have? Sen' 'im out, nuh – one man who can draw. Sen' 'im out!"

He stood rocking in the shifting sand, bawling out his challenge and squinting in the sun's glare . . .

The police raised their heads – but were frozen either by fear or disbelief at this apparition.

"What de raas unnu waiting for!" Maas Ray screamed. "Is him! Shoot!"

A sudden brief silence followed the echoes of his scream. Then, the fierce thunder of automatic rifles.[62]

The question remains to be posed, however, as to whether this netherworld of the imagination is a place of escape, a sort of 'opiate', as in Marx's notion of religion, or whether it is a place to nurture strategies of resistance for the eventual and inevitable re-engagement with reality. If the examples from

Dragon and *Harder* are to be considered useful, then the escape into the cinema, into the world of the star-bwai and the dragon, is less an avenue of evasion than a powerful incubator to nurture and reshape the texture of frontal resistance, if and when it does come.

Personhood as Common Ethos

9.   The underlying motive force in social and political life is the search for and preservation of personhood.

To return to Harris' appeal, but more particularly, Ahmad's argument with Jameson – Is there an underlying ethos that drives these novels? Is it nationalism, as Jameson suggests in his sweeping generalization about the nature of Third World literature? Nationalism, interestingly, is the one theme that is striking in its absence. In sifting through the rubble of the Dungle, the cacophony of Milk Lane, and the stark barrenness of the Hill, what emerges is the powerful motive force of what Lovelace refers to as "personhood". Aldrick's father, Sam Prospect, had given this tangible possession to his children: "Maybe that was his gift to his children, this sense of miracle and manness, this surviving on nothing and standing up still on your own two feet to be counted as somebody in a world where people were people, were human, by the amount of their property."[63]

Aldrick himself reclaimed his own personhood every year in the building of his dragon mas' from nothing and in the act of his vivid portrayal on the streets:

In truth, it was in a spirit of priesthood that Aldrick addressed his work; for, the making of his dragon costume was to him always a new miracle, a new test not only of his skill, but of his faith: for though he knew exactly what he had to do, it was only by faith that he could bring alive from these scraps of cloth and tin that dragon, its mouth breathing fire, its tail threshing the ground, its nine chains rattling, that would contain the beauty and threat and terror that was the message he took each year to Port of Spain. It was in this message that he asserted before the world his self. It was through it that he demanded that others *see* him, recognize his personhood, be warned of his dangerousness.[64]

Fisheye's respect came from a different source – the power of his right hand – but it was equally important in the consolidation of his position on the Hill:

That was his season, those years: the baddest man in town respecting him, and everywhere he pass on the Hill, people calling out to him, but out of a warm, embracing brotherhood and comradeship. Girls wanted to be his woman, schoolboys were pointing him out to their friends: "That is Fisheye! That is Fisheye!" saying, "Right-o Fisheye!" and he saying, "Right-o, how it going?" And if he like their looks, sometimes giving them six cents to go in the parlour and buy something.[65]

Ivan's personhood is established from a very young age by the repeated assertions from his grandmother. A careful reading of Maas' Nattie's reminder to the young Ivan after Miss 'Mando's funeral shows it as being rooted in family, place and manners:

"Bwai – you a somebody. You come from some whe'. All you generation dem is right yah." He gestured emphatically toward the earth. "You Granmaddah, you Granfaddah, you uncle Zekiel, whe' de bull kill down a Duncans – him dey yah too. All a dem right yah. Good people – respectable. People say all kin' a t'ing – some say dem did proud. Some say dem quick to anger an' love fight. But a nevah hear nobody say dat you people evah t'ief . . . And you raise up decent, to know what right an' to have manners."[66]

In the uprooted world of the city, however, there is no centre, no haven, no familial retreat. There is only the thinly constructed night world of the star-bwai or the equally tenuous warrior world of Fisheye's corner gang. When these are threatened or invaded, the entire structure upon which a fragile personhood is constructed comes crashing down and the ground is cleared for rebellion.

Unsheathing the Sword

10. Rebellion, at first defensive, occurs when the protective barriers of personhood have been breached.

Fisheye, Aldrick and Ivan all dwell in a seething cauldron close to boiling point. While hunger, unemployment and plain economic deprivation prevail, however, none are the accelerators that lead to the ultimate decision to break with the law. While the reasons in each case are specific and relate to personal narratives, there appear, nonetheless, to be critical underlying causes.

For Ivan, the causes of his eventual break with the law are cumulative. There is the deeply ingrained sense of right and wrong inherited from his rural peasant background. Then, there follow a series of tests in which his belief in the justice of the 'system' is severely undermined. Longah's appropriation of the bike that he had rescued, rebuilt and spent good money on was unjust, yet when he defended his rights, he came out the loser, whipped and humiliated for his stance. Hilton was exploitative and unjust in offering him pennies for his beautiful song, yet when he stood up for his rights in rejecting Hilton's offer, the song was, in effect, blacklisted. He was right in exposing the exploitative nature of the ganja trade and demanding more of its bounty for the small traders, yet when he stood up on this principle, he was isolated by Jose and Ray Jones, leading to the eventual confrontation with the motorcycle cop. All of these are important and adequate elements in explaining Ivan's eventual and tragic final break with the law, but Thelwell introduces one other factor of great significance.

Close to the time of his final confrontation, Ivan returns to Blue Bay only to discover, to his shock, that it is completely transformed. The beach that he and Dudus would frequently visit was now dominated by a hotel and locked off from local access. Unrepentant Garveyite Maas' Nattie's house was now occupied by a family of foreign, white 'Rastafarians'; but even more alarmingly, his own family plot of land was completely overgrown and unrecognizable:

In great agitation and bleeding from countless scratches, he retraced his steps to the road. He was breathing hard and felt hot and sticky with sweat. The scratches itched. He wiped the sweat from his eyes and climbed the hog plum tree. The little basin was unbroken bush. But it was the place, for he recognized the view from the valley and the opposite hill. There, he could see roofs shining through the trees, the smoke of cooking fires . . . This was the place . . . Desolation.[67]

It suddenly dawns upon him that his final link to the past, to continuity and a sense of belonging, has been shattered:

It was not easy to come to grips with the shock and desolation he felt. Ah shoulda did stay. Ah shoulda did stay an' tek care of de place, he thought. The worst insult that people had was the sneering "Cho, you no come from nowhe'." For the first time he was feeling what that really meant. Now he realized just how important that sense of place was to his most fundamental sense of himself.[68]

This sudden dawning that he comes 'from nowhere' is not the trigger that precipitates rebellion – that is to be located in the events previously discussed – but it is the necessary condition out of which his final vestigial connection with the world of manners is broken, facilitating other events to take their course.

The root causes of rebellion in *Dragon* are both different and similar. The embourgeoisification of carnival, the entry of 'white' bands and the commercialization of the steelbands, narrows the field for its traditional celebration as a symbolic spectacle of resistance. Both Aldrick and Fisheye, "Dragon and Badjohn", become, in this context, aggrieved and defensive "flagbearers of a disappearing warriorhood".[69] There are alternatives, of course. Aldrick could try to get a job; Fisheye could try to become a reformed badjohn and abide by the new, tamer rules of mas' playing. But it is nigh impossible, for both have staked their reputations on a certain constructed stance of rebellion. Then, immediately after carnival, when the police choose to raid the corners and rid them of "hooligans", the die is cast.[70] There is nowhere to retreat that will allow them to retain their thick sense of personhood, which has been crafted over the years:

Right after carnival the police felt secure enough to launch a campaign to rid the corner of 'hooligans', and they came into Calvary Hill now, no longer hesitant, respectful, but prepared to stop their jeeps and harass and intimidate and arrest at any show of resistance. Aldrick watched this happening. The power of the Dragon even to threaten was coming to an end. But he remained there on the corner out of a stubborn pride and loyalty, moving when the police came and returning at their leaving, so that Fisheye would watch him and say: You is man. All those fuckin' cowards run; you stand up. You is man.[71]

In the end, when the break is finally made, there is a common, carnivalesque sense of exhilaration, of power and control, as though, for a moment, the possibility might arise to correct all the accumulated hurt and slights. Ivan, for instance, newly graduated to the most wanted list, is ambushed in bed with Jose's woman; naked, both guns blazing, he 'drops' four policemen:

Babylon ragin', but dem get shock tonight – is how much I drop sah? For the first time he began to realize the enormity, the incredible reality of what had happened. It was history to raas. Wait until the breddah dem hear 'bout it. He wondered if the music men still sold songs in the villages . . . the feeling of power and invincibility flooded him again.[72]

And Fisheye, Aldrick and their crew, racing through town in the hijacked police jeep, suddenly anoint themselves the "People's Liberation Army" and call on the people to rise up for "Freedom, Liberty and Justice":

When Aldrick came to himself, he was hoarse, and perspiration was streaming down his face. He handed the megaphone back to Pistach and he didn't even know that they had been circling Woodford Square for the last hour until he heard the roar of the applauding crowd gathered in the Square: "Pow-er! Pow-er! Pow-er! Pow-er! Pow-er!"

And then he felt his whole body glow with a roasting heat and a cold flash move across his stomach, through his insides. People were shouting, crying out. They were looking to them in the jeep, expecting something.

"We have them!" Fisheye cried, and he leaned over the window and shot a bullet into the air.[73]

There is no final vindication for Ivan, however; and the unjust city, from the best vantage point on the slopes of the Hill, is not turned upside down. These small rebellions, then, do not amount to revolution. That rare event requires a different kind of conjuncture and deeper ploughing of the soil. Although the decision to break with order, to 'storm heaven', must occur in both instances, in the latter it must be on a scale many times greater. This, at least, would seem to suggest that the scrutiny of narrative, both fictional and real, might yet possess intrinsic value.

Endings and Beginnings

The aims of this brief incursion, then, have been modest. It has sought to 'cross the chasm', to initiate a conversation between the unnaturally separated schools of thought in the sphere of Caribbean Studies; it has tried to suggest the potential usefulness and value of the fictional text as a more central source of hypothesis formation in the social sciences; and it has sought to generate a number of preliminary hypotheses on the relative nature of the political spheres in Trinidad and Jamaica through a comparative method sensitive to notions of hegemony.

Two recent books, *The Repeating Island* by Antonio Benitez-Rojo and *Afro-Creole* by Richard Burton, in their method and substance, and on a far more ambitious scale, seek to accomplish what is attempted here. Both represent laudable efforts to erase the disciplinary boundaries and to find some harmony between the arts and the social sciences in the service of a better understanding of the Caribbean. Both are also praiseworthy in their generous definition of the wider Caribbean and their unwillingness to be constrained by the traditionally restrictive linguistic boundaries. Yet in critical respects, both disappoint.

Benitez-Rojo, operating within a self-described postmodernist frame of reference, defines the Caribbean by identifying its eclectic character and characterizing it as a "supersyncretic reference space".[74] In this context, he recognizes that the discourse of power and resistance has been a persistent binary opposition in the region, but he refuses to use it as the primary lens with which to approach the study of the Caribbean:

And yet the Caribbean is more than that; it can also be regarded as a cultural sea without boundaries, as a paradoxical fractal form extending infinitely through a finite world. Who can tell us that he's traveled to the origins of Caribbeanness? And this is why my analysis cannot dispense with any of the paradigms, while at the same time it will not be able to legitimate itself through any one of them, but rather only in and through their nonlinear sum.[75]

Burton, in a different and, in some respects, richer study, seeks to explore the politics of resistance through popular culture. In a broad sweep from Rastafari to carnival, Haitian vodun and beyond, he concludes that, even outwardly, radical cultural forms have been essentially means of refracting rather than focusing rebellion:

If Nicholls is right, then the radicalism and utopianism of the cultural forms discussed in this book appear to be less expressions of socio-political resistance than substitutes for it: it is as though West Indians have preferred to keep their radicalism in the cultural domain, where it can neither really threaten the power structure nor bring injury on them while pursuing oppositional ends day to day. Profoundly conscious, like all historically oppressed peoples, of the perils of challenging the structures of power (and still more of Power) head-on, West Indians have opted to create spaces within it where they can maneuver.[76]

If a reading of *The Harder They Come* and *The Dragon Can't Dance* might serve as a means of reopening debate on these two conclusions, then a response to Benitez-Rojo might indicate that even if he is right in suggesting that there are an infinite number of possible lenses with which to observe the complexity of the Caribbean, then the lens through which the binary of domination and resistance is observed needs necessarily to be given special attention. And, although Burton is evidently accurate in recognizing the paucity of rebellion when compared to symbolic act, the fact that revolt remains, nevertheless, a recurring decimal – individually and collectively, through Rhygins and gas price demonstrations, Black Power and Grenadian revolutions – merits a closer scrutiny of its causes and suggests that a premature closure on the 'conservative nature' of the Caribbean poor might not be truly merited.

4

Carl Stone:
Political Scientist as People's Tribune

One of the remarkable features of Carl Stone's tragically truncated career is that so little has been written about him. Despite his publication of some eight books and three monographs, co-editing of three others, and over fifty articles,[1] critical commentary on his oeuvre remains sparse and inadequate.[2] The work of Carl Stone remains a vast, rich and largely untapped hoard, yet to be effectively mined by political scientists, historians, sociologists and all those interested in the development of Jamaican politics in the late twentieth century.

This chapter seeks to make a small contribution to that effort by doing two things: first, it attempts to sketch a framework for Carl Stone studies by suggesting the secular drift of his thought, emphasizing the critical junctures and the overall process of evolution from the early seventies to his untimely death in 1993. This is also, by default, a reflection on Jamaican politics for this seminal quarter century. Second, it tries to tease out the underlying philosophy that guided his work and that, it is suggested, remained under 'deep cover' for most of his career. Three phases can be proposed in the development of Stone's thought. The first, which can be called Early Radicalism, is effectively captured in his book *Class, Race and Political Behaviour in Urban Jamaica*.[3] This was published just two years after his return from graduate school at the University of Michigan and was Stone's attempt to come to terms with the rapidly evolving and dynamic politics of urban Jamaica. The crucible of Kingston and lower St Andrew was about to give reggae music and Bob Marley to the world.[4]

Somewhat later it would donate the far less well-received 'posses' and 'yardies' criminal gangs. Stone saw in the tumultuous upsurge of the urban poor the possibility – if only tentatively – of a radical direction for Jamaican politics.

The second phase, which can be referred to as Stone Matured, is captured in his centrepiece work *Democracy and Clientelism in Jamaica*.[5] Here, the now confident senior academic and pollster presents his general theory of Jamaican politics, elaborated in the context of the cauldron of the 1976–78 period, in which Jamaica came as close as it has ever been to civil war. In this phase, Stone develops his thesis that Jamaican politics is based on a structure of patron-clientelism that makes it a distinct system and not simply a subtype of pluralist democracy.

The third phase can conveniently be called The Legacy Years. In the last years of his life the now highly respected Professor Stone, while maintaining his Herculean pace in the production of polls, newspaper columns and public speeches, wrote no definitive book with theoretical content.[6] Nevertheless, it is evident from various articles and speeches that, fully aware of his limited time, he sought to establish his legacy for Jamaican politics in the new conditions of unipolarity and globalization at the *fin de siècle*.

Embedded in all these phases was the evolving philosophy of the man, which is seldom stated up-front as 'policy position' but operates as an implicit, subliminal theme. The central argument is that Stone is the continuator of a tradition of radical Caribbean democracy. However, fully cognizant of the constraints and limitations placed on the independent thinker by the harsh Jamaican political climate, as the activist intellectual, he sought to locate himself on the unassailable high ground in order for his critique to be heard with maximum effect.[7] From this angle, Stone's empiricist methodology and peripatetic interventions into the public discourse cannot be seen as ends in themselves, but well-honed tools designed for a greater purpose; this was the strengthening of civil society through the forging of a counter-hegemonic discourse as the foundation for the emergence of a new, more democratic, political order.

The extent of his success, will, of course, be revealed over time and assessed in the inevitable deluge of biographies and theses that will appear. It is important to note here, however, that one of the areas of research that will require serious attention is that of Stone's enigmatic personality. From early in his career it was evident that Stone was self-consciously aware that he had a mission to perform. His was not the route of the 'doctor-politician', as in the manner of Eric Williams, nor of the 'opposition party intellectual', of the Trevor Munroe or Ralph Gonsalves type. Rather, Stone saw himself as an independent tribune of the people, a one-man counter-hegemonic force, single-handedly forging a new civic culture through his polls, columns and more academic interventions. To this end, in the tradition of West Indian politicians, he often brooked no opposition. Stone would ruthlessly cut down to size any lesser mortals who dared question his wisdom on the Jamaican political situation. Nevertheless, he could also be the nurturing senior academic, giving his junior colleagues useful advice and protecting them from the vagaries of campus politics.[8] Suffice it, at this time, to say that his famously accurate polling, his infusion and popularizing of a variety of concepts into the Caribbean lexicon,[9] his important contribution to the development of sugar workers' cooperatives,[10] land reform and worker participation and his consistent use of solidly grounded empirical techniques in journalism and political science research have all contributed to revolutionizing Jamaican political culture, with repercussions in the wider anglophone Caribbean.

Early Radicalism

Class, Race and Political Behaviour in Urban Jamaica was Stone's first concerted attempt to come to terms with Jamaican politics and remains, in many respects, his most thoroughly academic work.[11] Overtly, the study aimed at establishing the linkages between social stratification and political behaviour in urban Jamaica, but there were at least two other intentions.[12] While recognizing that public opinion in the Western sense – where issues were elaborated in a national discourse through the mass media – did not exist, he suggested that active, mobilized support was critical for the survival of the political system. Stone sought first to establish the character and extent of this support, but only as the initial step in a broader project: this was the identification and mapping of the social and political space for a 'third force' to emerge as an immediate competitor to the two dominant political parties.

In order to accomplish this first step, Stone began with an analysis of the Jamaican social structure that he strove to distinguish from two prominent schools of thought. The first of these, M.G. Smith's social pluralism,[13] had adopted an approach that divided Jamaican society into white, brown and black strata. These were differentiated by sharp cultural distinctions, relegating economic or class markers to secondary importance. According to Smith, the central factor generating political conflict was the absence of a value consensus and the failure of the social system to culturally assimilate the black strata. In questioning the accuracy of Smith's assessment, Stone raised four issues:

The first concerns the accuracy of its description of the determinants of social status; the second is its relevance to the subjective definition of contending strata in the society; the third is its accuracy in defining the main objectives and goals over which conflict occurs; and finally its explicit assumption that value consensus is the primary basis of political stability and integration.[14]

In a sophisticated analysis that is not open to easy summary, Stone concluded that the problem with Smith's typology was that it had remained frozen in the mode of classic plantation society. Smith failed to appreciate the (albeit uneven) diversification and modernization of the economy that had taken place after the World War II. While race, colour and occupational prestige were factors influencing social standing and life chances, after the war "material affluence and income"[15] were the main determinants. However, should his materialist approach be mistaken for Marxism, Stone immediately moved to counter any such assumption. The main thrust of his 'materialist' antagonism was not between wage labour and capital, that is, the proletariat and the bourgeoisie, but the 'haves' and the 'have nots':

The theory of class conflict developed by Marx emphasises the antagonistic interests between wage labour and capital in capitalist societies. An alternative approach to this view of class conflict suggests that the antagonism between rich and materially dispossessed strata is a more central source of conflict. The Marxist thesis dichotomises conflicting classes into capitalists and labour, which, however, overlaps with the rich and materially dispossessed categories.[16]

The weakness in the traditional Marxist position, he continued, was its failure to appreciate the relatively privileged position of the blue-collar worker in a society with endemic unemployment.[17] What was at play, rather, was an antagonism set in motion by the vast gap between the materially dispossessed and the wealthy, with the relative deprivation of the poor leading to frustration, alienation and, ultimately, aggressive behaviour.[18] Stone's subsequent presentation of his survey findings was to decisively substantiate this argument: on all the criteria for alienation and discontent, from hostility to voting and party politics through support for violence and interest in a third party,[19] it was invariably the lower class – defined as the most materially dispossessed – who proved to be most alienated and most militant.

What then accounted for the legitimacy and support that he admits existed for the system, if significant sectors of the population were alienated? He proposed a complex of institutional and psychological factors to explain this:

The first relates to the inheritance of the traditional legitimacy of the colonial bureaucracy by the leadership of the multiple-class coalitions; the second to the authoritarian and deferential attitudes towards elites and leadership which is rooted in the plantation history of the society; and the third to the extraordinary impact of the founding leaders of the multiple class coalitions, who have sustained faith in the system and thereby bestowed a residue of legitimacy for the political process.[20]

Functioning with this "residue of legitimacy", and in a context where the social classes are weak, the two political parties who, between themselves, alternate control of the state, operated a system of patronage, but one in which the benefits were severely limited. The patronage system enmeshed the people into a structure of dominance and subordination which by its very institutionalization served to maintain the authority of the ruling elites; but equally, the inability of these elites to satisfy the overwhelming demands generated cynicism and distrust from below. The result was a system that continued to survive but that had, at the same time, created the basis among the alienated poor of the city for a third, radical political force.[21]

Before examining in detail this central conclusion, however, it is appropriate to focus for a moment on a contradiction in the flow of Stone's thought. In rejecting Smith's analysis, Stone, as proposed, substitutes material factors for value consensus as the critical determinant in understanding the antagonisms in Jamaican society. Then, having sketched a picture of relative material deprivation, in an apparent *volte-face,* he suggests that the system is maintained precisely because the plantation values of hierarchy and obedience still hold among sufficiently wide strata to give the system functional legitimacy. Stone, aware of a tension, apparently seeks to address it by suggesting that the process is dynamic; a minority of the most materially dispossessed have moved beyond the culturally restraining values due to the imperative of their economic situation. Presumably, more will follow when they see the light, but even this concession serves to strengthen Smith's argument for the primacy of cultural determinants. Even if Stone wishes to differentiate between a cultural consensus and a purely political consensus, this does not solve the problem. Indeed, the colonial psychological values, which he invokes in explaining continued political legitimacy, resonate with Smithian echoes. This tension is never really resolved in Stone's work and reappears in his final years, in which he seems to concede a more elevated role for 'the cultural' in social determination.

Jamaican society, then, is fragile and fraught with tension resulting from its gross inequalities and, in the end, is held together by a political system that dissipates conflict and channels it horizontally, even as it perpetuates inequality. With this rather bleak prognosis, the young, radical Stone, expressing themes that would never again be so clearly stated, argues, in what is evidently the concluding thrust of the entire book, for a third force in Jamaican politics: "the possibility for the emergence of a third party in Jamaica is a real one".[22] Beyond the favourable social basis, which exists in the urban poor, four subjective factors would be required to make it a reality: first, a populist figure in keeping with Jamaican traditions would have to emerge; second, the party would have to focus on its constituency among the poor, instead of adopting the multiclass approach of the PNP and JLP; third, the requisite finances would have to be available to sustain a party organization, press and other necessary expenses; and fourth, it would have to possess a unified ideology that would have to combine a class-based appeal with a racial appeal.[23]

Following this, in the penultimate paragraph, Stone reveals his hand as clearly being on the side of a radical alternative – a position he would never repeat in quite the same way again: "Whatever happens, the hopelessness and manipulation of the masses will continue until the possibility arises for revolutionary changes within the social order."[24] Underlying the entire book is a deep suspicion of the elitist, closed framework of the Jamaican political system,[25] the analysis of which was only introduced here, but which appears as the main theme in his mature phase in *Democracy and Clientelism*.

Stone Matured

By the late seventies, Stone had matured immensely. No longer the young, inspired junior academic, he was now the increasingly respected national commentator, journalist and uncannily accurate pollster. By then, too, the Jamaican political scene had undergone quantum changes. Michael Manley's government, with its model of democratic socialism, had moved to the Left, with the most spectacular changes in its foreign affairs positions. As Stone would subsequently argue, the differences between the two parties remained fewer than their similarities,[26] but the antagonisms between the government and the increasingly conservative JLP and its private sector allies intensified. Michael Manley was to win the 1976 elections – then the most violent in Jamaica's history – but this would turn out to be only the dress rehearsal for the 1980 bloodbath in which upwards of eight hundred people died in pre-election violence.[27]

Stone's *Democracy and Clientelism in Jamaica*, written against the background of these momentous events, sought, ambitiously, to develop a model of Jamaican politics with relevance to the Third World as a whole. In the introduction, he again tries to locate and fine-tune his own theoretical position on the critical question of Jamaican social stratification. He defines his approach as class oriented, but non-Marxist and inductive:

My own treatment of class differs from many who write in the tradition of Marxist-Leninism, as well as those who write in the traditions of conventional Western sociology. I seek to combine a materialist framework of analysis that is divorced from both Marxist ideology and Marxist prescriptions for change. More importantly, the deductive and general theory approaches of Marxist analysis are rejected in favour of an inductive behavioural methodology that seeks to draw conclusions and inferences from empirical data and quantitative analysis.[28]

Interestingly, and perhaps in keeping with the charged and increasingly polarized political atmosphere of the period, he abandons overt references to a 'third force' or the occasional mention of the possibility for revolutionary transformation as he did in *Class, Race and Political Behaviour*. Rather, he sets very limited goals as to the purpose of the book, including the establishment of relevant data on Jamaican society and the development of a body of opinion about Jamaican politics to aid in the understanding of the wider Caribbean political process.[29] From this deceptively conservative position, he then proceeds to expound, once again, on his critique of M.G. Smith's plural society. However, beyond questioning Smith's use of cultural variables, he makes a new and noteworthy concession. Smith was wrong to give the primacy to cultural determinants, but "more than any other analysis of pre-independence Jamaica [his analysis] captured the essence of the fluidity, instability and fragility of the Jamaican power structure".[30]

The issue of 'fragility', while not absent in the earlier book, becomes a central theme in *Democracy and Clientelism* and is deserving of further comment. It is perhaps understandable that, in the context of the sanguinary power struggle of the late seventies, Stone should have wished to emphasize the notion of fragility, and, of course, it is only with hindsight that one can fully appreciate the significance of subsequent events. The 'fragile' Jamaican political system proved durable enough to survive the remarkable tests of the 1974–80 battles, the snap election called by the JLP government in 1983 that led to a boycott of the electoral process by the PNP, and the structural adjustment policies of the last two decades with all their implications for human suffering, without showing imminent signs of collapse. When this is contrasted with other Caribbean states that appear to have undergone far less overt stress, yet have experienced far more severe threats to their survival,[31] then Stone's notion of the fragile Jamaican state may have to be revised.

The perusal of the class structure then leads into the main purpose of the book, that is, the elaboration of the character of the Jamaican political system, which he describes as "patron-clientistic". Due to the weaknesses of the social classes in Jamaica, the state accretes power unto itself, but though its influence in the domestic sphere is far-reaching, it is ultimately checked by even more powerful international forces:

The implication is an increasing location of class power within the grasp of a bureaucratic, petty bourgeoisie that may in time emerge transformed as an administrative bourgeoisie or the dominant local class administering an oversized bureaucracy with external economic and political support. The future changes in Jamaican class structure depend very much on the balance between internal and external influences and the interplay of capitalist and socialist international interests in the Caribbean.[32]

The 'rules of the game' of Jamaican politics are then outlined in great detail: First, the political system is dominated by the two established parties; second, power is seen by the people as party determined; third, mass interest is based on the assumption that political support will lead to material benefits; fourth, due to the limited ability of the patrons to fulfil the demands of their clients, mass attitudes to party politics are fraught with distrust and ambivalence; fifth, no single class interest is able to control the state on a long-term basis, but instead, intense, intra-elite competition takes place for control over the nerve centres of power. In summary: "The main currents of Jamaican politics centre on a complex interplay of intra-elite power contentions and coalition building, with the mass public essentially providing critical audience supports."[33] But importantly, he also offers a relevant caveat: "On the other hand, the mass public is not without influence. This influence operates primarily through electoral politics."[34]

From this platform, patron-clientelism is defined. Jamaica's political system is not simply a variant of Western, pluralist democracy, but rather, a distinct prototype of an alternative system.[35] Patron-clientelism emerges at the time of the withdrawal of the colonial power; the new petty bourgeoisie, which is now in charge, uses the state's mechanisms as a means of competing with the traditionally powerful economic classes. However, because the local capitalists are relatively weak, at a certain stage they become entangled in a system of dependency in which they are subordinated to the state even as they do retain some measure of autonomy. As Stone graphically asserts: "In Jamaica, the 'political kingdom' assumed ascendancy over the domestic economic power structure in the immediate postindependence period under the JLP. These interests ran for refuge to the PNP only to find that the PNP accelerated the process towards state capitalism."[36] The only control on the power of the now-ascendant state bourgeoisie, he suggests, is international capital expressed through the IMF, which uses its power to bring deviant economies back into line. Stone then elaborates on the features of the mature, patron-client system in one of his richest and most disparaging sequences:

Party politics under clientelism is built around a network of personal allegiances between multiple patrons, brokers and clients. Patrons control the nerve centres of power and access to material and social rewards, while brokers or intermediaries provide the linkage between the rank-and-file clients or supporters and the political bosses . . .

The party boss or maximum leader is like a feudal monarch surrounded by a nobility who grow or diminish on scale of élite power depending on how he chooses to bestow favour. The maximum leader is able to keep the party together only if he constantly exerts personal authority over the party. The effective maximum leader can never be openly challenged, has the final word on most critical decisions (unless he chooses not to exercise that power), and is entrusted with the power to determine policy and overall directions in the party. Maximum leaders who show signs of indecisiveness, weakness and lack of control invite challenges and lose credibility because the role of maximum leader is defined in the political culture as demanding strength, appearances of personal domination, and decisiveness.[37]

The remainder of the book further develops this thesis on patron-clientelism and then departs into a more specific analysis of Jamaican party politics between 1976 and 1978. It is important to note, however, that *Democracy and Clientelism* concludes on a far different note than *Class, Race and Political Behaviour*. Rather than a radical option to break the chains of two-party dominance, he, quite probably cognizant of the abyss that the country faced in the late seventies, proposes, instead, a mutual withdrawal of forces and a reassessment of national priorities:

If it is accepted that the main ideological divisions in the Jamaican party system are more related to divisions on these international forces that have penetrated the society than to the domestic class issue, it follows that they are resolvable if a nationalist Jamaican perspective can emerge in both of the two parties to define an optimal basis on which to relate to these interests without becoming pawns of either. Only if such a new national consensus emerges can the necessary concerted action and collaborative action in the economic sphere restore growth where negative declines demoralise worker and capitalist alike.[38]

It would be premature and mistaken to assume that this relatively conservative conclusion indicated that Stone's entire perspective had shifted in a rightward direction. The thrust of *Democracy and Clientelism* remained an impassioned appeal against the injustices of the Jamaican political system, and his call for national alliance can therefore be seen as a tactical necessity to halt what was then a frightening downward spiral into violence and anarchy. This becomes apparent in the final years of his life when Stone, in a new social and political context, advanced his most concrete proposals for political and social renewal.

The Legacy Years

Three years after *Democracy and Clientelism* first appeared, the Grenadian revolution collapsed. For the Caribbean Left, the rout that had begun with the 1980 electoral defeat of Manley's PNP was sealed with Maurice Bishop's tragic death. The collapse of European communism and the ending of the Soviet state were, therefore, not totally unanticipated from a Caribbean perspective. The revolutionary shift that the younger Stone had hoped for in 1973 and the patriotic coalition against both superpowers that he had mooted in 1978 were no longer on the agenda of the new world order.

By the early nineties, too, Carl Stone knew that he was critically ill. While no definitive studies were published in the final years of his life, if one attempts to triangulate from the numerous speeches he gave and articles he wrote, it is evident that Stone sought to establish a legacy based on a rethinking of Jamaica's prospects in the new, emerging context. In doing this, he remained remarkably consistent to themes that date back to his earliest work.

Three issues were prevalent in Stone's final years. Beyond the stark critique of clientelism, he proposed, in both official[39] and popular channels, a thorough reform of the parliamentary system, for he was convinced that an important bottleneck preventing further democratic change lay in the archaic clauses of the constitution. Beyond merely structural reform, he was also increasingly convinced that central to the long-term economic crisis of the country was the stark reality of poor management acumen at all levels of the state. Closely connected to this was his relatively new emphasis on the need for a revolution in values in Jamaican society. It is striking that the final article in his last published collection should focus on the cultural values of the society in a way that the younger 'materialist' Stone would have considered heretical.

In his 1994 essay "The Jamaican Party System and Political Culture", Stone suggested how the party system had changed since the seventies and he proposed possible directions in which it might move for the twenty-first century. On the positive side, he argued, popular participation had increased geometrically, due largely to the mobilizing capacity of the two political parties. The access of the population to information had also grown tremendously due to the widespread availability of radio and television and also to the high levels of politicization. A further positive was to be seen in the gradual shift in election campaigns from personality to policy issues. Despite these gains, however, the middle classes still dominated politics; violence and 'garrison politics' – while less than at the peak in 1980 – were still endemic; and the political system, under the influence of patron-clientelism, had become even more centralized, with a corresponding decline in local leadership and community influence.[40] The growing popular dissatisfaction with members of Parliament in the early nineties, where the polls showed that between 1989 and 1991 negative ratings had increased from 40 percent to 70 percent, suggested a crisis of credibility and growing cynicism towards the system. This, Stone argued, did not indicate its imminent collapse, but unless important democratic issues and questions of economic management were addressed, cynicism and accompanying anarchy would probably intensify.

In response to these challenges, he proposed five measures to carry the country into the twenty-first century. First, internal party democracy had to be increased by

increasing the recruitment of party members from the middle strata and the more educated; by making internal party activities more visible, transparent and open to media scrutiny; by establishing more orderly and accurately documented membership lists to reduce thuggery and bogus voting in party elections; by encouraging rather than attacking independent thinking in the parties and by purging from the parties' leadership ranks persons associated with violence.[41]

Second, at the national level, a system of proportional representation needed to be instituted to eliminate the disproportionate share of seats that winning parties received under the first-past-the-post system and also to give third parties a fair chance at winning seats. Third, a presidential system should replace the Westminster variant because it would allow members of Parliament to concentrate on being legislators and provide them with sufficient time to see to their constituencies. Fourth, he proposed more decentralized systems of government, as over-centralization was one of the critical reasons why there was poor management in the delivery of health services. Further, on the question of management, he argued that members of Parliament were in vital positions but had received no specific training for their jobs and this had to change. Fifth, he suggested that ways needed to be found to divulge sources of party financing, and mixed systems of public and private financing of parties with appropriate disclosure mechanisms needed to be elaborated to circumvent the corruption of power by interest groups. Finally, Stone proposed that special punitive laws needed to be put on the books to deal with administrative and governmental corruption.[42]

In an important speech to members of the JLP in 1991, Stone returned to the issues of management and corruption as he raised more fundamental questions about the social values that had emerged after three decades of independence:

[T]he politician is often blamed for problems caused by weaknesses in the wider society. The capability to govern and run the country adequately has been impaired by rampant corruption, indiscipline, laziness, low work norms, a low sense of public responsibility and sheer rascality and rampant corruption in most of the public sector institutions in Government that are charged with responsibility to implement national policies . . . our people have become lazy and irresponsible and want something for nothing and these negative traits have become entrenched in our public sector.[43]

Stone, in this impassioned statement, while retaining his central thrust, seems to have changed focus in some respects. While searching for avenues to broaden and deepen democracy, he refrains from presenting the problem as primarily a structural one, deriving from a clientelistic political system rooted in economic deprivation. While this accounted for part of the explanation, another component lay in the psychology of a people whose dependent mentality – rooted in the plantation experience – had been strengthened by decades of clientelism. The question of dependency is captured poignantly in the same speech, where he notes, "We are waiting on politicians to solve our problems when it is we, the people who have the responsibility, the power and the capability to tackle these problems and solve them."[44]

These themes were driven home even more forcefully in Stone's last published piece, "Values, Norms and Personality Development in Jamaica". Here, Stone proposed that there was a crisis of values in Jamaica.[45] The old, authoritarian, colour-stratified and hierarchical plantation value structure had been undermined, but so too had other important values associated with the family and the community. In the context of the resultant disequilibrium, violence had emerged as a critical means of articulating power at all levels of the society. The result, presaging approaches to hegemonic dissolution discussed elsewhere in this volume, was a society on the verge of anarchy:

These profound changes in values, norms and modes of behaviour in all domains of social space have undermined the old authority systems without giving birth to a strong, new and legitimate social order. The old order is still crumbling, but new and coherent authority systems have not emerged to replace it.[46]

But even at this grave moment, Stone suggests that there is the dialectical possibility of recovery. The increased flow of information that is another feature of the new social order, could provide the basis for a deepening of democracy provided important democratic reforms were to be instituted. However, he concludes, somewhat pessimistically, that the elites and the 'political powerbrokers' have been unwilling to do this. Among the things that need to be done to deepen democracy, he proposes:

- Trying to create a meritocratic society where the most talented find opportunities and outlets for both achievement and self-expression

- Expansion of the country's economic base by opening up opportunities for entrepreneurship at the base of the society

- Expanding labour quality and human capital through more extensive and more diverse educational and training institutions, especially in technology and technical production skills and competencies

- Increasing collaboration and joint ventures between big and small scale capital by combining their diverse strengths in production and marketing

- Using a strategy of deepening democracy and decentralised public management (especially at the community level) to channel the creative energies of the people in the direction of managing their own affairs[47]

Locating Stone

Where, then, does Carl Stone stand amidst the panoply of modern, democratic thinkers? David Held has suggested eight historical and contemporary models of democracy.[48] In the contemporary period, the primary polarization is between the New Right thinkers, including Hayek and Nozick,[49] whose approach Held characterizes as "Legal Democracy", and the New Left, including Carol Pateman, Nicos Poulantzas and C.B. Macpherson with their notions of "Participatory Democracy".[50] Hayek et al., in opposition to contemporary liberalism, argue that political life, like economic life, should be a matter of individual initiative and they call for a laissez-faire society along with a 'minimal' state. The New Left, on the other hand, argues that individual rights, while important, are meaningless in a society based on vast inequalities. While opposing the Leninist prescription of party domination of the state, the New Left suggests various approaches that centre on the extension of democracy in the state, but also in the wider realm of 'civil society'.

Held suggests that, while there are obviously vast differences between the two positions, there is an underlying commonality of concern that may provide the basis for movement towards a synthesis:

The views of the New Right and New Left are, of course, radically different. The key elements of their theories are fundamentally at odds. It is therefore somewhat para-doxical to note that they share a vision of reducing arbitrary power and regulatory capacity to its lowest possible extent. Both the New Right and New Left fear the extension of networks of intrusive power into society . . . they both have ways of criticising the bureaucratic, inequitable and often repressive character of much state action. In addition, they are both concerned with the political social and economic conditions for the development of people's capacities, desires and interests. Put in this general and very abstract manner, there appears to be a convergence of emphasis on ascertaining the circumstances under which people can develop as 'free and equal'.[51]

Held argues that the common strand that links them together is the question of 'autonomy', and if the principle of autonomy is fully explored then the tentative construction of a synthetic approach to democracy might be possible. Among the elements in his framework, he first advances the more well debated formulae for the democratization of political institutions:

In the West the need to democratise political institutions has mostly been confined to questions of reforming the process whereby party leaders are selected and changing electoral rules. Other issues which are occasionally raised include public funding at elections for all parties meeting a minimum level of support; genuine access to, and more equitable distribution of, media time; freedom of information . . . deconcentration of the civil service to the regions along with its decentralisation; the defence and enhancement of local government powers against rigid, centralised state decisions; and experiments to make government more accountable and amenable to 'consumers'.[52]

These points by themselves, Held argues, are very important but insufficient to restrain the overarching powers of bureaucratized states. A new constitution and bill of rights would have to be instituted, but if it were to genuinely to deal with the question of autonomy, it would have to address a far broader range of rights than the 'formal' rights typically associated with liberal democracies. Thus, rights circumscribing the actions of the state would have to be instituted to preserve freedom, as, concurrently, social and economic rights would have to be entrenched to allow liberty to be genuinely enjoyed: "Without tough social and economic rights, rights with respect to the state could not be fully enjoyed; and without state rights, new forms of inequality of power, wealth and status could systematically disrupt the implementation of social and economic liberties."[53] This is the field on which Carl Stone's thought is located. A firm believer in competitive democracy and the limited, though important, autonomy granted the citizen under it, he was never confined within its framework, however. Rather, driven by the evident hierarchy and inequality of Jamaican 'democracy', he sought, in his own enigmatic way, to probe and explore its outer boundaries and arrive at some synthesis that would preserve liberty while confronting inequality.

But Stone, further, needs to be located on an entirely different grid. If, as Gordon Lewis suggests, a central impulse in Caribbean intellectual history has been the effort "– often groping and uncertain – after a culture to be regarded as genuinely Caribbean; in the course of which it borrowed, sometimes with almost servile acknowledgement and sometimes with embarrassed shame, from the achievements of the older world",[54] then Stone's work needs to be seen as not simply a part of a broader discourse on democracy but closely connected into specifically Caribbean imperatives. The question of a democratic renewal, he was increasingly convinced, could only occur with the strengthening of civil society that included the gradual erasure of the psychological shackles of dependency. To this end, Stone sought, not just in his policy statements but his very method, to escape from the dependency syndrome of relying on totalizing, imported frames of intellectual reference. Concerned not just with identifying the problem and searching for solutions, he was also intimately conscious of the need to find the right tools to begin the process of excavation.

In order to locate Stone, then, it might be useful to peruse for a moment the broad stream of the postwar Caribbean intelligentsia.[55] In the earliest period, before the consolidation of the University College of the West Indies, 'returnees' from the metropole almost invariably sought niches in the newly emergent party politics blossoming after universal adult suffrage in 1944.[56] Errol Barrow in Barbados, Forbes Burnham in Guyana, Michael Manley in Jamaica and, most significantly, Eric Williams in Trinidad and Tobago,[57] all represented a cadre of centrist, proto- and developed intellectuals who, influenced by British Fabian and Labour Party socialism, sought to assume what they considered as their rightful place in the newly emergent West Indian 'political kingdom'. A secondary cohort, closely related to them, including Nobel laureate W. Arthur Lewis and anthropologist M.G. Smith, operated from relatively secure metropolitan academic positions – though with occasional forays into the Caribbean – influencing the technical direction of their compatriots through academic debate and formal consultation.

The second trend emerged in the sixties with the consolidation of a critical mass of Caribbean-based and mostly Caribbean-born thinkers at the UWI. Gathering strength in the New World Group, intellectuals across a range of disciplines sought, from a radical perspective, to critique the efforts of the first decade of West Indian independence. With its strongest hand in economics, New World and its offshoots, led by iconoclastic thinking from Lloyd Best, George Beckford, Norman Girvan, Clive Thomas and many others, sought to advance a Caribbean 'dependentista' perspective,[58] with strong opposition to 'imperialism' and a regionalist, semiautarchic approach to economic development.

By the late sixties, New World, fraying at its edges, partly due to its failure to move beyond a narrowly intellectual discourse and the concurrent emergence of more possibilities for activism, had given way to Black Power, with Walter Rodney as its most powerful advocate.[59] But by the early seventies, Black Power, too, had conceded ground to various streams of Marxism after the failure of the Trinidad 'Revolution' of 1970.[60] With Rodney again emerging as a premier advocate, others in the variegated stream included Trevor Munroe in Jamaica; Tim Hector in Antigua;[61] Ralph Gonsalves in Barbados and, later, at home in St Vincent; Richard Jacobs, Michael Als and David Abdullah in Trinidad; Bill Riviere in Dominica; and Bernard Coard and Maurice Bishop in Grenada. With few exceptions (Hector and his Jamesian position in Antigua and the emergent praxis of the Working People's Alliance [WPA] in Guyana),[62] the newly emergent Marxist Left travelled the route of Leninist, vanguardist politics, with explicit assumptions about the comprador and repressive nature of their governing predecessors and the need for, and inevitability of, revolution as a means of improving the welfare of the Caribbean people.

Stone represents an emergent third trend. He was certainly not a part of the Marxist Left – though he borrowed unreservedly from Marxist class analysis and, indeed, often engaged in bitter and bruising polemics with its leading and relatively influential cadres at the UWI Mona Faculty of Social Sciences.[63] Equally, however, he cannot be considered as simply a dispassionate academic consultant or advisor to various Jamaican governments. Rather, his consistent advocacy of the poor and black, his reliance on popular opinion to help mould and influence his own perspectives, his trenchant critique of Jamaican government behind its facade of democracy, and his evident unwillingness to become the paid-up member of any existing political trend reveal him to be the prototype of a new category – that of the intellectual tribune. In this approach, then – reading the popular mood and paying serious attention to its expression – Stone, despite the evident lacunae in his work, prepares the way for the Caribbean subaltern approach sketched elsewhere in this volume.

Others have subsequently tried to follow Stone's model, though with much less success. Certainly, Trinidad and Tobago's Selwyn Ryan with his 'SARA' polls, daily columns and high media profile is one example, as, perhaps, was Ralph Gonsalves as a journalist in his Barbados sojourn before becoming a lawyer and full-time politician in St Vincent. Trevor Munroe, too, in his latest incarnation as media commentator, darling of the Jamaican lunch-speaker circuit and, now, independent senator, is seeking to travel Stone's route, though without the polls and its accompanying credibility that gave Stone wide readership and currency in his heyday.

This is not at all to say that Stone's philosophy and politics were unproblematic and free of contradiction, as, indeed, is suggested throughout this entire chapter. Thus, for example, his repeated advocacy of 'deeper' democracy does not, at first glance, sit smoothly with his shrill call for draconian measures, including capital punishment, to solve the problem of crime in Jamaica.[64] Nor is his metatheoretical position of positivist, inductive empiricism itself unproblematic, as was evident in his occasional and somewhat arbitrary mood swings from supporting the policies of one party to another as new polling results reflected the changing political opinions of the Jamaican people. But these are issues for subsequent scholarship. This chapter only opens the first page of the book on the career of a human being who, while often enigmatic, reveals, on closer inspection, a deep and abiding concern for his people, his country and his region. If one were then to summarize Stone in his own words, as he, with his profound sense of self would no doubt have appreciated, he was: "both actor and analyst, commentator and spectator, participant and observer"[65] on the slippery slopes of the Caribbean terrain.

5

Remembering Michael Manley: 1924–1997

Michael Manley straddled two eras. He was a brilliant product of the time of the heroic politician. Tall, handsome and a powerful speaker, his message of hope resonated in an entire generation of young people and found common cause with a previously gathering storm of discontent. Ronald Henry had risen against the regime of Manley's father, yet the muse of history had placed Michael alongside Ronald's father, Claudius, as allies in a new phase of popular upsurge. When that movement was ultimately defeated, Michael retreated for a decade then re-emerged victorious, though with a chastened programme in a new world order. But the people never forgot the earlier Manley, and when he died, the mourning was intense and widespread. His death signalled the end of an era when politics and the politician ruled. The popular outpouring of sympathy that accompanied the death of Michael Manley may be read as either the loss of something irrecoverable or the beginning of a new phase of popular awareness and autonomy.

My lasting memory of the man is a sepia-toned image taken from late October 1980 at a mass meeting in Spanish Town, site of the old capital of Jamaica. The long 1980 election was drawing to its bloody finale over the bodies of some eight hundred Jamaicans. Manley's governing PNP had been crippled by the collapsing economy, which had suffered debilitating loss of capital over the previous seven years, and by widespread violence, which had reached epidemic proportions. For more than two years, these harsh realities, driven home to the people in graphic detail by the premier and right-wing newspaper the *Daily Gleaner,* had contributed to the unpopularity of his government and the growing prestige of Edward Seaga's pro-American JLP.[1]

On this moonless night in October 1980, the party faithful had gathered in Spanish Town Square to sing together, to "stand firm" with their leader, "Joshua", and to tell the "Labourites", imperialists and Central Intelligence Agency (CIA) that they "knew where they were going". Tonight, however, was not going to be like hundreds of other meetings that had been taking place across the length and breadth of the small island. As Michael Manley rose to address the adoring throng, suddenly there was the unmistakable, heavy industrial rattle of submachine gun fire. It was pandemonium. People were running; shoes were everywhere. Local and national party leaders who had been sitting on the raised platform were flat on their bellies, except Michael. Three members of his personal security detachment were struggling to pull him to the floor, but he, with his full six feet-plus stature, refused to bow. Poised between heroism and foolhardiness, Manley in that moment, atop that stage, in that photographic still shot, became a metaphor for Jamaica and, simultaneously, a metaphor for himself.

Little can be understood about what brought Michael Manley to this point without an appreciation of his peculiar place in Jamaican society. Born in Kingston in 1924, the son of the Rhodes scholar and brilliant barrister Norman Manley and his vivacious English-born, first cousin wife and sculptress, Edna, the young Manley's childhood was in many ways typical of the privileged Jamaican upper middle classes. But this is only a partial insight. In the layered and colour-conscious hierarchy of Jamaican society, Michael was also a 'brown man', with the contradictory privileges assigned to this categorization. His mother, for all intents and purposes, could pass for white and his father, though swarthy, was in his overall phenotype distinctly 'brown'. But even these powerful markers of identity are insufficient to gain a handle on the young Manley. To understand his particular niche is to appreciate that his mother, though of partial Jamaican descent, was not a "product" of the island and did not bring to the Jamaican matrix that complacency of privilege and colour far more typical of someone of her social position. Instead, both herself and Norman – who had been educated in the trenches of the Great War and later at Oxford – brought with them egalitarian sensibilities,[2] if filtered through Fabian socialist lenses, which would have a profound effect on both Michael and his elder brother Douglas. This complex twist in the 'typical' middle class trajectory served both to somewhat marginalize Manley from the mainstream of his peers and to instil in him that sense of compassion and call to service which lasted through his life. He was thus from the middle class but not of it; and as Michael, the student at Jamaica College and then the London School of Economics, evolved into Manley, the militant trade unionist and finally, Joshua, the 'comrade leader', he was for the people, but never quite 'of' the people.

The tension between a patrician sensibility arising from the Camelot-like atmosphere of the Manley compound at Drumblair, and a democratic, egalitarian impulse, probably incubated more by his mother and nurtured on a close interaction with the harsh and unforgiving Jamaican class structure, was likely to have been the central factor explaining the course of his life. The tension contributed to a certain restlessness about his character:[3] he could, in mercurial fashion, appear at one moment aloof, contemplative and 'above' those around him and in another become the populist on whose every word tens of thousands of people hung, or rose with fists in the air, in tumultuous adulation.

After a brief stint at the BBC in 1951, Michael Manley returned to Jamaica at a critical time for his father. The left wing of the party, led by the "Four Hs",[4] had been purged in an inner-party struggle that was, at least in part, generated by the gathering Cold War pressures from the United States and Britain. The PNP was in disarray, for the Left had been, in great measure, responsible for the organization of the party, especially its powerful urban contingents and its working class support in the Trades Union Congress (TUC). Michael returned as a journalist for the weekly newspaper *Public Opinion*, but he soon left this job in order to build the party's new affiliate, the National Workers' Union (NWU). Under his leadership, the new union grew rapidly, outflanking the TUC and undermining any possibility of the Left establishing an independent political base outside the framework of the two dominant parties. On the one hand, then, his early intervention into Jamaican politics can be interpreted as antiradical, even anticommunist, given the flavour of the times. Yet at the same time, through the NWU, Manley built a trade union organization that, in its democratic structures and bargaining skills (which were evident in its organization of the new bauxite/alumina industry), far outshone its immediate rival, the hierarchical and personalist Bustamante Industrial Trade Union (BITU), founded by his father's cousin and nemesis, Alexander Bustamante.

This, however, was only the beginning of Manley's long and ambivalent relationship with the small, but vocal, Jamaican Left. In 1969, on his father's retirement, Michael became president of the PNP. A year before, the capital, Kingston, had erupted in an afternoon of violence. University students had staged a demonstration after the Hugh Shearer-led JLP government had declared Walter Rodney, a radical Guyanese lecturer at the multinational UWI, persona non grata. When the defenceless students were attacked by riot police with batons and teargas, things rapidly deteriorated. Thousands of unemployed young people commandeered the public transport system and took over the streets of Kingston. The violent protests were soon brought under control, but they signalled the upsurge of a new wave of black consciousness and social awareness, much of which remained unchanelled, though important individuals were coalescing around a radical newspaper called *Abeng*.

The PNP president was keenly aware of the new currents that were shaking the colonial and white-biased foundations of Jamaican society and acted astutely. Not only did he tap into the popular mood with his reggae and Rastafari-influenced campaign for the 1972 elections, but also he was able to convince key members of the newly coalescing Left to abandon an independent path and seek the political kingdom through the structures of the PNP.[5] Young radicals, such as D.K. Duncan, Arnold "Scree" Bertram and Hugh Small, came into the party and brought with them a level of energy and new thinking that, along with Manley's own process of evolution, would help transform the character of the PNP, and of Jamaican politics itself, in those tumultuous eight years in the seventies.

Manley won the election in 1972 with his "Rod of Correction" given to him by Rastafarian leader Claudius Henry and with the powerful slogan "Better Must Come". Hundreds of thousands of Jamaicans, who had listened with baited breath to his every word, in the ghettos of Kingston and in the poor rural districts in the hilly countryside, waited with great expectations for a change. And although it is easier to conclude, gazing backwards over the past two decades, that nothing has changed, what is evident on closer scrutiny is how much of what he set out to do was actually accomplished.

If one reads *The Politics of Change*,[6] which first appeared in 1972 – effectively his manifesto for his first term as prime minister – it can essentially be interpreted as a programme for 'nationalist modernization'. Manley sought to forge a broad alliance between the middle and working classes with what he saw as a new stratum of modern and forward thinking industrialists, to drag Jamaica from its colonial moorings and into the late twentieth century. Nothing at this stage in his thinking refers to socialism, so much as 'social justice'. In *The Politics of Change,* Manley deplores the poverty in Jamaican society, the widening gap between the rich and the poor, and calls for greater national control, if not ownership, of foreign capital. All of this, he argues – in a position that remained consistent throughout his career – should be addressed within the confines of parliamentary democracy, although he called for a more participatory politics and greater self-reliance. This, importantly, was linked to a foreign policy that he proposed should be more Third World oriented, with multiple linkages and alliances, instead of the traditional fealty to the West.

Eight years after, despite the defection of the 'new industrialists' and a significant part of the middle class, much of this had been achieved. Jamaica's educational system had been overhauled with a school feeding programme for primary school children and free education up to university level. New laws were approved to change the typical masculine bias of British common law. Thus, the old bastardy laws had been replaced by new legislation giving children born out of wedlock equal rights of inheritance, and so on. Women were granted equal pay for equal work, and an innovative maternity leave law gave new mothers job security and three months paid maternity leave. An energetic and unprecedented housing programme delivered more houses for the poor and middle classes than all previous regimes together had done. A new 'land-lease' programme was established, which accelerated the delivery of arable land to the rural poor. The Jamaica Adult Literacy (JAMAL) programme was implemented with significant success in reducing the country's high rates of illiteracy. And, the bauxite levy was negotiated, which at once dramatically increased the taxes earned by the country from its only significant mineral resource. Before the levy, the government's revenues from the transnationals had been a mere US$35 million per annum; immediately after, it skyrocketed to US$200 million.[7]

Many of the programmes were concentrated in the first three years of the new regime. Their effect was profound. For the first time in a decade, unemployment in Jamaica fell. Between 1971 and 1976, 35,000 new jobs were created and the numbers of unemployed decreased by some 11,000 persons.[8] There was also a significant redistribution of income from the top down, somewhat altering the previous, highly skewed picture. The share of wages and salaries as a percentage of national income, for example, increased from 58 percent to 64 percent between 1971 and 1976.

However, the costs that were paid for these noteworthy accomplishments were inordinate. From the earliest days of the Manley regime, capital began to leave the country. In an interesting debate with Canadian economist Kari Levitt shortly before his death,[9] Manley took her to task for suggesting that the reason capital flowed so rapidly out of the country was at least in part because of a heightened "rhetoric" that accompanied the party's "rededication" to democratic socialism in 1974. In an impassioned argument, Manley proposed that the drift had begun before, when the local upper classes got whiff of a relatively mild property tax adjustment that was to be made in 1973, after which applications to live in the United States rose dramatically. And, questioning the notion that active 'destabilization' of the country had begun only when the United States had been drawn into the picture, Manley again argues for an earlier, locally based resistance: "More importantly, beginning in 1975, the opposition began its calculated programme of violence. This was a full year before the CIA became involved as a punishment for our support of Cuba's defence of Angola against South Africa."[10]

Be that as it may, by the middle of 1976, Jamaica was in turmoil. Organized violence, primarily directed against strongholds of the ruling party in Kingston's inner city, had reached unprecedented levels. Entire communities, such as lower Jones Town and parts of Trench Town, had to be evacuated, creating internal refugee colonies, such as the appropriately titled "Sufferer's Heights" in St Catherine. Something had to be done. Manley's decision, since stridently condemned by his Opposition, was to call a state of emergency and arrest suspected perpetrators of violence including members of his own party, though the largest contingent came from the rank and file and some leaders of the JLP. In the national elections of that December, called even while the Emergency was still in effect, the PNP swept home to a second term with an increased parliamentary majority of eleven seats, gaining forty-seven to the JLP's thirteen.

The victory proved to be a pyrrhic one, however. Even as the party faithful were recovering from the celebration hangover, other events had conspired to bring the economy to the point of collapse. A growing panic that Jamaica was on the road to communism had consolidated among the already skittish

Jamaican upper middle and upper classes. Some fourteen thousand trained people had migrated to the United States and Canada between 1972 and 1974 alone – the earliest phase of the flight. By the end of 1976, it was discovered that some US$300 million had, by various means, left the country and the government was faced with a negative net foreign reserve situation for the first time in Jamaica's history. In a long series of negotiations, which stretched through 1977, the government at first appeared to be searching for some novel, radical alternative to address its debt problems, but eventually it succumbed and went to the IMF to negotiate the best possible loan terms. The eventual engagement with the IMF set the stage for the rapid and tragic downfall of Manley's government.

Even as Michael Manley's national prospects appeared increasingly dim, however, his prestige on the broader international stage continued to rise. Jamaica's support for the Cuban involvement in Angola, which Manley suggests brought the Americans into the destabilization campaign wholesale,[11] nonetheless served to increase the country's prestige in the Non-Aligned Movement. In Africa, in particular, Manley became a pivotal player in the negotiations for the independence of Zimbabwe and a leading spokesman against apartheid in South Africa. Manley, with his multiple contacts in the Socialist International, Africa, the Non-Aligned Movement and the Caribbean, for a critical period in the seventies, was a central player in advancing the debate for a new international economic order, with emphases on debt relief and enhanced economic and technical redistribution of resources to poor countries. In the Caribbean, he was a leading spokesman for deeper integration through the Caribbean Community (CARICOM) and, along with Trinidad, Guyana and Barbados, brought Cuba back into the fold by jointly recognizing that isolated Caribbean state in 1974.

By May 1977 the first IMF agreement, which proved to be surprisingly mild, was in place. In December, however, the regular 'test' was failed on a minor technicality and the screws were tightened. In May 1978 the new Extended Fund Facility was implemented and the real economic contraction began. Between 1978 and 1980, under the aegis of the IMF programme, the Cost of Living Index increased by some 40 percent; real wages declined by 20 to 30 percent and unemployment again began to increase. A figure of 22.8 percent unemployed in 1972 had increased to 26.8 percent by 1980.[12] By this stage, Manley and his party were in the pincers of a multipronged destabilization campaign. At the centre of it was the *Daily Gleaner,* which sought every opportunity to attack the government's relationship with Cuba and Manley's close personal friendship with Fidel Castro as indications that the country was about to 'go communist'. Although some members of the Left in the PNP and their erstwhile allies in the small Marxist-Leninist WPJ had visions of Jamaica on a path of "socialist orientation",[13] the mainstream of the population, including Manley himself, remained committed to a parliamentary democratic path. This was evidently not the only channel that his Opposition believed appropriate to achieve their political objectives, however.

In a series of sustained and increasingly heinous attacks, armed and trained gunmen, largely from the Opposition JLP, were able to undermine the rule of law and bring Jamaica to the brink of civil war. It is true that the PNP, with its significant mass base in the city, did indeed join the battle, but a close reading of the political geography of urban Jamaica quickly suggests, to all but the most naïve, that the brunt of the offensive was against PNP strongholds,[14] with the twin purposes of demoralizing the hardcore democratic socialist support and discrediting Manley's ability to govern.

The effect was devastating. In October 1980 the PNP tumbled to its worst ever electoral defeat, preserving only nine seats and conceding fifty-one to Edward Seaga and his JLP. It is of interest to note, for the historical record, that eight of the nine seats won were in constituencies where the violence of the previous months had been at its worst. At least here, the wanton shedding of blood seemed to have had the opposite effect of strengthening the resolve to resist against seemingly overwhelming odds. Manley, then, who had entered the decade of the seventies with so much hope for changing Jamaica, departed bitterly at the end of it, with the victorious bells of the JLP ringing in his ears along with the words of Seaga's inaugural speech in which he committed himself to "eradicating radicalism" from Jamaica, once and for all.

Nine years later, Manley was back in power, though this time with an agenda and a programme substantially different from that with which he had dominated Jamaican politics in the previous decade. By then, a paradigm shift had taken place. The Soviet Union was still months away from collapse, but a certain Reagan/Thatcher neoliberalism had swept the world before it. The new Jamaican government, in a manner not dissimilar to ideological shifts that would later lead to the ascendancy of Bill Clinton and Tony Blair, seemed to subscribe fully to the new paradigm. Manley, on many occasions, personally defended the efficacy of market relations and the government embarked on an energetic policy of privatization and import and currency liberalization. In the aforementioned debate with Levitt, Manley defended his 1989 policies on the grounds that he had few available options in a new world order and, in an adverse situation, had sought to maintain key egalitarian components, including a programme of worker participation, a push to spread ownership through the redistribution of shares to workers, the establishment of the Micro Industry Development Agency, out of funds obtained from the floating of public bonds, to help the poor establish small businesses, and the resumption of the land reform programme.[15]

Manley resigned as a result of ill health in 1992, and since then a PNP government led by P.J. Patterson has been in power, winning re-election in 1993 and 1997. Throughout this period, the market-oriented policies, initiated in 1989, have either remained in place or have been enhanced. While the debate in Jamaica rages on the effectiveness of these policies, this damning comment by Kari Levitt in her exchange with Manley, is worth considering:

I think it is now clear that the neo-liberal model has failed to deliver either stability or growth. Floating exchange rates and perpetual devaluations proved to be disastrous, and have mercifully been abandoned in favour of exchange rate stability. They failed to close the trade gap, which has now been aggravated by the reduction in duty on motor vehicles, and the encouragement of the importation of used cars, and is out of control. Last year, two thirds of bank credit was allocated to consumption expenditures. The manufacturing industry is in decline, unable to compete with imports from higher wage Caricom countries. Equipment is run down. Plants are closing. The 'mopping up of liquidity' by issue of CDs has acted as an engine of redistribution from the poor to the rich . . . the model is not working. Perhaps it can work in other countries where political democracy was suspended for long periods of time – as in Chile. Be that as it may, it is not working in Jamaica.[16]

In the last years of his life, Manley, now the elder statesman and remarried for the fifth time, never really slowed down. He played a somewhat low-profiled, though important, role in mediating the Haitian crisis and negotiating the return to power of President Aristide. He revised his passionate book on West Indian cricket,[17] reflective of his lifelong love affair with sport; he worked as a consultant on Caribbean tourism; and he maintained an interest in a variety of issues, including the cause of Caribbean migrants in the United

States, Britain and Canada, the African American struggle for civil rights, to which he had always paid keen attention; and he continued his own personal obsession with horticulture and music. For those who knew the vibrant Michael on the stage at his fiery best and were fortunate to encounter him in this new phase, it was indeed illuminating. Here was a humble, soft-spoken, almost shy person, with a willingness to listen to criticism, though also retaining a dogged ability to defend his former policies when he felt it appropriate. In these last years, many of which were spent in pain, bedridden with prostate cancer, Michael virtually disappeared from the Jamaican political stage, his name barely a whisper on the incessant talk radio circuit. Then, on 6 March 1997, the announcement of his death came.

It was as though a hidden well from deep underground had suddenly burst through the surface. For those who were there, and with whom I have been fortunate to speak, it is evident that the grief was genuine, widespread and palpable. Tens of thousands flocked to the National Arena to view Manley's body lying in state. Prominent among them were the poor of Kingston and the rural areas. Kumina dancers with their traditional African rhythms came down from St Thomas; 'nine nights' – the traditional ceremony in honour of the dead – were held by the dozen across the island. At the funeral, the people overwhelmed the official ceremonies and created, in the words of the *Daily Observer* reporter, a "security nightmare":

"The masses have come down," quipped a finely dressed woman in the formal procession while diplomats attempted to evade the throng. Meantime, large numbers of people, who complained about being kept away from 'the leader', scaled the fence to Heroes Park. "My Father bawl living eye water when he hear that Michael Manley dead," said a young woman from Vineyard Town in Kingston, "And look I come here and they keep me from Michael." Another declared, "Michael wouldn't check for this. He would say, "give my people way."[18]

The interviews in the papers – too many to list – spoke of deep affection:

The two middle aged women standing nearby said they too owed Michael Manley a lot. But wary of the violent possibility of Jamaican politics they declined to give their names. The one, of McIntyre Villa in East Kingston, Manley's former constituency, looks weathered beyond her 53 years. "He put me in a house," she said of Manley. "Manley did look out for poor people." She paused, looked around, then declared with assertion: "Me born in PNP. I have to come out to say goodbye to the leader." Tears welled in the eyes of her 51 year old friend, who lives on Mountain View Avenue, who herself did not get the home. Her mother did, in Waterford. Her children got free education and she had a "maternity leave with pay baby". "We lose a good man, a good leader," said this woman. She could not hold back the tears any more.[19]

The mourners from St Thomas, Mountain View, McIntyre Villa, Jones Town, North Gully and all across the island were grieving not only for the loss of the man, though this was a great part of it, but the loss of the seventies. They were grieving for an entire era when, for the first time poor, black people in Jamaica were beginning to have a voice, even though that voice, still muted, had to be amplified through Joshua's trumpet. It is in this very act of grief that there is the suggestion of a growing consciousness of what this loss of voice has meant and, perhaps, even as the wailing from the last 'nine nights' subsides, the beginning of a popular awakening. Henceforth, there will be no Joshua to bravely stand in the face of the deadly bullets and speak for the people. They will now, increasingly, have to speak for themselves.

6

Careening on the Edge of the Abyss:
Driving, Hegemony and the Rule of Law in Jamaica[1]

It all seemed overwhelming, out of control – the throngs lining the road, the noisy traffic, sometimes jammed bumper to bumper and barely moving, then suddenly in chaotic motion as though racing to the next jam-up. It was not exactly a different country: looked at individually the people seemed no different. But the number of them – so many, many more than he could ever remember seeing in one place. And collectively, the crowd, as an entity, seemed tense, nervous, and moved by a single and alarmingly unpredictable will.
> – Michael Thelwell, *The Harder They Come*

Early in the morning of Tuesday 19 September 1995, young Jeremy Small, all of six years old, got up with his eight-year-old sister, dressed and left his home as he did every weekday, for the St Francis Primary School. From his community in Peter's Rock – a largely peasant and working class dormitory village perched in the hills high above the city of Kingston – the teeming metropolis below appears pristine and calm at 6:00 a.m. But this is pure deception. Within an hour, the two had reached the crowded minibus stop at Barbican Square, where they regularly changed vehicles for the second and final stage of the journey. The rest of the story is reported in the *Daily Gleaner*:

The tragedy occurred shortly after 7:00 a.m. Jeremy and his sister Judith were waiting with scores of other people at the bus stop. When a bus arrived, persons eager to get into the bus began pushing and shoving. In the melee, the boy fell and ended up under the rear wheel of the bus. "The bus drive off and ran over him head, everybody bawl out and then the driver reverse and ran over him head again . . ." The protesters argued that if there were enough buses on the route, little Jeremy perhaps would still be alive.[2]

There is chaos and bloodshed on the streets of Jamaica. Since 1989, an average of four hundred persons have died and thirty-two hundred have been injured every year as a result of vehicular accidents.[3] In the early nineties, in terms of fatalities per hundred thousand cars, Jamaica ranked third in the world, behind Ethiopia and India.[4] In the pages of the daily newspapers and in the numerous talk shows that dominate the airwaves, there is a rising crescendo of complaint about a system where there is no respect for the law, of an "uncivil society",[5] of a war of all against all, of drivers veering dangerously, careening, as it were, on the edge of a social abyss.

Ted Dwyer, inveterate letter writer and headmaster of a local community college, describes what might be considered a stereotypical encounter in the daily life of the Jamaican motorist. This first case might be called, for classification's sake, that of "The Mad Minibus Driver":

We were not watching a Hollywood thriller filmed in Los Angeles or New York. We were watching, dumbfounded, a lawless hooligan driving a No. 83 Mountain View bus, on Friday, February 6. Either racing another bus or foolishly trying the impossible task of avoiding delay in clogged Trafalgar Road traffic, the lunatic turned off Trafalgar Road at Emmanuel Road, then unto Pawsey Road into Trafalgar Place, up St Lucia Avenue into Tobago Avenue and into the Texaco gas station area. Now under the canopy of the gas station, he tore off the covering of the vent of the bus badly damaging the canopy.

We watched in disbelief. After a brief stop, the conductor retrieved the cover of the vent out of the debris of the canopy, hardly seeming to recognise that damage had been done to other people's property or the need to stop for a word on the matter.

God is good. The bus could have plunged into the bay area, just a few feet away to cause a fiery explosion. And I would have witnessed the death of some of my college students.[6]

Then, there is the second case, easily recognizable to even the visitor who has driven for a short time in Kingston. The appropriately pen-named "Miserable Motorist" describes it:

Don't you just hate it when you are moving along in bumper to bumper traffic at snail's pace and the person behind you 'draws gear' and plants his posterior in front of you? I find that on these occasions, my usually calm demeanour is transformed into rage . . . and I become . . . 'The Miserable Motorist'! On this particular morning, having left home at the late hour of 6:35 a.m. (when you live in Stony Hill you must leave at 6:15 a.m.), I managed to remain calm all the way to Russell Heights. There I was, sitting in a line of traffic. Well behaved and calm. The line moved forward slowly, and a motorist, driving in a red what-it-was, decided that he just had to be in front of me, and so he flung his car in front of mine with great relish.

Well, you know what happened next. I was transformed into 'The Miserable Motorist' and decided that I wanted back my space in the line. I pulled up beside Mr Red Car with thunder in my face and insisted that he return to me what was mine – MY space – and to my utter distress he refused . . . eventually, the motorist in front of my nemesis waved at me to drive in front of him. By then I was blocking oncoming traffic and transforming other usually calm people into 'miserable motorists'.[7]

And the third case, perhaps best illustrative of the fleeting regard for law, is the case of the "Anonymous Vehicles and the Police Patrol Car":

A police patrol car with a siren on was seen driving fast along Maxfield Avenue. Motorists in the lane in which the police car was travelling gave it access, but I noticed that two cars were following the police car and travelling at the same speed. When a check was made, these two cars were not police cars, nor were they in any way connected with the emergency on hand. This is the typical behaviour of some motorists.[8]

Common to all three examples and, indeed, to the numerous daily incidents, is a frenetic urgency to move. It is almost as though in a situation where the Jamaican economy has remained virtually stagnant for two decades, and where social mobility is increasingly stymied by these conditions, that the urge for spatial movement takes on greater significance. Allied to this is the critical importance of the horn. In Jamaica, the horn is a weapon of physical offence. Long before the traffic light has changed from red to green, the cacophony of horn blowing begins, and should the unaccustomed or unalert motorist not immediately accelerate, then he is met with a prolonged, piercing blast. Movement, at whatever cost, is a priority.

The second, and more important, commonality, of course, is the scant regard for the law. In the case of the minibus driver and his conductor/salvager, 'law' is encapsulated in the recovery of one's own damaged property and simultaneously in the disregard for that of the gas station owner; for the evidently middle class 'miserable motorist', law is to be asserted through retribution, the recovery of space and respect, even at the expense of the oncoming, legally positioned traffic; and for the resourceful, anonymous drivers trailing the police car, the law, on this occasion physically manifest in patrol vehicle with wailing siren, is but a means to break the law and to move more quickly to one's destination.

As with the many and detailed descriptions of the problem, there have been numerous formal and informal attempts to understand the causes for the chaos and to propose solutions. Thus, a letter from "Concerned Commuter" in October 1997 locates the problem as beginning with the proliferation of privately run minibuses following the demise of the state-owned Jamaica Omnibus Service (JOS) some two decades ago. The suggested answer is to return to a state-owned system with some private input:

> With a proper feasibility study, inclusive of good management and foresight, we could once more boast a state-owned transportation system. Eliminating the private bus owner would not be the only alternative, since competition usually improves standards, provided, of course, they want to remain in business.[9]

Conrad Reid, a physical planner writing in 1997, takes a different tack, arguing against the commonly held view that there are too many cars on the road. Cars, he suggests, are a necessary and inevitable part of the landscape and their numbers will continue to increase. What is necessary is to move from the government's policy of ad hoc measures to a consolidated approach of building a new, efficient network of roadways:

> Dual carriageways, one way road, traffic lights, roundabouts, more police, *cul de sacs* and bypasses are the order of the day. These attempts, as good as they may seem, will not deal with the inevitable growth in vehicle population . . . the traffic problem of the KMA [Kingston Metropolitan Area] is not due to the myth of 'too many cars', but to the failure over the years to implement a sensible network of roadways. Money currently being spent on band-aid measures would be better utilised if the authorities would fit into their plans freeways to accommodate traffic movement between the hubs of city activity.[10]

And writer Hentley Allen, while agreeing with the notion of overcrowding, adds a new and important dimension when he advances the need for a new atmosphere of discipline and civility:

> I welcome the news that new buses will soon be on the road. However, I am quick to point out that more buses does not necessarily mean a solving of the problems. In fact, it may very well aggravate the situation. What we need is more discipline on our roads by bus crews, commuters and the general motoring public . . . bus drivers and

conductors/conductresses need to attire themselves in the uniforms stipulated for the service. A new attitude toward civility by both bus crews and commuters needs to be adopted. Pushing and shoving to get on to a bus smacks of what obtains in the jungle![11]

There are no shortages of analysis or proposals to solve the problem of gridlock and its effects. Indeed, since the December 1997 re-election of the PNP, for an unprecedented third term in office, there is a new and vigorous minister with sole responsibility for transport and he is keenly aware of the crisis and intent on combating it with new technical and organizational initiatives.[12] Supporting him, there is a relatively new senior superintendent of police for traffic who, in his zeal to enforce the law, has already earned the ire of taxi men for insisting that they pay their overdue traffic tickets and, in effect, from their selfish perspective, enforcing the law too much to its letter.[13]

What, then, in the face of past and current measures, accounts for the unabated lawlessness and carnage on the roads? The conclusion here is that, unlike the thrust of many analysts, the problem of transportation in Jamaica cannot simply be relegated to narrowly defined niches associated with more efficient urban planning or public administration, if such pure modes might, for the moment, be imagined. Rather, what is happening on the roads is a reflection, indeed, a metaphor, for a profound social and political crisis. This writer has suggested elsewhere that this crisis can be called "hegemonic dissolution".[14] It is occurring at a time when the old, dominant social alliance is no longer able to assert itself over Jamaican society; yet the popular resistance to this domination does not have the organizational capacity, world view, or favourable international conjuncture to replace it. This tense and fraught moment, then, has the possibility of moving in a number of possible directions. The first mooted possibility is that of an authoritarian solution, either within or outside the constitution; the second is the possibility of democratic renewal; and the third is a direction called, after Marx, "the common ruin of the contending classes".[15]

From such a perspective, it can be inferred that gridlock on the roads mirrors and simultaneously buttresses gridlock in the social and political arena. This chapter, then, seeks to move beyond the broad description of hegemonic dissolution – a sort of "low-level equilibrium"[16] that permeates all spheres of living – to map its contours and sketch the details and character of the ennui that is pervasive in Jamaica today.

The background to all of this is a small island moving rapidly from the rural to the urban. Kingston, the capital, throughout the century, but especially after World War II, has expanded from its position on a narrow grid north of its famous protected harbour to its present occupation of the entire vast Liguanea Plain, eventually spreading over to occupy flat land to the south and west in the adjacent parish of St Catherine.[17] In this respect, it is the quintessential Third World city, with sharp and geographically delineated wealth differentials, unplanned growth, large squatter communities on its outskirts and inadequate, overburdened infrastructure. At the heart of it all is the urban transport system, the flawed transmission line, the corrupted blood in the bloated organism.

This transport system has gone through several metamorphoses that reflect the peculiarities of Kingston's rapid growth as well as the character of its marginal insertion into the global system of late capitalism and the dynamic of the confrontation of social forces in the country itself. From such an angle, the policies that have been tried – all patently unsuccessful – traverse the gamut of imagined approaches to social organization in the twentieth century. They can be listed as follows:

1. Local capital as monopoly
2. Foreign capital as monopoly
3. Bureaucratic state monopoly
4. Free competition with limited regulation
5. Free competition further modified

The failure of all of these approaches, and that of the collective imagination, to provide a safe, timely, clean and civilized service leaves room open, via an admittedly crude process of elimination, for unimagined approaches, of which the proposal to be advanced here is that of a democratic and social solution. To arrive at such a conclusion, however, a history needs to be traced.

The History

Chaos is not new to the city. After World War II, the exploding demand for automobiles accompanied rapid geographical expansion and soon led to an eclipsing of the limited tram system:

In the immediate post World War II period, with the removal of petrol rationing and other wartime restrictions, there was a rapid increase in automobile transport, clogging the main streets which were shared with the old tramways operating under a license taken over by the Jamaica Public Service Co. Ltd. This was coupled with an increase in the number of taxicabs and minibuses – the so-called 'scrambolas' – which actively competed with the tramcars by running before them as stage carriages, or tapping the new suburbs which were growing out of the vacant cattle pens, or small estates, on the fringes of the built up area.[18]

Local Capital as Monopoly

It was evident to all that a new transport system was required. In 1947, a Jamaican, H.J. Lindsay, was granted the exclusive monopoly for twenty years to run bus routes in the east and centre of the city previously serviced by the tram, provided he was able, within twelve months of start-up, to significantly increase the capital outlay of his service to the then princely sum of £325,000. Lindsay failed to do this, however, and within two years, the service offered by his Jamaica Utilities Ltd was under attack and he himself was accused of corruption, having granted exclusive selling rights for petrol and parts to his own subsidiary, the Jamaica Motor Car Co. Ltd. A commission of enquiry, established to examine the operations of the new concern, ruled in 1951 that it was not viable and that Lindsay's licence should be revoked. Swaby's 1974 study suggests that the local man never had a chance: some members of the commission had conflicting interests in that they were representing a transnational corporation that, even as Lindsay still held his contract, was already negotiating with the government to take over the apparently lucrative public transport business.[19]

The conclusion from this brief episode is that in the late colonial atmosphere of the 1940s, where even though there were sitting, elected members of Parliament, the governor still held ultimate power, the chances of a local entrepreneur surviving in the face of British capital allied to local interests were minimal. Lindsay's effort was a failure, though his Jamaica Utilities Ltd set the foundation for the entrance of a monopolistic transnational corporation into the picture.

Foreign Capital as Monopoly

In 1953, British Electric Traction (BET), a large transnational conglomerate with worldwide investments in transport systems, took over the franchise from Lindsay's Jamaica Utilities Ltd. With strong support from those local businessmen and lawyers who had played a key role in discrediting his operation, the new JOS was soon consolidated. The subsequent three-decade history of the JOS presents a study in contrasts. On the one hand, the JOS provided, for most of its period (though with notable complaints from time to time), a relatively decent and efficient service; on the other hand, the legal dirty tricks, profit gouging and general lack of concern for the long-term interests of the country, which characterized BET's reign, hastened the crisis and ultimately led to the collapse of the public transport system in the early eighties and the mess that exists today.

The highlights of BET's involvement in Jamaica can be adumbrated as follows:

1. Handsome Profits: Between 1953 and 1969, in its period of greatest profitability, BET, from an initial investment of some £800,000, had managed to increase this eightfold to a total of £6,530,892.[20]

2. Revenue from Dirty Tricks: Further to these direct profits, BET paid itself a management fee of some 7.5 percent of its gross revenues. This was hidden from its public accounts, precisely because it went against the letter of the agreement under which it had been granted the franchise to run the JOS. In the first six years of operation, these hidden management fees totalled some 40.2 percent of net revenue, or £727,000, compared with income tax for the same period of £184,802 and dividends of £371,374.

3. Arbitrary Reduction in Depreciation Rate: In 1964 BET, faced with more organized and aggressive public sector monitoring, was 'persuaded' to reduce the unethical and probably illegal management fee to a flat rate of £100,000 per annum but, in order to maintain and increase its profits, this concession was accompanied by an arbitrary reduction in the depreciation rate. From 1953 to 1964, depreciation had been calculated at 20 percent of revenue. In the latter year, it was reduced to 8.3 percent.[21] To the casual observer, such an action can be understood as, over time, having a potentially catastrophic effect on the ability of the company to replace its capital, in particular, its rolling stock. This is correct and this action, by itself, played an important role in the ultimate collapse of the JOS, but it needs to be seen in the context of the following point.

4. Exclusive Use of Local Funds to Buy Buses: Instead of relying on its own retained earnings, or new injections from Britain, the JOS financed the

replacement and expansion of its fleet through overdrafts from the local banking system.

In summary, the JOS, under BET, provided a functioning service for at least two clear decades but at great expense, depleting the country of the reserves that might have financed the transport system through harder times. When the operating environment did become more difficult in the seventies, BET, having taken its profits, simply left. Swaby, in his detailed analysis, is therefore justified in his conclusion that: "Short of outright nationalisation, nothing but a well-staffed regulatory authority with effective powers under the laws of a developing nation, which is aware of the risks of entrusting its infra-structural to foreign multinational corporations can maintain a balance in the country's interest."[22]

Bureaucratic State Monopoly

If in its first fifteen years of operation the JOS had provided handsome profits to BET, it is also true to say that, by the early seventies, a number of the fundamental features in the economic environment were moving against the profitability of the company. New routes had been opened up but the number of 'bus miles' increased at the expense of the number of 'passenger miles'. In 1959, for example, passengers/bus mile stood at 14.5, whereas in 1970, the figure had fallen to 11.5.[23] To offset falling revenues, the JOS had applied for a rate increase to the Public Passenger Transport Board. An increase was eventually granted in 1969, but it was less than the figure requested.

With no reduction in the level of the management fee that had been fixed in previous years, dividends fell. When BET eventually left and the Government of Jamaica took over the company in 1974, it was already beset by severe difficulties that undermined its ability to function effectively. Among the main problems were:

1. The company had no 'war chest' to either purchase new buses or to underwrite losses in lean years, as the accumulated profits of the previous two decades had gone with the BET.
2. The energy crisis of 1974 had a profound impact on the entire economy of Jamaica and was felt most acutely in transport, with its high reliance on fuel and lubricants. This served to further undermine whatever limited margins of profitability still existed.

3. The limited financial resources and the soaring cost of parts led, in the period between 1974 and 1979, to a drastic fall in the number of buses available for service on the roads. Whereas in 1974 the average turnout was some 70.6 percent of available stock, by 1980 this had fallen to 45.9 percent.[24]

4. As inflation followed in the wake of the energy crisis, JOS workers, like other employees throughout the country, demanded wage increases to keep up with the cost of living. The cash-strapped company was particularly hard hit and unable to offer significant increases, and this led to a drop in morale and further decline in the efficiency of the service.

5. Finally, what eventually led to its demise was the emergence, in response to the diminishing number of buses on the road, of a fleet of 'robot' minibuses that illegally plied the bus routes, robbing the JOS of further revenue, leading into a downward spiral of shortages, further drops in the numbers, greater competition and eventual collapse.

Free Competition with Limited Regulation

The year 1980 was the last in which a state-owned transport system dominated in the city of Kingston. It was also, not coincidentally, the year in which the PNP government, headed by Michael Manley and based on the principles of democratic socialism, gave way to the pro-American, pro–free market JLP under Edward Seaga. It is important to note that in early 1980, even before the handing over of power, the PNP, faced with extreme competition, had been forced to come to terms with the robot operators by establishing a route-sharing agreement. This was ultimately to the detriment of the JOS which, hampered by an ever-diminishing fleet, simply could not compete. By 1982, when the company was finally dissolved, minibuses accounted for a full 79.6 percent of total passengers transported with only 19.1 percent to the JOS.[25]

In October 1980 the JLP came to power on an antisocialist wave, immediately ahead of the ascendancy of Ronald Reagan to the US presidency. At the heart of the new government's ideological position was the neoliberal maxim that the state should not be involved with commercial activity but should allow the private sector to flourish and the market to play its 'natural' role of maximizing economic efficiency. While it is true that the free market rhetoric of the JLP was far greater than the actual policies it followed,[26] significant attempts were made to privatize and the transport sector, which appeared to be as good an example as any of inefficient and corrupt state mismanagement, was ripe for the picking. Among the key aims of the transport policy of the new government were:

1. To provide an acceptable level of service at a minimum economic cost
2. To ensure that the new system required no government budgetary subsidies
3. To reduce the possibilities of the system being disrupted by industrial action
4. To ensure that democratic ownership of the vehicle fleet continues
5. To ensure that the fleet contains genuine and permanent competitive elements[27]

The new system came into effect in August 1983, with ten package holders, each having the legal right to ply the routes in ten demarcated zones in the city. These package holders bought a subfranchise from the still existing corporate body of the JOS and, in turn, sold the right to actually drive the routes to individual owners of minibuses. In Pat Anderson's 1989 study, a single person who was also the driver owned most of these minibuses.[28] The resulting arrangement was considered by many minibus operators as highly exploitative. They were forced to work long and difficult hours to pay what many considered penurious sums to subfranchise holders who appeared to do very little else beside collect this rent. For those cases in which the owner of the bus employed a driver, it was the latter person who had to hustle in order to bring in the daily quota, without which there was no pay. But if these arrangements were poor, the actual quality of the service was abysmal.

In Anderson's important survey of bus workers and passengers, she found that 90 percent responded that there was no timetabling. According to one passenger, "Everybody does their own thing – no regulation. They stop when they want and start when they want."[29] Many buses simply failed to complete their routes: the bus would simply run on the lucrative part of the journey and then turn around, ejecting and stranding the commuters who expected to continue along the route; buses would not stop at designated stops, but would make arbitrary and dangerous stops wherever passengers were to be found. Fewer than six percent of those interviewed indicated that they received tickets after paying their fare; and most alarming, many drivers and conductors refused to accept lower paying fares for schoolchildren, senior citizens and invalids. Only 13.3 percent of the passengers interviewed said that schoolchildren were accepted willingly, while 16.7 percent suggested that the buses refused to accept senior citizens at all.[30]

The rule of the market, with limited regulation by the package holders and the government, descended into what can only be called the rule of barbarism on the roads. The conclusion of the Anderson study on the quality of the new service and the state of workers in the sector is fitting, if only because its measured tone more accurately underlines the extent of the disaster:

The stated objective of Government's transportation policy to "ensure that the system contains genuine and permanent competitive elements" seems to have been fully met in the conditions of deregulation which now exist in the mini-bus service. It should be clear from the foregoing review of quality of service that service objectives have taken second place to the overriding objective of increasing money intake; and that the pressure to increase revenue is most severe among the smaller and more marginal vehicles.

Whereas passengers experience both the negative and positive aspects of competition, minibus workers seem to experience mainly the negative consequences, as they are subjected to extreme and continuous stress in the performance of their work . . . For drivers, the pressure to perform is expressed in their need to drive aggressively to collect passengers . . . The mini-bus system was described by one working proprietor as a cut throat system in which competing buses blocked each other at the terminus to delay departure.[31]

Free Competition Further Modified

In April 1989, some nine years after his historic defeat at the polls, Michael Manley returned to power, though no longer advocating the somewhat radical and statist programme that democratic socialism had been in the seventies.[32] In one of its early policy initiatives, the PNP government abandoned the package-holder system in late 1989 and the franchise fees, previously paid to the JOS and then to the Transport Authority, were paid directly to the authority. This new arrangement, which did little to alleviate the situation, was seen as temporary, but the new system would take some seven years and a further election to come fully into operation. The final system can best be described as 'free competition further modified'. The essential features of the 1983 model, that is, the absence of subsidy from the government and continued private ownership of the fleet, have been maintained, but there has been a greater attempt at regulation and central control.[33] In 1993, as one of the first initiatives, the National Transport Co-operative Society was established as a service cooperative to help the rationalization of the entire system; a more manageable system of five franchise zones has replaced the original ten; new articulated buses have been introduced to help ease congestion; and a dedicated school bus system has helped, though not entirely, to undermine the earlier, brutal rejection of schoolchildren.[34]

But even before a proper assessment of the current system can be made, it is faced with a new and all too familiar crisis. In a manner reminiscent of the 'robot' crisis of the 1970s, and not unlike the 'scrambola' crisis of the 1940s, the new system is coming under severe pressure from an unexpected direction. Spurred on by the increasing availability of cheap, second-hand Japanese cars, generally referred to as 'deportees',[35] hundreds of unlicensed taxis have taken to the streets, undercutting the profitability of the minibus drivers and intensifying the aforementioned cut-throat atmosphere on the roads.

The dramatic mushrooming of these deportees is indicative of the paradox of urban Jamaican transport and its convoluted connection to the social. The deportees represent liberation for an entire stratum of modest, black Jamaicans, who, under the old dispensation, were forced to ride in the cramped and sweaty quarters of the minibuses.[36] And, predictably, they have come under fire from the 'better-offs', who, in letters to the editor and veranda conversation, berate them as entirely responsible for the crisis on the roads. Undoubtedly, they represent independence and an escape from wage labour and the grind off poverty; but simultaneously with this, by virtue of their numbers and, more so, the intense competition for passengers, they exponentially increase the chaos on the already overburdened roads, where driving is ever more a question of survival. It is in this phase, then, in which there is ironically embedded the (illusory) hope of social emancipation, that the country as a whole descends to the threshold of a state of war of all against all.

Three Focal Lengths of Vision

Using distance and vision as metaphors, it is possible to think of the transport system, itself a manifestation of the emergent crisis of hegemony, as visible through three focal lengths. These are the global, the local/political and the hegemonic/individual.

The Global

Subscribing to Watson, we can agree that global capitalism in the last quarter of the twentieth century is gripped by a "techno-paradigm" shift of immense proportions:

The Techno-paradigm shift leads to wrenching structural change in the technology foundation. It necessitates reforms in outdated science and technology policy in the private and public sectors, and in international business and international relations. The Techno-paradigm shift and the globalization of high-technology production are integrally linked. The globalization process alters the structural configurations within the global economy by creating new contradictions in the motion of the productive forces: it disarticulates the international division of labor, propels new areas toward the center of the global economy, and tends to marginalize areas like the Caribbean.[37]

The disadvantages that Caribbean countries face in the new international dispensation come from their traditional and continued reliance on a strategy of attracting investment on the basis of low wages and the existence of ample raw materials:

It is now clear that the traditional comparative advantage based on low wages and large reserves of raw materials, like bauxite, do not offer security in the new environment. Guaranteed markets for agricultural exports are weakening or disappearing as a result of global trade reforms and the new regionalization, both of which are influenced by the new technologies. The new technologies are giving (industry specific) competitive advantage to companies, outdating (location specific) comparative advantage. This works against the Caribbean. Merchant capital in the region is still largely tied to circulation (use values) rather than productive activity (exchange values).[38]

In using this analysis as an illuminating lens, it can be suggested that the broadest framework for transport options has been 'overdetermined' by Jamaica's failure, along with most of the rest of the Caribbean, to emerge as a 'player' rather than a 'victim' of the techno-paradigm shift. Had Jamaica, hypothetically, taken the route of a Singapore after independence, it can be argued that the problem of urban transport might have been solved by throwing money at it. In a buoyant, successful economy, many options, such as a monorail system or subway, might have been tried and proven successful.

In an economy in which real poverty has increased in the last twenty years, however, such possibilities remain beyond the financial means of government or the private sector. And the failure to build a brand new system does not address the fact that in other Caribbean countries – Trinidad and Barbados, for example – urban transport, despite evident problems, is far superior to that which exists in Jamaica.

But even while the global perspective underwrites one of the central and obvious reasons why transport in Jamaica is bad, this broad, tectonic picture obscures the particular moments of engagement with the global environment that help to explain the crisis. Among the most important:

1. The entire marriage with BET, a particularly voracious example of the mid century transnational corporation, proved to be detrimental. BET, as suggested, single-handedly siphoned off profits and so depleted the war chest as to completely expose the JOS to the financial crisis when it hit in the seventies. Had the government of the time sought to secure the national interest by resisting BET's policies, through either a more effective regulatory body, as Swaby suggests, or an earlier nationalization while the business was still profitable, the entire outcome might have been different. As it turned out, when BET decided to leave, the system had already been sucked dry, leaving only its shell.

2. A second and certainly critical factor, which needs no elaboration, was the 1974 oil crisis, which dealt a particularly vicious blow to the JOS as well as, ultimately, to Manley's electoral prospects.

3. A third global factor was the eclipse of Keynesian economics in both theory and practice and the rise of neoliberal assertions in the 1970s. This affected Jamaica and the transport sector through two avenues. The first was through the well-known structural adjustment policies of divestment, devaluation and deregulation that followed the fiscal and foreign exchange crises of the mid seventies. The negative (and positive) effects of these policies have been documented elsewhere,[39] but the underlying ideological imperative, that private ownership is a necessarily more efficient and superior approach to organizing the economy, has remained dominant for two decades.[40] The second avenue was as a direct result of the victory of the JLP at the polls in 1980. This sealed the local political lid on the view that the free market was the only way forward, though it is suggested that as the JLP regime lengthened, it became apparent to the lending agencies

that Seaga was not the disciple of the market he had projected himself as in Opposition.

4. A final factor, which can be directly linked to end of century globalization, is the effect of the rapid extension and consolidation of global markets. Thus the supply of second-hand, reconditioned automobiles, unknown in the Caribbean only a decade ago, has found a happy marriage partner in the many frustrated passengers and potential entrepreneurs who seek salvation in the purchase of a cheap private car.

The Local/Political

However, if the marginalization of Jamaica and its economic effects, together with the specific ways the country was affected by global capital, determined the broad framework for the transport crisis, there is still a closer focus needed to see the picture. Little can be understood without trying to come to terms with the character of the Jamaican state.

If one interprets Carl Stone's model of clientelism liberally,[41] then its essential feature is the extent to which the Jamaican state has, historically, maintained its legitimacy by securing its relative autonomy from the dominant economic classes. Central to both PNP and JLP governments in the postwar period, then, has been this priority task of retaining and enhancing a populist appearance, which was especially necessary because of the insurgent character of the popular support from below.[42]

Specific policies that have worked against the consolidation of an effective transport system have arisen from an ideological perspective that appears to genuflect to popular interests, while never really conceding significant change. Three examples come to mind. First, the resistance of the government to rational increases in the fare structure of the JOS in the 1960s and 1970s pandered to 'the people' but served to undermine that company's viability, even as it is recognized that the real blame lay with BET's profit-gouging policies, which were never seriously confronted. Second, the persistent failure to combat illegal taxis and minibuses in all phases of the modern history of urban transport in Jamaica cannot be seen as simply the result of an inefficient or corrupt police force. It is suggested, rather, that the answer lies in that same misplaced populism in which the implicit policy of successive governments is to give ample leeway to the 'small man' so that he can hustle for a living in the absence of real economic growth or substantial social welfare policies. Many other instances of this type can be documented, including the failure to promptly remove squatters from government lands and the subsequent attempts to grant them legal deed after the squatting colony is deeply entrenched or, more recently, the failure to promptly halt the proliferation of illegal cable television operators until years after they are established. The decision in recent years to open up the market to the mass importation of refurbished cars is a third instance that many believe may have played a role in boosting the PNP's popularity before the elections in 1997. In addition to the aforementioned effect of intensifying the crisis on the roads, these cars have undoubtedly contributed to the foreign exchange drain and, since they will require spare parts at an accelerated rate, will continue to do so in the near future.

But equally, and by definition, these populist policies have existed alongside the toleration of sweatshop working conditions for minibus drivers and conductors. In Anderson's survey, 79 percent worked more than thirteen hours per day, 60.6 percent were not paid extra for work done overtime and 69.35 percent did not receive notice before being fired,[43] leading to her conclusion that:

one can state with a high level of certainty that workers in the minibus service do experience adverse working conditions which spring from the informal and unprotected nature of their work activity. Earnings are unattractive compared to the long working hours for all workers, with inadequate and arbitrary break times; there is a non-contractual form and method of payment for workers . . . abuse of workers' labour seen in the lack of any established pay policy regarding work done overtime; long work weeks; inadequate provisions for allowances, benefits, paid leave; and arbitrary dismissal practices for the majority of workers in the service.[44]

And, for a decade and a half, despite demonstrations, disasters and largely ineffective changes, both parties have presided over a system that has tolerated brutish behaviour, especially toward the young and the weak, and therefore both are responsible for policies that might be called populist but could not be considered popular or, by any stretch of the imagination, democratic.

In identifying the broad, undergirding ideology that has guided both parties, however, it would be remiss in the extreme not to appreciate a historical fact: even though the problems in urban transportation date back to at least the 1940s, the critical turning point, when things fall apart, is in the 1980s. It is the ideological and political victory of unmitigated market forces, the abandoning or, more appropriately, sidelining, of the old party-union alliances, that signal the start of the present phase. The collapse of a popular movement in 1980, led by, but not confined to, Manley's PNP, opened the floodgates. The unionized, uniformed JOS driver and conductor of the previous decades – orderly and reasonably, if never perfectly, polite – gave way to the 'lunatic' minibus driver and his "ductor', with his slave-driver–like insistence to his already cramped passengers to "small up oonu self"[45] in order to fit one more victim beneath the deck. And yet, as in the analogy, the 'ductor is simultaneously violent victimizer and suppliant victim; for his hostility and anger to his passengers and the public on the road derives, at least in part, from his dire conditions of work and living. The breaking of a national movement thus opened the barrier not to efficiency and profitability but to chaos and barbarism.

The Hegemonic/Individual

To appreciate the global and the local/political is to see most of the picture, but the puzzle is only complete with the final close-up. The anarchy on the roads, the traffic jam, the gridlock and those who seek to escape its confines represent a broader retreat from law, from order and from what can be termed the "rule of manners". Norbert Elias' reflections on the use of manners as a critical and powerful tool for the maintenance of power by the consolidating medieval upper classes has more than passing import. Referring to the dilemmas of the *nouveaux riches* in the Middle Ages, Elias notes:

At the same time their predicament shows, from a new angle, the importance which a strict code of manners has for the upper class. It is a prestige instrument, but it is also – in a certain phase – an instrument of power. It is not a little characteristic of the structure of Western society that the watchword of its colonising movement is 'civilization'. For the people of a society with a high division of functions, it is not enough simply to rule subject peoples and countries by force of arms like a warrior caste, although the old, simple goals of most of the earlier expansionist movements, the expulsion of other peoples from their land, the acquisition of new soil for cultivation and settlement, doubtless plays no small part in Western expansion. But it is not only the land that is needed but the people; these must be integrated, whether as workers or consumers, into the net of the hegemonial, the upper class country, with its highly developed differentiation of functions.[46]

If the acquisition of manners, then, including when to blow one's nose and one's horn, how to sit in public and when to be quiet, is not natural, but a function of power, then the breakdown of power will be accompanied and, equally, encouraged by a collapse or inversion of manners.[47] It is difficult to empirically defend such a claim, though an example might help to explore the point. O. Johnson, a senior citizen writing in the *Daily Observer* in late 1997 makes this appeal:

I am writing to express my discomfort and frustration as a sick senior citizen who has to go about every day businesses and, having to travel on these sound system buses.

The sound systems on these buses are outrageous and are driving us old people to the madhouse or to our graves. Twenty-five per cent of these buses on every route have sound systems that don't play at the bus terminus or if a police is nearby.

As soon as the driver or conductor start the journey, they turn on the sound system and up goes the volume to the point where it becomes unbearable. They abuse any person that asks them to turn down the noise. They say we should come off the bus and take the taxi; so if we don't want to hear music, we should not take the bus. Many times I leave that bus and take another but the next one is also the same. There is no certainty that the next bus doesn't have a sound system on it. I must ask here why isn't the law against such systems not being enforced so as to stop this indiscipline. We are appealing to the authority to enforce the law so that we senior citizens can travel on these buses with some peace and comfort.[48]

The example is useful because it addresses questions of music and culture along with broader issues related to transport. In the first instance, it illustrates the relationship to the law, in that it is heeded only and literally within earshot of the law enforcer. In an interview, Senior Superintendent of Police for Traffic Keith Gardner suggested that whenever his marked patrol car appeared in a congested area, the traffic would suddenly, as if by miracle, begin to move. His interpretation of this is that the people wanted to be policed and, by implication, that more patrols would solve the problem of congested traffic.[49] This, it is suggested, is a slight misinterpretation of the phenomenon. The people, or significant numbers of them, have abandoned an adherence, however tenuous it might previously have been, to a statal and upper class understanding of both law and manners. The notion of a public space, in which all have a right to some measure of peace and quiet, respect and consideration, is jettisoned. Indeed, there are no longer public spaces, nor is there public transport but 'poor black people's transport', or even 'my transport', in which manners and the civil have been inverted. The loud noise in the minibus, then, is as if to say that, "even though you seek to control my world, in this space, I am dominant, and anyone who dare question my notion of manners, will be severely ostracized".[50] The minibus, then, even as it is symbolic of the collapse of a certain sense of order at the end of a global economic process, is also an instrument of protest against that upper class world, both in the aggressive driving of its crew and the deafening sound of its loudspeakers.

Any attempt to bureaucratically or, from a policing perspective, technically 'fix' the current problem is probably doomed to failure without this grasp of how the law has come to be abandoned and how 'uncivil society' has trumped the society of manners. Illegality and incivility on the roads are not to be confined under the rubric of indiscipline, for they are also matters of resistance to power. Any effective reconstruction of the transport system will, it follows, have to reconfigure these questions of power in order to reinstate a (revised) notion of manners, or crush this resistance completely.

Toward a Conclusion: Reasoned Utopias

That which applies to transportation applies equally to life in all its myriad dimensions in today's Jamaica. The headline of the *Daily Observer* of 29 December 1997 reads:

Ugly End to Mid-Season Final

The first ever national Premier League mid-season final played between Waterhouse and Arnett Gardens ended prematurely at the Harbour View mini-stadium yesterday after an irate crowd threw bottles and stones on the field of play, forcing referee Peter Prendergast to call the game with 33 minutes remaining.[51]

The same paper, reporting on the annual Boxing Day reggae show Sting, carried this equally dismal account: "After the expected face-off between Bounti Killa and Merciless failed to materialize, patrons at the boxing day Sting show became incensed. The result was a bottle throwing melee that brought the show to an end."[52] And in what, on the surface, appears to be a completely unrelated incident, two months later the *Daily Gleaner* had as its headline "Shipping Threat":

Illegal fishing in Kingston Harbour is posing danger to docking vessels and their pilots and shipping agents are threatening to stop their ships using the channel if the authorities do not clamp down hard on the activity, shipping sources say.

Both Harbour officials and the marine police confirmed the problem but said that small fines and short jail terms did not provide a sufficient deterrent.

In fact, since December, 58 people have been arrested for illegal fishing in the channel used by ships entering the Kingston Harbour.[53]

What unites all these disparate examples is the absence of consensus, the contentiousness, the disregard for law, and the negation of the civil. Jamaica is careening on the edge of an abyss. There is gridlock on the roads, in the economy,[54] in the political sphere and in the hearts of men and women.

In the narrow arena of public transport, all that has been tried has failed. The single, local entrepreneur as monopolist was tried but failed due to insufficient capital and the inclination of the powerful to choose the foreign over the local. The giant, transnational company provided a modicum of orderly transport, but so sucked the lifeblood out of the system that it could not survive; and when hard times came, it quietly fled. The government as bureaucratic monopoly, if the truth be told, was never given a genuine chance to prove its ability to run an effective system, for it acquired a company already mired in financial crisis. Yet it is fair comment to say that the system that the government ran was not without merit and continued to possess a measure of order and decency. Then, well within the space of a decade, the unmitigated free market approach drove the transport system, and before it, the people of the city, to an unprecedented state of decadence and barbarity. The modified system that has succeeded it, before it has had a chance to prove its merits, has, in turn, had to face a new danger as unlicensed taxis have worsened the situation.

Not every possibility has been exhausted. It could be that, as in Argentina, a privately owned, genuine oligopoly, with large, well-organized subfranchisees, with efficient garages and bus terminals, might prove effective;[55] nor is it impossible that a Trinidadian-style system with a central, government-managed public bus route supported by numerous, privately owned taxis, could turn out to be the right one.[56] But if the specifics of the Jamaican case are to be incorporated into any solution, then such an approach has to be both technical and political.

In approaching the question of possible solutions, I take seriously Pierre Bourdieu's comment that intellectuals in this period have suffered from a "banker's fatalism" that leads us to believe that the world cannot be any different than the way it is. What is therefore required to combat this is a 'reasoned utopianism' that would connect with objective trends while seeking to think through possible scenarios for future humanitarian and emancipatory projects.[57] From such a perspective, the first thing that must be acknowledged is that after fifteen years of privatization, it is evident that there is the need for a centrally organized, locally controlled,[58] government-subsidized system. Such an approach, supported, if feasible, by private vehicles on feeder routes, is necessary if scheduling, cleaning of vehicles, regularization of uniforms and training of staff is to be taken seriously. And such a centralized approach is also critical for the bulk purchase of vehicles, parts and fuel. It is also imperative that there be a central corporation that trade unions can bargain with on behalf of the staff. If the drivers and conductors are to be treated as human beings, and in turn are to recover their humanity, then they must be removed from the exploitative sweatshop atmosphere that developed after the demise of the JOS and still prevails today.

But this cannot be all. If the notion that the current crisis is, at least in part, a result of a popular negation of the law then, for a new system to work, there must be some policy to address the alienation that lies behind it – that sense of being outside the diameter of society and the legal. It would seem that, gazing back over the last half century, the only thing that has not been considered is the question of popular influence and power over the choice of system, its monitoring and regulation, with worker control over the actual day-to-day operations.

Beyond the narrowly representative notion of an elected minister doing his democratic duty by organizing together with a group of technocrats the better scheme, there has been no consideration of ways of incorporating the people into active management.[59] While the conclusion of this chapter is not the place to elaborate an entire programme, two pointers toward a future direction might be mentioned here:

1. Local Transport Councils: These would be composed of all adult citizens in a designated zone of the city. They would meet initially to discuss technically simplified alternatives as to the best approach and then vote for their favoured choice. Beyond the launching of the new system, these councils could play a critical monitoring role. A smaller, elected group might be responsible for reporting on whether buses were keeping to the established schedule; another might function like the existing and successful Neighbourhood Watch groups, to ensure that criminal and vandal elements who often 'hijack' minibuses are discouraged.

2. Popular Ownership: One possible approach would be to issue transport shares to communities, with ceilings on individual and family ownership. Such an approach, wedded to the local transport councils, would give a sense of real control to a wide cross-section of the population. With this format, annual general meetings could discuss profits and losses, make decisions with regard to the purchase of new vehicles, ratify route expansion and hire and fire managers on the basis of performance. One approach could be to split share ownership between the bus workers themselves, the local transport councils and the government in equal blocs.

These proposals, if viewed together, would give the workers and the community a new sense of proprietorship over one of the most important things in their daily lives – the means for getting from here to there. Implementation of these proposals would undermine the need to hustle, evident in the present approach; it would remove the opacity of monopoly control, whether by the government, the local wealthy or foreign interests, thus minimizing the possibilities for corruption; and, by reincorporating the people within the diameter of the civil, it would lay the basis for the reformulation and reincorporation of notions of law and manners on a more equal, less weighted, more democratic foundation.

But can such a notion even be mooted in a society and world dominated by ideas of the superiority of the market and the final triumph of (limited) representative democracy? Meiksins-Wood, for example, while arguing for new, more democratic ways to organize the workplace, underlines the view that even drastic forms of worker ownership may lapse into the workers becoming equally exploitative employers under an overarching capitalist system.[60] The answer may very simply be 'no', but in the specific history of Jamaica, in the light of the failure of everything else, it is at least legitimate to place it on the agenda.

Postscript: Robotham's Vision Through a Different Prism

While writing the first draft of this chapter, I came across Don Robotham's booklet, delivered as the prestigious 1998 Grace Kennedy Foundation Lecture, *Vision and Voluntarism: Reviving Voluntarism in Jamaica*.[61] The essay seemed to touch on many of the issues raised here. Although Robotham addresses the question of how to increase voluntarism in Jamaica, he describes the decline of a "moral feeling for each other",[62] precisely the notion at the heart of this chapter.

Robotham identifies four periods in Jamaica's history when voluntarism was at its peak: immediately following the abolition of slavery, the black nationalist period under Marcus Garvey in the twenties, the period of the growth of the nationalist movement in the thirties, and the socialist period in the seventies.[63] His comment on the seventies is a useful point of departure to initiate a critique of his important intervention:

Jamaica's fourth peak of voluntarism occurred in 1972 with the election of Michael Manley to power on the slogan "Better Must Come" . . . But this also was not to last. By 1974, a change had begun to occur in the vision, turning it in the direction of socialism. By 1976, the vision was the doctrine of class struggle. The argument put forward was that improvement in the circumstances of life for the majority of Jamaicans required that the wealthier groups be subordinated. This doctrine of class struggle, of which I myself was a strong and ardent advocate, wrought great harm on the country. It inspired a very wide range of voluntary activity, but, on the other hand, it so divided the nation that it threatened to destroy the very framework on which the society depended for its existence.[64]

Disavowing a doctrine of social confrontation, Robotham seems to be searching for a route of compromise, of social unification, founded on what he sees as an underlying sense of 'Jamaicanness', in order to build a new social order based on voluntarism and trust. There can be little argument that an ending of antagonisms, a healing of the nation, and a retreat from the abyss of social confrontation is a pleasing and appealing vision. Where the problem appears to reside is in Robotham's method of getting to this favoured resolution.

Robotham wants a retreat from what he sees as new and old racial and colour-based antagonisms. The old anti-black chauvinism is now being accompanied, perhaps even superseded, by chauvinism directed at Jamaicans of fairer complexion. For Robotham, "chauvinism is chauvinism, whether it is white brown or black. It needs to be denounced because it is wrong."[65] Beyond the moral assertion of this fact, he promotes the idea that nonideological, nonpartisan community organizations should be formed around people's needs in their communities and voluntarism should be encouraged and taught in schools.

Two things seem to be wrong in Robotham's framework. First, he seems to misinterpret the causes for the deep antagonisms that pervade Jamaican society, and from this, his 'solution' is seriously flawed. If the example of the 1970s is to be used, then it is difficult not to come to the conclusion that what Robotham is saying is that the entrance of "class struggle advocating ideologues" is the critical factor in bringing Jamaica to the edge. My reading is quite the opposite. Deep antagonisms based on class and colour have been characteristic of the "Two Jamaicas", as Philip Curtin appropriately described the society in his famous text. In the 1970s, the alliance of middle class radicals with the poor and black helped, in part, to give legitimacy and voice to the long-suppressed antagonisms, the "hidden transcripts",[66] that came to the fore in the favourable atmosphere for popular expression that marked the peculiar conjuncture. And it was the dashing of hopes after the 1980 election that has contributed in great measure to the contemporary alienation, in which the text has once again retreated to the basement.

It is not the presence of ideologically flawed exhortations that generated social antagonism, then, but the feeling of alienation, of powerlessness, that those with power and wealth, viewed from within the passing minibus in their air conditioned cars, did not care less, a feeling that continues to afflict so many in Jamaica today.

Ken Carter's useful book *Why Workers Won't Work* is rich in its empirical description and analysis of the state of worker alienation as perceived by the workers themselves, supporting a far longer and richer genealogy. The following commentary from an office maid in a large banking institution, so reminiscent of the well-known 'poisoning tactic' practised during slavery, poignantly reveals the depth of these antagonisms:

Mi dear, ah don't have the education fi answer all dem fancy questions yu have ina yu paper. But let mi put it ina mi own words fi yu, an mi no care if yu go back an tell di big man dem for mi a leave di work anyway. But yu see dem shiny-teeth hypocrites ina di bank who a sit behind dem big desk and a flash dem false smiles, an a ask yu how yu pickney do, while all di time dem a order yu round like dawg and a treat yu like yu a no sombady too? A fix dem business every morning. A just 'awk and spit' ina dem coffee before a serve dem it. Dem so blasted 'fool-fool', when dem si di curdle pon top, dem gobble it down tink a cream.[67]

Similarly, these two comments, taken randomly from a list of recommendations from union delegates and workers, speak volumes as to the perceived nature of the problem and the sense of being profoundly disrespected, which ordinary people in Jamaica feel every day:

1. Management must see workers as human beings and not just as tools of production. If workers are seen as human beings, then it is more likely they will be treated as human beings . . .

16. Learn to say 'Good Morning', 'Thank you', 'Please', 'Miss', 'Mr', 'Mrs'. Some of us are old enough to be your mothers and fathers. It is just circumstances. We are not as rich or as educated, but we are people too. We earn a little respect.[68]

The problem is one of the absence of power and respect, which can only be addressed by their recovery. Robotham calls on the poor and black to dismantle their hidden text of resistance and to come to the table on the basis of Jamaicanness and the need for social peace. But there is no quid pro quo. After the supper, the wealthy leave in their limousines and the poor wait for their (late and overcrowded) minibuses. At least, in the course advocated here for the reform of a single sector, there is the possibility of a reincorporation of the people on the basis of some measure of real control and, perhaps, along with it, a new degree of respect. Voluntarism without power, however, is a recipe for frustration and further alienation.

Conclusion

The Caribbean Left at Century's End

If one imagines the Caribbean region in the last half-century not as a disparate group of sun-drenched islands but as distinct peoples, identifiable by history, culture and sensibility, different but more like each other than anyone else, then two dominant images have from time to time prevailed. If, at the end of the century, it is what can be termed the Naipaulian[1] image that is predominant; a vision of humid, mosquito-ridden less-than-paradises, where "few prospects please and every man is vile",[2] inhabited by mimic men with little meaningful history and therefore no vision of the future, where former State Department bureaucrats now seeking shelter in academia can, without tongue in cheek, call for the recolonization of the islands in their own best interests,[3] then it might be comfort, albeit a somewhat cold one, to remember that this has not always been the case.

Three decades ago, despite his own very peripheral role in the events that were unfolding, it was a different approach, what might be coined the Jamesian perspective, that was ascending. C.L.R. James, in the classic appendix to his seminal *Black Jacobins*,[4] had traced the outline of a West Indian essence and persona. Never confining himself to any narrow corridor of language, James' brush swept across the archipelago, from Cuba to the Guianas, from Garvey to Martí, Césaire to Padmore and Williams to Naipaul (yes, particularly in light of their differing perspectives, he included Naipaul, whom he considered in his iconoclastic style to be quintessentially West Indian).

At the heart of James' picture was a people forged in the furnace of slavery, disconnected from the confining traditions of their old world past, strategically located as gatekeepers between East and West, and postmodern long before the term was invented and then vulgarized. Most importantly, they were capable, therefore, despite their diminutive size, of making the most original and profound contributions to civilization, as he saw it, in its real meaning, as a counterpoint to barbarism. Central to this reading was the notion of a people driven by resistance to slavery, confinement, hierarchy and all of the features of that brutal, sordid past. This experience, he wrote four years after the triumph of the Cuban Revolution, had impelled Fidel Castro to attack Moncada and had, 150 years before, driven Toussaint L'Ouverture, in that prolonged and brilliant struggle that eventually gave birth to Haiti, the first free black nation in the New World.

It was in the 1970s that this tradition of resistance temporarily cohabited with the notion of revolution in what can be considered as the most important decade in the twentieth century history of the Caribbean peoples. For the Caribbean, like Dickens' narrator of another revolutionary era in *A Tale of Two Cities*, the seventies were "the best of times and the worst of times". For many, in countries such as Jamaica, it was a time of shortage, of inexplicable violence, and of personal abuse. For many more, however, it was a time of possibility and hope. Anyone who doubts the latter assertion need only turn to the popular culture of the time. One is amazed, for example, in a cursory search of the popular reggae tunes of the period, to find even love ballads without overt references to struggle, black dignity, redemption and, not infrequently, revolution. The words of Jimmy Cliff's "Harder They Come", released at the beginning of the decade, from the classic movie of the same name, resonate with the spirit of the time:

Well the oppressors are trying to keep me down
Trying to drive me underground
And they think that they have got the battle won
I say forgive them Lord they know not what they've done
Because as sure as the sun will shine
I'm gonna get my share now, what's mine
And then the Harder they come the harder they fall
One and all[5]

To a great extent, Cliff's hope for a better day was encapsulated in four events, or rather, two new events and two stages in older events. The first of these was the consolidation of the Cuban Revolution. Until the early seventies, Cuba had remained a pariah, particularly in the anglophone Caribbean, but on the basis of booming sugar prices, windfalls from the resale of Soviet oil and visionary social policies, it had emerged, despite the continued question marks concerning democratic procedure, as, at minimum, a rough facsimile of what Utopia might look like.

The second event was the leftward turn in the Michael Manley government in Jamaica after 1974 under the banner of democratic socialism. While Manley and the PNP were never able to consolidate an alternative social and political model, the initiatives taken between 1974 and 1977, especially the mobilization around the People's Production Plan in the early part of 1977,[6] suggested that the movement for change and 'better', linking into a longer genealogy going back to Garvey and Rastafari, had momentum. After Manley's resounding defeat of the right-leaning JLP in the 1976 general elections, the momentum seemed, for a moment, to be strengthening.

The third and fourth events were the Grenadian and Nicaraguan revolutions, respectively. Grenada, in particular, with its black, anglophone credentials, spoke to the English-speaking Caribbean, the Caribbean diaspora in North America and Britain and, critically, the African American population. For most of the four and a half years of its existence, the message from the Grenadian revolution was that radical change, including innovative educational policies and new, if embryonic, approaches to popular involvement were feasible and radical policies could work.[7] Nicaragua, before the sanguinary civil war blunted any possibility of an alternative model, suggested, often in spite of the intentions of the Sandinista leadership, that revolution could coexist with notions of pluralism in ways quite apposite to the classic example of the monolithic state and party of the Cuban Revolution.[8]

But in 1980 Manley was defeated in a bloody general election strewn with more than eight hundred bodies, and in 1983, the leadership of the Grenadian revolution devoured itself, with the murder of Maurice Bishop, Jacqueline Creft and others of his closest associates opening the door for the US invasion and the symbolic reassertion of its hemispheric hegemony for the first time since the Vietnam War. Then, in 1990 the Sandinista government, faced with a relentless and economically devastating war with the US-backed Contras, lost the national elections, though remaining the single largest party. Finally, after 1989 and the rapid collapse of Eastern Europe and then the Soviet Union, Cuba, no longer buoyed by its umbilical connection to the USSR, faced with continuing boycott from the United States, and mired in a catastrophic economic depression, survived, but diminished as either model or hope.

Francis Fukuyama in his neo-Hegelian essay and subsequent book *The End of History and the Last Man,* interpreting some of these events at the end of the last decade, argued that history had ended and that the liberal idea had triumphed.[9] And Jorge Dominguez, in his in many ways insightful collection *Democracy in the Caribbean,* writing from mid decade, recognized and lauded the survival of representative democracy in the Commonwealth Caribbean and (guardedly) argued for its potential to survive.[10] But has history ended? And what really is the state of Caribbean democracy?

It would seem, from the evidence, that forecasts as to the absolute triumph of a certain interpretation of democracy and the decisive defeat of popular modes of resistance have been too early and too optimistic. Tellingly, in 1990, Yassin Abu Bakr, operating not on the traditional terrain of the Left but through Islamic and Trinidadian notions of prophecy and judgement, tried unsuccessfully, but with considerable economic and political collateral damage, to take the Parliament in Trinidad and Tobago.[11] Riots over the damaging policies of structural adjustment wracked Venezuela after the social democrat Carlos Andres Perez returned to power in the early part of this decade. In Mexico, which has decided to cast its lot with the United States and Canada in the North American Free Trade Agreement (NAFTA), two major guerrilla movements have arisen in the space of five years and continue to survive. First, the Zapatistas in Chiapas and now the Ejercito Popular Revolucionario have taken to the field. The Zapatistas, notably, and with some success, have introduced to the array of weaponry of twentieth century guerrillas the Internet and World Wide Web.[12] In the early nineties, the rise and electoral victory in Haiti of Jean Bertrand Aristide and his Lavalas movement suggested a new and initially successful local and metropolitan 'pincer' approach to popular mobilization. Yet, his overthrow by the military and ultimate return to power, though now 'tamed' and at the behest of the United States, rammed home the immense limitations of insular sovereignty in the early phases of the new world order.[13] Further afield, despite the arrest of its charismatic leader Guzman, the ominous threat of Sendero Luminoso still hangs over Peru and the civil war in Colombia,[14] which has never really ended since *La Violencia,* has recently entered a new and more deadly phase. And, while no radical, overtly political movement has emerged in Jamaica, Rastafari, which, as suggested in the introduction, even at the start of this decade seemed to be on the wane, is waxing strong again.

With this evident if sporadic and contradictory movement, it is reasonable to conclude that the present moment is not the beginning of some new political millennium. The entire history of subordination and domination, of exploiters and exploited, of national and racial humiliation, imperial aggrandizement and accompanying hubris, has not suddenly and magically been synthesized under the aegis of a benign capitalism and a newly inclusive constitutional, liberal, democracy. Struggles for popular assertion are gaining momentum and will continue. And, where the avenue to peaceful participation is decisively closed, the struggles may occasionally take less than peaceful forms. They will inevitably have to play themselves out on a new field with new, severe global and national limitations, however, as well as new, if far less evident, possibilities.[15] In this new dispensation, what can be learned from the experience of the Caribbean Left over the recent past?

First, as one gazes back over the past half-century, it might be useful to ask, What has changed in the Caribbean as a result of the revolutions and other forms of popular upsurge of the previous thirty years? One can begin by stating the obvious. Everywhere, the ideology of neoliberalism has triumphed. In formal, official politics, the Left, or indeed, any notion of egalitarian, structural transformation of the hierarchical societies of the region, is dead. Any academic wishing to test Kuhn's hypotheses as to how paradigms inexorably assert themselves might benefit from a cursory observation of what has happened in the last decade in the Caribbean and Latin America.[16] It would, however, be an error to focus only on formal paradigms. Not far beneath the structurally adjusted surface, there is contestation. Much is happening, and a lot of it is coming out of the legacy of the popular movement of the recent past.

Everywhere, there is an insurgent populism, an assertion of identity and of self that, while chaotic, might also be the foundation for a new, more participatory form of democracy. This is most evident through the medium of the talk show, which, similar to trends in North America, has expanded immensely in the last two decades.[17] Radio talk shows have become a daily tribunal through which people criticize governments, make unprecedented interventions on wide-ranging national issues and seek remedy for perceived bureaucratic abuse. There is, in this new phenomenon, both a victory in the mushrooming of popular participation and in the act of toleration of that involvement. There is also, certainly in the anglophone Caribbean, a peculiar thing happening that can only be described in this way: While the Left has lost decisively in the economic debate, has failed to reformulate feasible, popular, alternatives for the new period and has, for the most, part unravelled organizationally, much of its political argument has returned to centrestage, though not necessarily as a cohesive package and not always voiced by the old Left itself.

Thus, when the Eastern Caribbean islands were considering a new political union in the early nineties, the issues were discussed in constituent assemblies in each territory, borrowing, though without recognition, from the methodology used to discuss the annual budget and other issues in local and national assemblies during the Grenada revolution.[18] And in Jamaica, over the last five years, the on-again, off-again constitutional reform exercise,[19] while yet to arrive at a consensus, is debating issues such as proportional representation, local government empowerment and, though with little chance of approval, the possibility of recall for nonperforming members of Parliament. These were all central elements in the programmatic platform of the Left in the seventies. In many territories, even as the political Left has withered away, the grass-roots Left in the nongovernmental organizations (NGOs), feminist and other organizations has grown and, in some respects, flourished.[20] And the trade union Left, focusing attention on its core constituency, has held its own as in Trinidad and Grenada, or even grown significantly as in the case of the University and Allied Workers' Union (UAWU) in Jamaica. The UAWU, in the period since the collapse of the WPJ, to which it was closely affiliated, has moved from being a minor player to being one of the major unions, with representation in all the key economic sectors.[21] Most strikingly, Fidel Castro, the bane of the Caribbean Right in the first three decades of the Cuban Revolution, is now fêted not only by governments, but, ironically, the private sector, as elder statesman and even hero, throughout the region.[22]

The most interesting development, however, is quite possibly the re-emergence and consolidation of a popular discourse of resistance. This, as suggested in the Introduction, is evident in recent developments in reggae music, where so-called consciousness is replacing the previous emphasis on 'slackness'. Is this a return to the themes of struggle and resistance so typical of the seventies? History never quite repeats itself, and even then, it would be too early to come to such a conclusion. In order to continue the trend of thought, however, it might be significant to explore what can be considered as the lessons that emerged from that remarkable decade.

If one thinks not only about the Cuban, Nicaraguan and Grenadian revolutions but the myriad groups and fractions of parties that inhabited the sphere of the Left in the seventies, two strengths and four critical, though not necessarily all-inclusive, weaknesses inherent to the theoretical framework and praxis of these movements can be proposed.

The strengths of the era included, first, the assertion of principles of voluntarism reflected in, for instance, the early attempt to put voluntary work into Labour Day in Jamaica, after Manley's 1972 electoral victory. This effort brought sections of the middle and working classes into political life in new and unprecedented ways as it began to forge for the first time a broader political community. Similar attempts were mirrored in the road-building programme in Grenada, which encouraged grass-roots mobilization for self-help and community work. Undoubtedly, though, the stellar model for popular mobilization was the literacy drive in Cuba in the early phases of the revolution. This forging of a national community worth living in and dying for was evident and palpable and is the critical feature that has kept the Cuban Revolution alive in its darkest days.

The second strength of the era was unquestionably the unprecedented assertion of pride in self. In those territories with large populations of African descent, the assertion of black dignity, emerging out of Garveyism and the nationalist movement, but taking new purchase from Rastafari and Black Power, was significant and empowering. It is one of the least tangible, yet perhaps, most important features as it is remembered from the regrettable perspective of the late nineties when much of the old self-negation has reasserted itself.[23]

It is more important, however, in a moment of critical reflection to focus on the negative features of the time. The first was a dangerous approach, which can best be called 'triumphalism'. The view that history was on our side and that our opponents were not simply wrong but against the very course of history led, as suggested in chapter 2 on NUFF, to serious and damaging consequences. This derived, at least in part, from a certain Caribbean Marxism-Leninism. A distinction, as suggested in that chapter, has to be made between the Jamesian stream, which, outside of Antigua and the early pre-revolutionary period in Grenada, never took on mass proportions, and the

Marxism-Leninism of the WPJ, the later NJM, Yulimo in St Vincent, the People's Progressive Party in Guyana, the Dominica Liberation Movement and others. The dogmatic application of Lenin's Russian experiences that led to his theory of the vanguard as a tool for the taking of power was applied uncreatively to the running of states, and led, ultimately, as in the case of Grenada, to the alienation of parties from the people.[24]

But more so, the Left adopted an abstract Marxism. This was due to a political immaturity that was at least in part the result of the very recent re-emergence of a vibrant, radical praxis in many territories. Maurice Bishop, for instance, had only begun to read Marx seriously after the NJM had become a significant national force in the mid seventies. Many persons were shocked, after the collapse of the Grenadian revolution, to discover that the colonels and majors who were prominent in the People's Revolutionary Government (PRG) and People's Revolutionary Army (PRA) were still mainly in their mid twenties. This youthfulness and inexperience might, in part, account for the failure to grasp the nuances in Marxian dialectics and to approach it as a methodological tool instead of a set of recipe-like prescriptions. In his *Notes on Dialectics,* James said that what he had come to understand most was how things were never finite, but always in motion.[25] This simple but profound insight was missing from the praxis of much of the Caribbean Left. The question was never how to use a method to grasp a particular history with its own roots and seminal contribution to modernity, but how to apply an already known set of prescriptions. A further contributing factor to the character of the Caribbean Left was the prestige of the Soviet Union as it blossomed in the sixties and seventies. For young Caribbean radicals with little knowledge of the purges and collectivization of the Stalinist era, the Soviet Union was a powerful magnet, due to its strategic support for the African liberation struggles, for revolutionary Cuba and the anticolonial struggle in Vietnam. This led to the easy availability and attraction of not only Soviet interpretations of Marxism but also the flawed Soviet notion of noncapitalist development.

Youthfulness and intellectual immaturity contributed to an evident militarism, discussed in this volume in relation to NUFF, but also present in many other instances. Invoking the power of history and truth as being on the side of the people meant that any means were deemed appropriate to justify the activities of the vanguard both in the taking and, if successful, in the retention of power.

Finally, as a corollary of all these, a rampant authoritarianism prevailed. This was captured in the common notion that procedural democracy was essentially a veil designed to obscure the power of the bourgeoisie and imperialism, and that true democracy could be encapsulated in a basket of economic rights and 'participatory democracy' and not necessarily through (indeed, often without) competitive electoral forms.

While these generalizations are useful and reflect the central feature of the time, it is also important to recognize that this is only part of the story and one needs also to probe the extent to which Cuba, Nicaragua, Grenada, and the rest of the Left that did not achieve state power, departed from some abstract, polar notion of authoritarianism.

From such a perspective, it can be suggested that in the case of Grenada, despite the highly centralist character of the party and the dogmatic application of Leninism that characterized the entire process, ultimately leading to its collapse, there were important popular initiatives. The three annual budget debates,[26] in which the opinions of an entire cross-section of the population were taken into consideration for the final presentation, remain a signal achievement of that process. The parish councils, which brought citizens together in local bodies to discuss wide-ranging municipal, national and international issues, were another important innovation, as were the numerous creative policies to achieve full literacy and transform the education curriculum.[27] Together, these and other policies contributed to a spirit of popular renewal and hope that, at least in the first few years of the process, was palpable, but has since been lost in the blood and rubble of Bishop's death and the immediate US invasion. Yet, as has been suggested elsewhere, dogmatism and centralism dominated and served, of these three processes, to place Grenada at one polar extreme.[28]

At the other end, the Sandinistas, who in many, though not all, instances seemed predisposed to a centralist model, were forced by popular insurgency, often from their own mass base, to yield significant ground to plurality, and finally, in the act of conceding power in 1990, to transcend the notion of historical inevitability, with its dangerous consequences for democracy.[29] In between the two, the Cuban process, with its singular focus on the leader and long history of suppression of opposition,[30] stands closer to the Grenadian pole, but is differentiated by the unprecedented process of popular involvement, social improvement and, most profoundly, resistance to imperial diktat,[31] which, if not fulfilling the qualifications for democracy, certainly cannot be discounted as irrelevant to the discussion.

In retrospect, then, none of these three revolutions can stand as pristine models for the future, though at the same time, there are positive lessons to be learned from them all. Cuba has, after all, created the best social welfare system in the Third World and its educational and health accomplishments remain remarkable and unblemished.[32] The process of discussion and drafting of the national constitution in Nicaragua remains a model as to what real, electoral democracy can mean when the people are mobilized, aware and able to make studied choices around substantial issues.[33] And the Grenadian budget debates and parish councils, though embryonic, have helped to chart paths of popular involvement that can only fully be appreciated by anyone who has sat through the afternoon drone of the minister of finance in a hot Caribbean House of Representatives, with most of the parliamentarians nodding off to sleep in the back benches.

The Left, then, despite evident contra flows, has been decisively defeated. But where does that leave the Caribbean at the end of the century? While, as suggested in the introduction, there have been different experiences, on the whole, growth has been minimal and in some instances negative.[34] More critically for the future, new capital inflows have been minimal, as the small, resource poor markets of the Caribbean can hardly compete individually with the new, much larger emergent markets in Eastern Europe or further south on the continental land mass.[35] As Norman Girvan succinctly suggests, the Caribbean region is comprised of "societies at risk": "We may sum up the dangers facing Caribbean societies in terms of possible *marginalisation* from the growth points in the world economy, further political and social *fragmentation* intra-nationally and intra-regionally, and creeping *loss of autonomy*, defined as the capacity actively to shape their future development."[36]

The classic case, of course, is Jamaica, which actually began its process of structural adjustment under the Manley regime two decades ago in 1976. When Manley lost power in 1980, two Jamaican dollars could buy one US dollar; today it is hovering above the figure of forty to one. Vast income inequality gaps have grown worse in Jamaica under the deteriorating foreign exchange regime. The IMF-inspired policy of high interest rates has, arguably, tended to mop up liquidity and inflation, but it has made life unbearable for the poor, the lower middle classes and anyone seeking to invest in productive enterprise. The devastating and prolonged economic crisis, which has witnessed Jamaica experiencing the worst drop in standards of living of any middle income country with the sole exception of Romania, has so undermined the once deeply entrenched elitist system of patron-client representative democracy that it is now far more fragile than any time since its emergence in 1944. And, precisely because no serious political force has arisen to contest the loosening arrangements at the top, the absence of leadership and direction, the dissolution of hegemony, is leading to repercussions throughout the society, evident in rising crime rates, the erosion of traditional notions of manners and, everywhere, an increasing contestation, through popular language, music and other cultural forms at all levels of the social matrix.

Jamaica, as is suggested elsewhere, has three possible, though by no means inevitable, options.[37] The first, is the emergence of new authoritarian arrangements, either within or outside the constitution that would seek to reimpose 'order' and 'manners' on an increasingly ungovernable people; the second is the gradual slide into anarchy, or what Marx and Engels referred to as the "common ruin of the contending classes"; and the third is a democratic renewal. The last part of this conclusion is devoted to exploring the notion of democratic renewal and what its contents might include, as it is proposed that critical aspects of the Jamaican narrative are not exceptional for other small states of the archipelago.

Much of the literature from the Left in the post-Cold War era has focused, and rightly so, in the wake of the collapse of "really existing socialism", on the lessons to be learned from the Eastern European debacle, the theoretical implications for the Left and the practical arrangements that might be appropriate to any future (though not immediately anticipated) "progressive" state.[38] From a hemispheric perspective, the most important work has been Jorge Castaneda's monumental study of the Left in Latin America, *Utopia Unarmed*.[39] In the second half of his vast and difficult to summarize study, Castaneda proposes a political and economic platform for the Left in the new conditions at the end of the century. He argues that the old notions of 'revolution' and 'military combat', so dear to the heart of an earlier generation, are no longer on the agenda. Among the salient points he proposes are:

1. a platform of consistent representative democracy for the Left;
2. a new attitude to the United States, no longer to be regarded as a monolithic enemy but a layered society within which Latin American

states must seek allies and lobby officials in order to, following the Israeli and Cuban exile pattern, influence foreign policy in the interests of the region;

3. a new flexible notion of nationalism that, while retaining the concept, would broaden it into deeper patterns of regionalism along the lines of the European Union;

4. and a new economic policy based on tax reforms, debt forgiveness, sustainable development and export-led development.[40]

While there is much to be recommended in Castaneda's model, including the stress on productivity and export competitiveness, the focus on human rights as not a tactical but a foundational necessity, and a resistance to the current trend to sell off national resources at bargain basement prices, there are glaring lacunae that seriously undermine its feasibility. These centre not so much around the question of democracy, but his proposed economic pro-gramme for the Latin American Left. In order to approach this critique, and borrowing loosely from Castaneda,[41] a certain routine can be proposed that might be considered typical not only for Latin America but also the Caribbean, over the last three decades. This can be termed the Routine of the Reforming Regime.

In the first phase, a new populist/Left regime comes to power either electorally or via revolutionary overthrow, and in order to fulfil the high expectations from its mass base, invests heavily in social welfare and human development programmes. In the second phase, in order to meet the inevitable budgetary requirements, the government – with or without a prior ideological inclination – is compelled to impose heavy taxes on the local wealthy or to nationalize transnational corporations, or both. There is, as a result of the early social measures, an initial improvement in the quality of people's lives, but the necessary focus on outstanding needs is not balanced by increases in economic productivity. In the third phase, then, a rapid process of disinvestment begins, as capital flees to Miami along with many members of the initially small cadre of skilled persons. Accompanying this phase is the planned sabotage of the economy (double invoicing, hoarding, artificial shortages) along with more traditional forms of political and military destabilization from conservative parties and the CIA, both now convinced that the government is on the path to communism and alliance with the Soviet Union. In the fourth phase, with capital fleeing and productivity plummeting, inflation ensues and, increasingly, money is printed in a vain effort to retain the flow of benefits to the popular base. This only exacerbates the situation, however. Scarcities become endemic; there is growing disenchantment; increasing sectors from the middle and even critical elements among the lower classes join the ranks of the Opposition. In the fifth phase, the governing party, while retaining its core constituency, which, aware of the intricacies of the process, is now invariably even more committed to the road of reform or revolution, is now in a clear minority and is defeated either by elections or counter-revolutionary coup. Finally, in the sixth phase, a government more supportive of open market, neoliberalism comes to power. Deflationary policies are practised, with damaging effects on the poor. High interest rates are used to mop up liquidity. National assets are sold off for short-term budgetary needs. Public infrastructure in health and education – already severely overburdened – begins to collapse. The economy is, after decades of protectionism, suddenly opened up to competition with the world.

The result, in isolated cases, is growth and competitiveness, as with Chile (though even in this case, it is accompanied by new indices of poverty in vulnerable sectors of the population). In most instances, however, the devastation of agriculture by cheap imports, the destruction of local manufacturing, and the vast speculative profits generated by high interest rates, which further discourage local investment in the productive sector, lead to a disastrous outcome.

If the initial assumption of any future radical project is that the Left, by definition, must address as its central platform the question of poverty[42] and of the vast inequalities of wealth pervasive in the region, then it seems, in this critical respect, as though Castaneda's proposals are at best very vague, at worst guilty of the very utopianism that he identifies as the self-indulgence of the old Left. What Castaneda proposes is that at the end of the Cold War, without the threat of communism as its major geopolitical opponent, the United States government will be willing to, first, play a major role in debt forgiveness and, second, assist in the repatriation of national assets when, in the taxation phase of the typical routine, the local wealthy export their resources to the United States as a safe haven against national appropriation.[43] Further, Castaneda is hopeful, in the context of the closure of this typical escape route, to convince the national wealthy to support the appropriate reforms as an alternative to social upheaval, or, worse yet, Sendero Luminoso – unrest.[44]

While this appears to be a sincere attempt to address a genuine dilemma faced by any reforming government, it is too flawed to be considered as workable. The approach fails to address the reality in the larger Caribbean territories, as in Latin America, of the tremendous imbalance in ownership patterns and how this inevitably undermines any notion of democratic will, or the creation of relatively balanced economies with the potential for growth and development. The likelihood of a major, altruistic shift in US foreign policy is also far-fetched. This is already evident in the case of short-term, small-minded instances, such as US opposition to the protection of Eastern Caribbean bananas,[45] in a context where entire economies are dependent on the special arrangements with the European Union and where the United States has very little to lose in supporting the continuation of these special arrangements.

Further, while Castaneda's suggestion that force of circumstance (Sendero-as-alternative) might convince the local rich to support a reforming government is thinkable, it hinges on a level of US compliance that runs in the face of present trends to attract foreign capital to the United States in order to help offset the national balance of trade imbalances. The hard reality is that Castaneda, in his highly optimistic proposals, ignores, or at best drastically underestimates, the power of the market, the power of capital, in both its local and global dimensions, and ends up relying essentially on the ephemeral goodwill of the local wealthy and the hegemonic power.

In the present conjuncture, it would appear that the realistic possibilities for an alternative path of popular development might have to proceed on a somewhat different course. In the first instance, there is a hegemonic imperative that requires the rethinking both at the scholarly and popular levels of a number of critical issues. The first of these, following a central theme of this study, is the reimagining of Caribbean politics from below. The epistemic process of placing the people at the centre of Caribbean history is still very embryonic. The exercise, as Wilson Harris proposes,[46] of rethinking popular culture on its own terms and not from the perspective of a Western gaze, would have to be at the heart of any radical revival. It is the arrogance derived from the view that the people and popular culture could not be trusted to know what they really wanted that needs to be relegated to the past. Indeed, it might be mooted that the most persuasive argument for a rethinking of episteme is economic; for, in poverty-stricken and resource-poor states, the likelihood of economic recovery is greatest when there is the fullest mobilization of human resources. This is more likely to emerge from an inclusive politics that is sensitive to the history, culture and needs of a particular people.

A second and related question, as Perry Mars suggests,[47] is the development of an adequate theory of race-class relations in the Caribbean. This is not only appropriate in the instances of Guyana and Trinidad, where the likelihood of African/Indian social confrontation has increased, but equally, in relatively monolithic societies such as Jamaica. It has been the constant feature of social movements in Jamaica in the last hundred years, that while the leaders may define the movement in terms of national, class or social goals, the people have invariably redefined it in terms of race. What are the unresolved issues of language, colour and psyche that distort people's lives and life chances and lead to bizarre effects such as the upsurge of skin bleaching? What would be the policies of a state that sought to address these issues in a way to help overcome the psychological corrosion of the past? What, as Mars intimates, would the state form of a genuine multiethnic, multiracial state look like, in comparison to one that, as in the present order, pretends that it is above such questions? Any future radical movement hoping to gain credibility and, ultimately, popular support would have to begin to answer some of these still outstanding questions.

The second issue of hegemony concerns the admittedly idealistic exercise of proposing alternative models of future development. Radical thinkers in the Caribbean have been hypnotized by the fixed stare of neoliberalism and have inadequately engaged in the theoretical exercise of proposing alternatives.[48] In contrast, the debate in Europe and the United States on alternative approaches to socialism is alive and well.[49] What is to be rescued from the political and economic experience of the recent past? How is the significant work on gender in the Caribbean to be incorporated into policy measures for an alternative agenda? Where does the market function effectively and where does it not? Are markets inevitably wedded to capitalist forms of appropriation, or are they useful tools that might be utilized in different types of social formation? Is it possible in late, global capitalism to even think in terms of sovereignty in a Westphalian, or even postcolonial sense? What would the better society and polity look like? The Left has, in an approach harking back to Marx himself, in which the future would resolve its own problems, largely elided these basic questions. Without such a vision of a better world – a 'feasible socialism" – there will be little foundation for the accumulation of popular support.

Beyond the hegemonic exercise of proposing alternatives for the future and of mooting the possibility that there is an alternative, at least two more overtly political issues need too be resolved by a new Left. The first concerns the character and form of the political organization that will advance an alternative, radical agenda. The arguments are well known, but the approach to a solution remains unresolved. The classic, Leninist vanguard, with all its capacity for concentration of forces in a mobile, revolutionary situation, is a dangerous instrument once it is ensconced in power. The very same secrecy and exclusivity that facilitate insurrection work to exclude the people from participating in the exercise of power. This is further enhanced in the Caribbean, where the tendency towards the elevation of charismatic leaders to god-like status has been prevalent. The obvious antidote would seem to be a democratic federation of grass-roots movements, with clear principles for the election and rotation of leadership. The relevant question would then be as to whether or not such an organization would have sufficient coherence and cohesion to offer itself as an alternative to a population jaded by decades of broken promises.

If this were to be achieved, then at the heart of the political programme of such an organization in power would have to be a flanking movement for democracy on all fronts. This would have to be carried out not as tactical measure, but arising from the imperative that it is only on a footing of popular involvement and popular awareness that any programme of social renewal can take place.

There are real openings for pressing democratic reform in the context of the present national and international focus on representative democracy. Where a new Left might make significant headway is not only at the level of the theoretical debate as to how to redefine democracy,[50] but the far more practical effort to make 'representative democracy' more consistent, meaningful and democratic. To include and extend beyond Castaneda's proposals, this would involve:

1. strengthening the power of local government to give people in their communities greater control over their lives and undermine the asphyxiating power of the centre;

2. amending, where appropriate, the first-past-the-post-system to include mixed systems of proportional and constituency-based elections, in order to undermine tribalism, yet retain the principle of constituency-based

representation and simultaneously allow smaller parties and differing interests to flourish;

3. in those territories practising export variations of the Westminster system, separating the executive from Parliament in order to reduce the dictatorial powers of the current party-dominated, prime ministerial arrangements;

4. entrenching, as Castaneda suggests, the entire gamut of human rights provisions, an issue which is, needless to say, impatient of debate;

5. regularizing all electoral matters in a body constitutionally empowered to include all significant political trends.

6. fair and equal access to electoral resources and media time, in order to undermine the arbitrary power of money in swaying the electorate and frustrating the democratic right to choose fairly between clearly elaborated options;

7. instituting the provision of recall of nonperforming members of Parliament, with specific sanctions for broken election manifesto promises and clear procedures and provisions to avoid frivolity;

8. establishing term limits for all elected parliamentarians, with the possibility of one term in, one out and a return;

9. constitutionally required popular discussion and ratification of budget debates and other specified traditionally executive and legislative prerogatives; and

10. the active establishment of Caribbean lobbying groups in the United States, United Kingdom, and Canada to mobilize support at the grassroots level and in Congress/Parliament for the gamut of Caribbean causes.[51]

If these proposals are coupled with Castaneda's suggestion of deeper regional integration,[52] though with the important proviso that the Caribbean is a distinct civilization with its own interests and not a backwater of Latin America,[53] then such an approach might have spin-off benefits, including a more coherent foreign policy, common and consistent approaches to the environment, an integrated labour market, and regional courts sharing costs and undermining the potential for small town corruption. If some national sovereignty is shared in the interest of a larger Caribbean of some thirty-five million persons – roughly the demographic size of Canada – which could then speak more cohesively about human resources and market share; and if this were coupled to the political mobilization of the large pan-Caribbean communities in North America in the interest of both political lobbying and the election of pro-regional congressmen, then, in the long term, Castaneda's proposal of a modified US foreign policy with greater sensitivity to Caribbean interests might be imagined and even achieved.

Such an exercise must necessarily be linked to a practical attempt to forge counter-market links with trade unions, environmental and community-based organizations and lobbies in the United States, Europe and elsewhere in order to undermine the momentum of a certain capital-driven notion of globalization. The slogan cannot simply be against globalization but, rather, a globalization that is driven by the needs of the people and not the voracious necessity of capital.[54]

Without addressing the first issue, that is, the struggle for democracy, the second, the struggle against the market, is impossible. But without the second, the first becomes empty and meaningless. Without a concerted attempt to deepen democracy[55] and include the powerless in a flanking movement, around traditional wealth and entrenched power, then any short-term project of social renewal will follow a familiar trajectory, spiralling to disaster.

Two proposals seem to emerge from the experience of the recent past: Without democracy there can be no genuine social renewal; and without greater focus and consideration of the Caribbean, writ large, there can be little hope of insular national salvation.

Both the Naipaulian and Jamesian visions are written into the historical imagination of the pan-Caribbean peoples, and the unforeseen twists of history could yield either further marginalization and inconsequentiality, or unprecedented openings for democracy, popular empowerment and human flourishing. But the latter vision will not occur without a concerted attempt to understand the pitfalls of the past, of which the history of the revolutionary path is a central concern. If, however, there is any single factor that weighs in favour of a brighter future for the Caribbean, it is that formerly enslaved peoples will not kindly submit for long to 'Shiprider solutions', namelessness and relegation to the appendices of history. As Kamau Brathwaite, in his insurrectionary poem "Negus", puts it:

It is not
It is not
It is not enough

to be pause, to be hole
to be semicolon, to be semicolony,
fling me the stone
that will confound the void
find me the rage
and I will raze the colony
fill me with words
and I will blind your god[56]

Poverty, marginalization and dispossession demand a response. The Caribbean, in the twilight of the twentieth century, cries out for a new, invigorated popular movement.

Notes

Preface

1. Hegemonic dissolution is described in my earlier volume in this way:

   The economic crisis, the collapse of the political project, the growing psychological independence of the subordinate classes are the conditions under which a moment of hegemonic dissolution has emerged. Using hegemony in the Gramscian sense to mean effective leadership and control of the direction of society, we can argue that the social bloc in charge of Jamaican society is no longer ruling over a people convinced of its social superiority and its inherent right to 'run things' – to use the popular Jamaican phrase.

   See Brian Meeks, *Radical Caribbean: From Black Power to Abu Bakr* (Kingston, Jamaica: The Press, University of the West Indies, 1996), 131.
2. See Alasdair MacIntyre, "Ideology, social science and revolution", *Comparative Politics* 5, no. 3 (April 1973): 321–42.

Introduction

1. *Daily Observer*, 24 September 1998.
2. *Daily Observer*, 26 September 1998.
3. *Daily Observer*, 16 April 1999.
4. In both 1979, under an earlier People's National Party (PNP) regime headed by Michael Manley, and in 1985, under Edward Seaga's Jamaica Labour Party (JLP) government, there were islandwide protests following steep increases in the price of gasoline. These were recent and well-remembered precedents, of which any politically savvy regime should have been keenly aware.
5. *Daily Observer*, 20 April 1999.
6. Roughly translated: "We all suffer as a result of these policies and the demonstration [to roll back the prices] is in favour of all of us, so everyone should stop working" (*Daily Observer*, 20 April 1999).

7. It is important to note, as an indication of the complexity of the present moment, that the single area of the city that remained free of roadblocks in April was precisely that part over which Zeeks and his supporters 'ruled'. By keeping the peace in his zone, he demonstrated his power more effectively than any protest could have done. It also suggests a continuing willingness to accede to some measure of legitimacy from the ruling regime, though, undoubtedly, on terms that would grant him a wider ambit of autonomy.

8. The so-called Moses Committee – named after its chairman, Private Sector Organization of Jamaica (PSOJ) president, Peter Moses – included independent senator, university professor and trade union activist Trevor Munroe; the president of the Civil Service Association; a representative of the Jamaica Council of Churches; the president of the Association of Nongovernmental Organizations; and other representatives from the trade unions, private sector, "young people's organizations" and labour groups. See *Daily Observer,* 22 April 1999.

9. See *Daily Observer,* 28 April 1999.

10. See Carl Stone, "Assessing our democracy: 1991 JLP's Central Clarendon Dinner", in *Carl Stone Speaks on People, Politics and Development,* ed. Rosemarie Stone (Kingston, Jamaica: Rosemarie Stone, 1995), 200.

11. See Don Robotham, *Vision and Voluntarism: Reviving Voluntarism in Jamaica,* Grace, Kennedy Foundation Lecture (Kingston, Jamaica: Grace, Kennedy Foundation, 1998), 15.

12. See Brian Meeks, "The political moment in Jamaica: The dimensions of hegemonic dissolution", in *Radical Caribbean: From Black Power to Abu Bakr* (Kingston, Jamaica: The Press, University of the West Indies, 1996).

13. An appropriate and dismaying indicator of the state of law and obedience is captured in the comparative homicide statistics for Kingston and other cities in the world. The British Home Office survey of homicide rates per 100,000 citizens among a select group of European and North American cities showed that American cities had far higher rates of homicide, the highest being Washington, DC, with 69.3. Kingston, for the same period, (1995–97) averaged 107.6. European cities, in comparison, had generally low rates. London, for example, was 2.1; Paris was 3.3. See "Kingston's homicide rate high among world's cities", *Sunday Gleaner,* 18 October 1998.

14. See William Zartman, *Collapsed States: The Disintegration and Restoration of Legitimate Authority* (Boulder: Lynne Rienner, 1995).

15. Robert H. Jackson, *Quasi-States: Sovereignty, International Relations and the Third World* (Cambridge: Cambridge University Press, 1990).

16. Jennifer Widner, "States and statelessness in late twentieth century Africa", *Daedalus* 124, no. 3 (1995): 129–54.

17. See chapter 3 on Carl Stone.

18. See *Report of the Director of Elections: General Elections, 1997* (Kingston, Jamaica: Electoral Office of Jamaica, 1998), 26.

19. It may be too early to write off the National Democratic Movement (NDM) as stillborn, though its performance in the last election – receiving only 4.76 percent of the vote – is a strong indicator. See *Report of the Director of Elections,* 26.

20. In the February 1999 Stone Polls – still the benchmark of political popularity in Jamaica – the PNP's national support stood at 25 percent of the electorate, compared to 20 percent for the JLP and 7 percent for the NDM. In December 1997, just before the last national elections, the PNP had enjoyed 32 percent of the vote, and the Opposition JLP 20 percent. Thus, both parties are supported by shrinking minorities, though the PNP's support is shrinking faster than that of the JLP. See "PNP still ahead but weaker in the third term", *Sunday Observer,* 14 March 1999.

21. I am in agreement here with the position taken by Trevor Munroe. See Trevor Munroe, *Renewing Democracy into the Millennium: The Jamaican Experience in Perspective* (Kingston, Jamaica: The Press, University of the West Indies, 1999).

22. See Francis Fukuyama, *The End of History and the Last Man* (New York: The Free Press, 1992).

23. See Samuel Huntington, *The Third Wave: Democratization in the Late Twentieth Century* (Norman and London: University of Oklahoma Press, 1991).

24. See John Gray, *False Dawn: The Delusions of Global Capitalism* (New York: The New Press, 1998); and Mark Berger, "Up from neo-liberalism: Free market mythologies and the coming crisis of global capitalism", *Third World Quarterly* 20, no. 2 (1999): 453–63.

25. For an extensive discussion of this thesis, see Robert Wade and Frank Veneroso, "The Asian crisis: The high debt model versus the Wall Street-Treasury-IMF complex", *New Left Review,* no. 228 (March/April 1998): 3–24.

26. Ibid, 20–21.

27. *Newsweek,* 7 September 1998, 8.

28. See Fareed Zakaria, "So much for globalization", *Newsweek,* 7 September 1998, 19.

29. Robert Samuelson, "A world meltdown?" *Newsweek,* 7 September 1998, 14.

30. Michael Elliott, "Coming apart", *Newsweek,* 12 October 1998, 30.

31. George Soros, "The crisis of global capitalism", *Newsweek,* 1 February 1999, 9–12.

32. United Nations Development Programme, *UNDP Human Development Report 1996* (New York and Oxford: Oxford University Press, 1996), 13.

33. See Frederic L. Bender, ed., *Karl Marx: The Communist Manifesto* (New York and London: Norton, 1998).

34. For a useful discussion of this, see Ernest Mandel, "Marx's theory of wages in the *Communist Manifesto* and subsequently", in *Karl Marx: The Communist Manifesto,* ed. Frederic L. Bender (New York and London: Norton, 1998)

35. Kari Levitt, "Lessons of the seventies for the nineties in international context" (Paper presented at the symposium Jamaica in the Seventies, University of the West Indies, Mona, 24–26 August 1998), 8–9.

36. I rely here heavily on Levitt, "Lessons", with whose approach I am largely in agreement.

37. See ibid., and Derick Boyd, *Economic Management, Income Distribution and Poverty in Jamaica* (New York: Praeger, 1988).

38. See World Bank, *World Bank World Development Report: Knowledge for Development 1998–9* (New York: Oxford University Press, 1999), 198.

39. See ibid., 210.

40. United Nations Development Programme, *UNDP Human Development Report,* 168.

41. Ibid., 148.

42. Ibid.

43. Ibid.

44. In 1991, foreign aid amounted to some 5 percent of the Jamaican gross national product, by 1996 it had been reduced to 1.4 percent. See World Bank, *World Development Report,* 230.

45. In the 1990s, levels of unemployment have hovered at the impossibly, though typically, high level of 16 percent. See Planning Institute of Jamaica, *Economic and Social Survey: Jamaica 1997* (Kingston, Jamaica: Planning Institute of Jamaica, 1998), iv.

46. For a useful study of the winners and losers in the structural adjustment phase of the 1980s, see Patricia Anderson and Michael Witter, "Crisis, adjustment and social change: A case study of Jamaica", in *Consequences of Structural Adjustment: A Review of the Jamaican Experience,* ed. Elsie Le Franc (Kingston, Jamaica: Canoe Press, 1994), 1–55.

47. Laurie Gunst's interviews and description of life among the Jamaican posses on the US East Coast and elsewhere is still the most convincing – though incomplete from a scholarly perspective – assessment of the phenomenon. See Laurie Gunst, *Born fi Dead: A Journey through the Jamaican Posse Underworld* (New York: Henry Holt, 1995).

48. See Planning Institute of Jamaica, *Economic and Social Survey,* table 2.2.

49. I adhere to this view that the transition to dancehall derives out of a specific sociopolitical conjuncture, though I acknowledge Cecil Gutzmore's point, raised in a short though fascinating discussion, that the very mechanics of deejay music – with emphasis on the spoken word – encouraged the linguistic transition to Ja-

maican. An essay devoted strictly to this question would have to address this nuance in greater detail.

50. See Planning Institute of Jamaica, *Economic and Social Survey*, 17.5.

51. Ibid.

52. Munroe, *Renewing Democracy*, Table 4.2, 122.

53. See *Report of the Director of Elections*, 26.

54. See Munroe, *Renewing Democracy*, 118.

55. Buju Banton, "Love me brownin' ", *Mr Mention* (Polygram PH 1994).

56. Buju Banton, "'Til I'm laid to rest", *'Til Shiloh* (Polygram 314–524 119–2).

57. See, for a similar reading of this new, militant upsurge, Carolyn Cooper and Cecil Gutzmore, "Border clash: The politics of location in Jamaican popular culture" (Paper presented at the conference African Diaspora Studies on the Eve of the Twenty-first Century, University of California, Berkeley, April 1998).

58. *Daily Observer*, 9 August 1999.

59. See, for an insider's description of the debates within the Manley regime during this fascinating moment, Norman Girvan, " 'Not for sale': Three episodes in the life of democratic socialism" (Paper presented at the symposium Jamaica in the Seventies, University of the West Indies, Mona, 24–26 August 1998).

60. With the exception of Beckford and Witter's critical assessment of the fall of the Manley regime, there is no significant major study that emerges from this trend in the 1980s. See George Beckford and Michael Witter, *Small Garden, Bitter Weed: Struggle and Change in Jamaica* (London: Zed Books; Morant Bay, Jamaica: Maroon Publishing House, 1980). It should be noted, however, tl at further south in Guyana, one of the more important contributions to Caribbean political thinking in this decade came from C.Y. Thomas, whose party – Walter Rodney's – the Working People's Alliance (WPA) had gone through its own process of rethinking after Rodney's death and the Grenada events. See C.Y. Thomas, *The Rise of the Authoritarian State in Peripheral Societies* (New York: Monthly Review Press, 1984).

61. See Workers' Party of Jamaica, "Contribution to rethinking: Issues in the communist movement" (Mimeo, Kingston, 1987).

62. See Judith Wedderburn, ed., *Rethinking Development* (Mona, Jamaica: The Consortium Graduate School of Social Sciences, University of the West Indies, 1991).

63. See Alistair Hennessy, ed., *Intellectuals in the Twentieth Century Caribbean*, Volume 1, *Spectre of the New Class: The Commonwealth Caribbean*, Warwick University Caribbean Studies Series (London and Basingstoke: Macmillan, 1992).

64. See Brian Meeks, ed., *New Currents in Caribbean Thought*, special issue, *Social and Economic Studies* 43, no. 3 (September 1994).

65. Robotham, *Vision and Voluntarism*, 64.

66. See chapter 6, "Careening on the Edge of the Abyss".

67. Robotham's emphasis on national community and the papering over of historical and contemporary social cleavages is reminiscent of the post-Marxist populism of Paul Piccone and others around the journal *Telos*. Frankel identifies the danger of this perspective easily folding into a form of right wing chauvinism. See Boris Frankel, "Confronting neoliberal regimes: The post-Marxist embrace of populism and realpolitik", *New Left Review,* no. 226 (November/December 1997): 57–92.

68. See especially, Munroe, *Renewing Democracy,* 112–14.

69. See David Scott, "The government of freedom" (Paper presented at the conference New Currents in Caribbean Thought: Looking Towards the Twenty-first Century, Michigan State University, 4–5 April 1997); and David Scott, "Revolution, theory, modernity: Notes on the cognitive-political crisis of our time", *Social and Economic Studies* 44, no. 3 (June 1995): 1–23.

70. See Brian Meeks, *Caribbean Revolutions and Revolutionary Theory: An Assessment of Cuba, Nicaragua and Grenada,* Warwick University Caribbean Studies Series (London and Basingstoke: Macmillan, 1993).

71. Scott, "Revolution, theory, modernity", 12.

72. See , for example, the interesting early debate between Geoffrey Hawthorn, Gayatri Spivak, Ron Aronson and John Dunn, "The post-modern condition: The end of politics?" (17–34), where Dunn expresses a similar opinion, with which I am in complete agreement. See G.C. Spivak, ed., *The Postcolonial Condition: Interviews, Strategies, Dialogues* (London: Routledge, 1990).

73. See Scott, "Revolution, theory, modernity", 18.

74. See, for example, Hilbourne Watson, Introduction, "The Caribbean and the techno-paradigm shift in global capitalism", in *The Caribbean in the Global Political Economy,* ed. Hilbourne Watson (Boulder and London: Lynn Rienner; Kingston, Jamaica: Ian Randle, 1994), 4–5.

75. See Brian Meeks, "Re-reading *The Black Jacobins*: James, the dialectic and the revolutionary conjuncture", in *Radical Caribbean: From Black Power to Abu Bakr* (Kingston, Jamaica: The Press, University of the West Indies, 1996).

76. See Hilbourne Watson, "Themes in liberalism, modernity, Marxism, postmodernism and beyond: An interpretation and critique of Brian Meeks' 'Re-reading *The Black Jacobins*: James, the dialectic and the revolutionary conjuncture' " (Paper presented at the conference New Currents in Caribbean Thought: Looking Towards the Twenty-first Century, Michigan State University, 4–5 April 1997).

77. See ibid., 44.

78. C.Y. Thomas, in particular, maintained an impressive rate of publication in the eighties, and his *Rise of the Authoritarian State* remains a singularly important contribution to the debate on democracy in 'transitional' societies.

79. See Kari Levitt and Michael Witter, eds, *The Critical Tradition of Caribbean Political Economy: The Legacy of George Beckford* (Kingston, Jamaica: Ian Randle Publishers, 1997).

80. See *Marronage*, no. 1 (1998).

81. See Bjorn Hettne and Magnus Blomstrum, *Development Theory in Transition: The Dependency Debate and Beyond, Third World Responses* (London: Zed Books, 1984). For a recent critique of the New World/Plantation school, see Cecilia Green, "Caribbean dependency theory revisited: A historical-materialist-feminist revision" (Paper presented at the conference New Currents in Caribbean Thought: Looking Towards the Twenty-first Century, Michigan State University, 4–5 April 1997).

82. See Norman Girvan, "Reinterpreting the Caribbean" (Typescript, University of the West Indies, Mona, 1999); and Norman Girvan, "Social consensus, democratic socialism and the market economy" (Paper presented at the PNP Sixtieth Anniversary Symposium, 17 September 1998, Kingston, Jamaica).

83. See C.Y. Thomas, "On reconstructing a political economy of the Caribbean" (Paper presented at the conference New Currents in Caribbean Thought: Looking Towards the Twenty-first Century, Michigan State University, 4–5 April 1997).

84. See Levitt, "Lessons".

85. C.L.R. James, *Beyond a Boundary* (New York: Pantheon Books, 1984).

86. Walter Rodney, *A History of the Guyanese Working People* (Baltimore: Johns Hopkins University Press, 1981).

87. James Scott, *Domination and the Arts of Resistance: Hidden Transcripts* (New Haven: Yale University Press, 1990); and James Scott, *Weapons of the Weak: Everyday Forms of Peasant Resistance* (New Haven: Yale University Press, 1985).

88. Gayatri Spivak and Ranajit Guha, eds, *Selected Subaltern Studies* (New York: Oxford University Press, 1988). And, for an interpretation of the approach to Latin American conditions, see John Beverley, *Subalternity and Representation: Arguments in Cultural Theory* (Durham and London: Duke University Press, 1999).

89. As Stuart Hall ("The toad in the garden: Thatcherism among the theorists", in *Marxism and the Interpretation of Culture*, ed. Cary Nelson and Lawrence Grossberg [Urbana and Chicago: University of Illinois Press, 1988]) counters,

> The moment you give the ideological dimension of the analysis its proper place, people invert the paradigm, accusing you of thinking that things work by ideology alone. Ideology is tremendously important, and it has its own specificity, its own kind of effects, its own mechanisms, but it doesn't operate outside the play of other determinations; it has social, political, economic conditions of existence. One has to take the question of the nucleus of economic activity seriously, as Gramsci said, even when using a hegemonic approach. (35)

90. See Barrington Chevannes, *Rastafari: Roots and Ideology* (Syracuse: Syracuse University Press, 1995).

91. See Horace Campbell, *Rasta and Resistance: From Marcus Garvey to Walter Rodney* (Dar Es Salaam: Tanzania Publishing House, 1985).

92. Rupert Lewis, *Walter Rodney's Intellectual and Political Thought* (Kingston, Jamaica: The Press, University of the West Indies; Detroit: Wayne State University Press, 1999).

93. See, for example, Pat Mohammed (guest ed.), *Feminist Review,* no. 59 (June 1998).

94. See Obika Gray, "Global culture and the politics of moral deregulation in Jamaica" (Paper presented at the Caribbean Studies Association Conference, Panama City, May 1999).

95. See Anthony Bogues, "Singing songs of freedom: Freedom and the black tradition in the Americas" (Paper presented in a colloquium at the Afro-American Studies Programme, Brown University, 14 July 1998). For a parallel perspective, see Clinton Hutton, "Notions of freedom in popular Jamaican music" (Paper presented at the Caribbean Studies Association Conference, Antigua, May 1998).

96. A notable exception to this is Tony Bogues' initiative, through the Department of Government at the University of the West Indies (UWI), Mona, to establish an interactive programme of mutual research and education, involving UWI graduate students and residents of the inner-city community of Craig Town. Reminiscent of Walter Rodney's earlier efforts to link town with gown, the project is still too young to be properly assessed; its potential is obvious, however.

Chapter 1

1. There have been only two significant attempts to initiate guerrilla warfare in recent times in the anglophone Caribbean. Henry's was the first. The second occurred in the early 1970s in Trinidad and Tobago and is explored in chapter 2. I owe a special note of thanks to the late Huntley Munroe, QC, former Jamaican director of public prosecutions, for making available to me his meticulously kept private file from the treason felony trial of Ronald Henry and his comrades. All documents from that file are hereafter referred to as "HM's file".

2. *Daily Gleaner,* 27 June 1960.

3. Considering the fact that this is the only guerrilla movement of its kind to have emerged in modern Jamaica, so little has been written on Henry's rebellion as to be interpreted as an instance of serious neglect by Caribbean academics. See, among the few, Terry Lacey, *Violence and Politics in Jamaica: 1960–1970* (Manchester: Manchester University Press, 1977), A. Barrington Chevannes, "The repairer of the breach: Reverend Claudius Henry and Jamaican society", in *Ethnic-*

ity in the Americas, ed. Frances Henry (The Hague: Mouton Publishers, 1976), 263–89; and Obika Gray, *Radicalism and Social Change in Jamaica: 1960–1972* (Knoxville: University of Tennessee Press, 1991).

4. *Daily Gleaner,* 7 April 1960.

5. Ibid.

6. I rely heavily on Chevannes' pioneering essay for the narrative on Henry's background. See Chevannes, "The repairer of the breach", 265–66.

7. See A. Barrington Chevannes, *Rastafari: Roots and Ideology* (Syracuse: Syracuse University Press, 1995).

8. Chevannes, "The repairer of the breach", 275.

9. Ibid., 276.

10. *Daily Gleaner,* 6 May 1960.

11. Adolphus Christie's cautioned statement, HM's file.

12. Eldred Morgan's cautioned statement, HM's file.

13. Titus Damon's cautioned statement, HM's file.

14. Donald Harper's cautioned statement, HM's file.

15. Al Thomas' cautioned statement, HM's file.

16. Ronald Henry to "Dad", letter number 1, HM's file.

17. Ronald Henry to "Dad", letter number 2, HM's file.

18. See, in particular, Superintendent Mullin's sworn statement about his visit to the First Africa Corps in the Bronx, where Ronald alludes to the fact that he was in the US Air Force and Eldred Morgan's cautioned statement where he suggests that he had been in the army. No corroborating evidence has as yet been found.

19. Donald Harper's cautioned statement, HM's file.

20. Albert Gabbidon's cautioned statement, HM's file.

21. See Private Stanley Barnes' sworn statement, HM's file.

22. See, for example, then minister of home affairs, William Seivright's comments in the *Daily Gleaner,* 25 June 1960 where he refers to the troublemakers as "pawns in a bigger game".

23. See Timothy Wickham-Crowley, *Guerrillas and Revolution in Latin America: A Comparative Study of Insurgents and Regimes since 1956* (Princeton: Princeton University Press, 1992); and Jeff Goodwin, *State and Revolution in the Third World: A Comparative Analysis* (Berkeley: University of California Press, forthcoming).

24. See John Foran and Jeff Goodwin, "Revolutionary outcomes in Iran and Nicaragua: Coalition, fragmentation, war and the limits of social transformation", *Theory and Society* 22 (1993): 209–47.

25. See Farideh Farhi, *States and Urban-based Revolutions: Iran and Nicaragua* (Urbana and Chicago: University of Illinois Press, 1990).

26. Theda Skocpol, *Social Revolutions in the Modern World* (Cambridge: Cambridge University Press, 1994).

27. Forrest Colburn, *The Vogue of Revolution in Poor Countries* (Princeton: Princeton University Press, 1994), 104.

28. See Bernard Yack, *The Longing for Total Revolution* (Princeton: Princeton University Press, 1994).

29. Antonio Gramsci, *Selections From Prison Notebooks* (London: Lawrence and Wishart, 1986), 377.

30. Harvey Kaye, Introduction to *The Face of the Crowd: Studies in Revolution, Ideology and Popular Protest: Selected Essays of George Rudé*, ed. Harvey Kaye (Atlantic Highlands, NJ: Humanities Press International, 1988), 25.

31. George Rudé, *The Face of the Crowd: Studies in Revolution, Ideology and Popular Protest: Selected Essays of George Rudé*, ed. Harvey Kaye (Atlantic Highlands, NJ: Humanities Press International, 1988), 197.

32. Ibid., 198.

33. Abigail Bakan, *Ideology and Class Conflict in Jamaica: The Politics of Rebellion* (Montreal and London: McGill-Queen's University Press, 1990), 14.

34. Ibid., 134.

35. Ibid., 135.

36. James Scott, *Domination and the Arts of Resistance: Hidden Transcripts* (New Haven and London: Yale University Press, 1990). In searching for hidden messages and encoded meanings as forms of resistance, Scott draws heavily on the corpus of contemporary cultural studies from Bakhtin and Barthes through Stallybrass and White to Stuart Hall. What is novel is his consistent and sustained critique of the inadequacies of Gramscian 'hegemony' and the application of his theory of veiled resistance to the specific terrain of revolt. See M. Bakhtin, *The Dialogic Imagination* (Austin: University of Texas Press, 1981); Roland Barthes, *Mythologies* (London: Jonathan Cape, 1972); Peter Stallybrass and Allon White, *The Politics and Poetics of Transgression* (Ithaca: Cornell University Press, 1986); Stuart Hall, "Encoding, decoding", in *The Cultural Studies Reader*, ed. Simon During (London and New York: Routledge, 1993), 90–103; and Dick Hebdige, "From culture to hegemony", in *The Cultural Studies Reader*, ed. Simon During (London and New York: Routledge, 1993), 357–67.

37. Scott, *Domination and the Arts of Resistance*, 86.

38. Ibid., especially 70–82.

39. Ibid., 14.

40. Ibid., 191.

41. Ibid., 192.

42. It is important to note that Scott makes room for what he calls a "paper thin theory of hegemony". Where a good many subordinates may see the possibility

of one day occupying positions of power or, alternatively, where the population is atomized and kept under strict resistance then hegemony, in the willed sense, may occur. See ibid., 82–83.

43. I thank Fred Cooper for his sharp critique of Scott and this chapter in an earlier draft, which led to this comment. Cooper considers Scott's approach too flawed and unidimensional to be very useful. He argues that Scott fails to grasp the distinctiveness of different social contexts and the subsequent implications for the nature and character of resistance. He is also sensitive, in the tradition of E.P. Thompson, to the interpenetration and interconnectedness of ideologies and cultures and therefore critical of what he sees as Scott's simple dichotomization of 'those above' and 'those below', as well as the failure to see that social movements develop over time, with different dynamics at different stages of their development.

While largely agreeing with his nuanced critique, I still think that Scott's persistent argument for a relatively autonomous space, in which a subordinate discourse is cultivated, inches the debate beyond Gramsci and helps to explain the persistence and resilience of popular forms of resistance in contexts such as Jamaica. For an elaboration of Cooper's positions on some of these issues, see Fred Cooper, "Conflict and connecting: Rethinking African colonial history", *American Historical Review*, 99 (1994); and Fred Cooper, *Decolonization and African Society: The Labor Question in French and British Africa* (Cambridge and New York: Cambridge University Press, 1996).

44. An untouched dimension of Ronald's 'disconnectedness' surrounds the fact that he and a number of his comrades were fair skinned, spoke with American accents, or were American. In the layered social structure of pre-independence Jamaica, the code transmitted would have been that they were from the elite, which might or might not, depending on how it is read, have been an obstacle in their further progress had the revolt taken off. This was decisively not the case with Claudius, who was unmistakably black, a son of the soil and rooted in Afro-Jamaican religious tradition. I thank Lorna Goodison for a comment that prompted this note.

45. See Friedrich Engels, *Germany: Revolution and Counter-revolution* (Moscow: International Publishers, 1933), 100.

46. The Henry Rebellion is an enigma. It certainly does not fit into Eric Hobsbawm's careful analysis of "Primitive Rebels", which he disaggregates into "social bandits", "mafia-type movements", "millenarian movements", "city mobs" and "labour sects". Hobsbawm's main thrust is to locate these movements as forms of resistance appropriate to stages in the transition from early to modern capitalism. Thus, the closer the society approximates a modern, industrial type, the less likely it is for instances of social banditry to occur and the more

likely for working class/industrial forms of militancy to predominate. Henry's movement, however, appears as a pastiche, defying simple categorization. It is at once millenarian and falls within the ambit of Hobsbawm's analysis but it is also highly modern in its use of aircraft, the ports, transnational communication and, more critically, its multinational, pan-African objectives. Perhaps it requires a category of its own: "Black Atlantic Rebels", moving within a notional space between the Caribbean, the North Atlantic and Africa, and operating with their own tools of resistance and mythology of redemption. See Eric Hobsbawm, *Primitive Rebels: Studies in Archaic Forms of Social Movement in the Nineteenth and Twentieth Centuries* (New York: Praeger, 1959). For an elaboration of the notion of "Black Atlantic", see Paul Gilroy, *The Black Atlantic: Modernity and Double Consciousness* (Cambridge, Mass.: Harvard University Press, 1993).

47. Louis Simpson, *North of Jamaica* (New York: Harper and Row, 1972), quoted in Douglas Hall, *Grace Kennedy and Company Limited: A Story of Jamaican Enterprise* (Kingston, Jamaica: Grace Kennedy, 1992), 27–28.

48. Carl Stone's rich study of political attitudes in urban Jamaica, conducted more than a decade after Henry's rebellion, is instructive. Among the 10 percent of Kingston's population whom he defines as 'lumpenproletariat', that is, those who are unemployed and no longer seeking work, some 74 percent were hostile to the official Jamaican credo of multiracialism; 63 percent were hostile to both the major political parties; 56 percent were hostile to whites; and 65 percent supported "violence by the poor". In his broader sample of the entire urban community, this militancy necessarily diminished, but he still found that a significant minority was "militant in demanding an end to race privilege and white foreign economic domination, and in articulating black solidarity rather than multiracialism". See Carl Stone, *Class, Race and Political Behaviour in Urban Jamaica* (Mona, Jamaica: Institute of Social and Economic Research, 1973). For lumpenproletariat statistics, 147; the quote is from 106.

49. Bakan, *Ideology and Class Conflict*, 80.

50. See ibid., 95.

51. See Rupert Lewis, *Marcus Garvey: Anti-Colonial Champion* (Trenton: Africa World Press, 1988).

52. See, especially, Horace Campbell, *Rasta and Resistance: From Marcus Garvey to Walter Rodney* (Trenton: Africa World Press, 1987).

53. Patrick Kerr's sworn statement, HM's file. The references to the gates of the prison and "Swallowfield" are commonly held Rastafarian beliefs that give Garvey certain divine and prophetic qualities. Both references, years later, became incorporated into many different reggae songs. Thus Swallowfield as the battlefield appears in the Mighty Diamonds "Right time", and the prison gates is a theme in Culture's "Two sevens clash". See Mighty Diamonds, "Right time",

Go Seek Your Rights (Virgin CDFL 9002); and Culture, "Two sevens clash", *The Story of Jamaican Music* (Island CD 518 402-2).

54. One of the nagging questions that kept recurring while reading Ronald's file was: How was he able to fairly easily procure recruits off the streets of New York for a tenuous and ill-explained scheme of revolution that, needless to say, was life-threatening? And who were these young African Americans and West Indians who were willing to commit their lives to Ronald's cause at the proverbial drop of a hat? This can only be answered if it is appreciated that New York, and Harlem in particular, is at the hub of the African diasporic experience in the New World. At least since the 1920s and Garvey's Universal Negro Improvement Association (UNIA), Harlem, by virtue of its size and strategic location, has been a fecund community for the generation of intellectual and political notions of black nationalism. While the Harlem of the 1950s was far removed from its nationalist heyday under Garvey's sojourn, this was, in its own right, a period of increasing militancy. Malcolm X was preaching at Mohammed's Mosque No. 7 and creating his own mass following; there was increasing awareness of, and growing militancy for, the civil rights movement in the South; African independence was in the air, and a new generation of pan-Africanists was emerging, with heroes such as Ghana's Kwame Nkrumah and Kenya's Tom Mboya; and groups with esoteric names such as the "Hearts of Africa Committee", "The Provisional Committee for a Free Africa", "United Sons and Daughters of Africa", and "The Yoruba Temple of New Oyo" were springing up and distributing pamphlets on every corner. Harlem, in this sense, acted as a source of dry powder, providing a ready charge for the larger ignition that was planned for Jamaica. But Jamaica was not ready for revolution. For a discussion of nationalist movements in Harlem in this period, see E.U. Essien Udom, "The Nationalist Movements of Harlem", in *Harlem: A Community in Transition,* ed. John Henrik Clarke (New York: Citadel Press, 1964). For an interesting sketch of Malcolm X in his last year of life, and an insight into the Caribbean contribution to African American militancy, see Jan Carew, *Ghosts in Our Blood: With Malcolm X in Africa, England and the Caribbean* (Chicago: Lawrence Hill Books, 1994). I thank Winston James for his comments, which led to this footnote. His book on Caribbean radicals in New York eloquently examines some of these aspects of Harlem's remarkable history. See Winston James, *Holding Aloft the Banner of Ethiopia: Caribbean Radicalism in Early Twentieth Century America* (London, New York: Verso, 1998).

55. See *Daily Gleaner,* 16 September 1960.

56. See Lacey, *Violence and Politics,* 84.

57. A central issue of the 1972 electoral campaign surrounded the "rod of correction" and the "Henry Pamphlet". After the 1960 incident, Claudius, convicted

of treason felony, served a sentence of ten years hard labour. On release, he established a highly successful, largely self-supporting commune on the plains of southern Clarendon. Henry reputedly commanded a large following in that parish and, in the weeks before the election, issued a pamphlet endorsing Michael Manley's PNP. It featured pictures of Henry with a rod purportedly given to him by Haile Selassie, Manley and Selassie himself. The JLP, completely misreading the mood of the electorate, sought, in subsequent newspaper advertisements, to lambaste Manley for consorting with known and convicted subversives, but this campaign largely backfired. Among many voters, particularly the young, the association between the PNP, Rastafari and black consciousness gave the party a certain credibility and élan and contributed to its resounding victory at the polls. See, for example, Olive Senior's account in *The Message is Change: A Perspective on the 1972 General Elections* (Kingston: Kingston Publishers, 1972).

58. Both myself and Obika Gray, separately, and with different emphases, explore the intense and barely veiled struggle for cultural and social dominance that is gaining momentum in Jamaica today. See Obika Gray, "Discovering the social power of the poor", *Social and Economic Studies* 43, no. 3 (September 1994): 169–89; and Brian Meeks, *Radical Caribbean: From Black Power to Abu Bakr* (Kingston, Jamaica: The Press, University of the West Indies, 1996).

Chapter 2

1. I wish to thank the late Thelma Henderson, friend and fighter for the rights of workers and women in Trinidad and Tobago, who helped immeasurably in the realization of this chapter. To her memory it is also dedicated.

2. Clem Haynes, interview with author, Cocorite, Trinidad, 5 June 1996. Henceforth, Haynes interview.

3. Terrence Thornhill, interview with author, Petit Valley, Trinidad, 20 December 1996. Henceforth, Thornhill interview.

4. The first, to my knowledge, is the 1961 guerrilla movement organized by Ronald Henry in Jamaica. Henry, however, though successful in infiltrating arms and personnel from the United States, was intercepted before initiating combat in the field. See chapter 1, "The Henry Rebellion".

5. Research on the 1970 Black Power revolution has been significantly augmented by Selwyn Ryan and Taimoon Stewart, eds, *The Black Power Revolution 1970: A Retrospective* (St Augustine, Trinidad: Institute of Social and Economic Research, 1995), which brings together a number of otherwise unavailable articles and commentaries. See also Brian Meeks, "The development of the 1970 revolution in Trinidad and Tobago" (MSc thesis, UWI Mona, 1976); Susan Craig, "Background to the 1970 confrontation in Trinidad and Tobago", in *Contemporary*

Caribbean: A Sociological Reader, ed. Susan Craig (Port of Spain, Trinidad: Susan Craig, 1982), 385–423; and Paul Sutton, "Black Power in Trinidad and Tobago: The crisis of 1970", *Journal of Commonwealth and Comparative Politics* 21, no. 2 (July 1983).

6. For two somewhat different perspectives on the political strategy the PNM employed to carve out its electoral majority through various ethnic alliances, see Ralph Premdas, "Ethnic conflict in Trinidad and Tobago: Domination and reconciliation", in *Trinidad Ethnicity,* ed. Kevin Yelvington, Warwick University Caribbean Studies Series (London and Basingstoke: Macmillan, 1993), 136–60; and Percy Hintzen, *The Costs of Regime Survival: Racial Mobilization, Elite Domination and Control of the State in Guyana and Trinidad* (Cambridge: Cambridge University Press, 1989).

7. The most important single study on NUFF is David Millette's undergraduate dissertation, "Guerrilla war in Trinidad: 1970–1974", which appears as a chapter in Selwyn Ryan and Taimoon Stewart, eds, *The Black Power Revolution 1970: A Retrospective* (St Augustine, Trinidad: Institute of Social and Economic Research, 1995), 625–60. Other references are scant and appear in the general literature on the 1970 revolution, or take the form of recent journalistic reminiscences on the 1970 era.

8. Shah and LaSalle were the two young lieutenants who led the army rebellion. They were subsequently tried for treason, convicted and later pardoned by the Williams regime.

9. Malcolm "Jai" Kernahan, interview with author, Gonzales, Port of Spain, Trinidad, 4 June 1996. Henceforth, Kernahan interview.

10. Ibid.

11. Ibid.

12. Ibid.

13. *Daily Express,* 1 June 1972.

14. For a report of Valentine's funeral, see *Daily Express,* 12 July 1972.

15. See *Daily Express,* 22 February 1973.

16. See *Daily Express,* 1 June 1973.

17. See *Daily Express* and *Sunday Express,* 6–18 August 1973 for reports and commentary on the two raids and the guerrilla movement.

18. Thornhill interview

19. See, for example, James Madison, "Federalist papers no. 10", in *The Federalist Papers,* Alexander Hamilton, James Madison and John Jay (New York: Mentor, 1961), 78: "By a faction I understand a number of citizens, whether amounting to a majority or minority of the whole, who are united or activated by some common impulse of passion, or of interest, adverse to the rights of other citizens, or to the permanent or aggregate interests of the community."

20. See, for example, Gordon Lewis' far from frivolous comments in *The Growth of the Modern West Indies* (London: McGibbon and Kee, 1968), 197.

21. See Brian Meeks "Re-reading *The Black Jacobins*: James, the dialectic and the revolutionary conjuncture", *Social and Economic Studies* 43, no. 3 (September 1994): 75–103.

22. Hilbourne Watson, "Themes in liberalism, modernity, Marxism, postmodernism and beyond: An interpretation and critique of Brian Meeks' 'Re-reading *The Black Jacobins*: James, the dialectic and the revolutionary conjuncture' " (Paper presented at the conference New Currents in Caribbean Thought: Looking Towards the Twenty-first Century, Michigan State University, 4–5 April 1997), 1.

23. Ibid., 43.

24. See, for a similar conclusion, Charles Mills, "Getting out of the cave: Tension between democracy and elitism in Marx's theory of cognitive liberation", *Social and Economic Studies* 39, no. 1 (March 1990): 1–50.

25. The approach taken here is perhaps closest in spirit to that of Eric Olin Wright, Andrew Levine and Elliott Sober (*Reconstructing Marxism: Essays on Explanation and the Theory of History* [London and New York: Verso, 1992]) who suggest that a model of "historical trajectories", sensitive to the explanatory strength in race, culture, leadership and other variables, should replace the approach which overstates the role of economic structures in determining history:

> If agents capable of transforming relations of production are not always forthcoming when production relations stagnate, it is obvious that production relations may not always develop optimally. The road map of historical development can thus have forks and detours, junctures in which more than one option is historically possible and in which suboptimal outcomes can occur. The cumulative quality of the forces of production still makes retreats on the map less likely than stasis or progression . . . but eliminating the thesis of optimal selection of economic structures opens the possibility of multiple routes into the future. (90)

26. John Elster, *Making Sense of Marx* (Cambridge: Cambridge University Press, 1985), 360.

27. See, for example, Antonio Gramsci, *Selections from Prison Notebooks* (London: Lawrence and Wishart, 1986), 377; and George Rudé, *The Face of the Crowd: Studies in Revolution, Ideology and Popular Protest: Selected Essays of George Rudé*, ed. Harvey Kaye (Atlantic Highlands, NJ: Humanities Press International, 1988).

28. See James Scott, *Domination and the Arts of Resistance: Hidden Transcripts* (New Haven and London: Yale University Press, 1990) and chapter 1, this volume.

29. See Barrington Moore, *Social Origins of Dictatorship and Democracy: Lord and Peasant in the Making of the Modern World* (Harmondsworth: Penguin, 1987); and Eric Wolf, *Peasant Wars of the Twentieth Century* (London: Faber and Faber, 1971).

30. See, for example, Charles Tilley, *From Mobilization to Revolution* (New York: Addison-Wesley, 1978); Theda Skocpol, *Social Revolutions in the Modern World* (Cambridge: Cambridge University Press, 1994); and Timothy Wickham-Crowley, *Guerrillas and Revolution in Latin America: A Comparative Study of Insurgents and Regimes since 1956* (Princeton: Princeton University Press, 1992).

31. This is Wickham-Crowley's coined term for "Patriarchal Praetorian Regimes". See Wickham-Crowley, *Guerrillas and Revolution*, 9.

32. See Jeff Goodwin, "A theory of persistent insurgency: El Salvador, Guatemala and Peru in comparative perspective" (Paper presented at the Seventeenth Latin American Studies Association Conference, September 1992).

33. Kernahan interview.

34. Thornhill interview.

35. Haynes interview.

36. See, for a useful discussion of 'subcultures', Albert K. Cohen, "A general theory of sub-cultures", in *The Subcultures Reader,* ed. Ken Gelder and Sarah Thornton (London and New York: Routledge, 1997), 44–54.

37. Earl Lovelace, *The Dragon Can't Dance* (Harlow: Longman, 1979), 172–73.

38. Anthony Emrold Phillip, *Life Is a Stage: The Complete Calypsoes of Brother Valentino,* comp. Zeno Obi Constance (Port of Spain, Trinidad: Zeno Constance, 1996), 12

39. Ibid., 11.

40. See Brian Meeks, *Caribbean Revolutions and Revolutionary Theory: An Assessment of Cuba, Nicaragua and Grenada,* Warwick University Caribbean Studies Series (London and Basingstoke: Macmillan, 1993).

41. I agree with Wallerstein's identification of 1968 and its aftermath as the flash point of a peculiar historical conjuncture of revolutionary activity. See Immanuel Wallerstein, Terrence Hopkins and Giovanni Arrighi, *Antisystemic Movements* (London: Verso, 1989).

42. See Meeks, "The development of the 1970 revolution", 230–32.

43. For a critical chronicle of this period, see Selwyn Ryan, *Revolution and Reaction: Parties and Politics in Trinidad and Tobago, 1970–1981* (St Augustine, Trinidad: Institute of Social and Economic Research, 1989).

Chapter 3

1. Wilson Harris, "History, fable and myth in the Caribbean and the Guianas", in *Selected Essays of Wilson Harris: The Unfinished Genesis of the Imagination,* ed. Andrew Bundy (London and New York: Routledge, 1999), 159.

2. Ibid., 156.

3. Ibid., 159.

4. Dennis Benn, *The Growth and Development of Political Ideas in the Caribbean: 1774–1983* (Mona, Jamaica: Institute of Social and Economic Research, 1987), 167.

5. Ibid., 167.

6. Ibid., 168.

7. Though it is true that Stone, toward the end of his life, sought to move away from his strong empiricist-behaviouralist moorings to take matters of culture into greater account. See chapter 4, "Carl Stone".

8. See, in particular, Rex Nettleford, *Mirror, Mirror: Identity, Race and Protest in Jamaica* (London: William Collins, 1970); Rex Nettleford, *Caribbean Cultural Identity: The Case of Jamaica* (Kingston, Jamaica: Institute of Jamaica, 1978); and Rex Nettleford, *Inward Stretch: Outward Reach* (London: Macmillan, 1993).

9. The blurb for the course "Sports, Politics and Society" (GT21M), for example, begins with the statement that "This course exposes students to the sphere of sport as a legitimate area for social science research and analysis", and the course "Popular Jamaican Music: 1962–1982" (GT23M) begins with the statement that "This course explores the folk and popular music as socio-political, cultural and philosophical instruments and expressions in the making of the African Diaspora in the Americas." See *Welcome to the Department of Government, UWI, Mona* (Mona, Jamaica: Department of Government, University of the West Indies, 1995), 57; and Clinton Hutton, "GT23M – Popular Jamaican Music: 1962–1982: Roots lyrics as socio-political and philosophical text", course handout, University of the West Indies, Mona, 1998, 1.

10. See Carolyn Cooper, ed., special issue on Reggae Studies, *Social and Economic Studies* 47, no. 1 (March 1998).

11. See, for example, Richard Burton, *Afro-Creole: Power, Opposition and Play in the Caribbean* (Ithaca and London: Cornell University Press, 1997); Antonio Benitez-Rojo, *The Repeating Island: The Caribbean and the Postmodern Perspective* (Durham and London: Duke University Press, 1996); and Stefano Harney, *Nationalism and Identity: Culture and the Imagination in a Caribbean Diaspora* (London and New Jersey: Zed Books; Kingston, Jamaica: The Press, University of the West Indies, 1996).

12. Konrad Jarausch and Kenneth Hardy, *Quantitative Methods for Historians: A Guide to Research, Data and Statistics* (Chapel Hill and London: University of North Carolina Press, 1991), 191. The highly developed approach of content analysis and the use of manifest and latent variables to reveal a "richness of detail not evident from quantitative analysis alone" are some of the avenues through which quantitative methodologists are travelling in order to escape the label of being "too abstract". The approach taken here does not frontally address these

hard, data questions but sketches a general orientation to the problem of literary analysis, over which such methodologies might prove useful. See, for example, Judy Gray and Iain Densten, "Integrating quantitative and qualitative analysis using latent and manifest variables", *Quality and Quantity* 32, no. 4 (1998): 419–31.

13. See Frederick Jameson, "Third World literature in the era of multinational capitalism", *Social Text* 15 (Fall 1986).

14. Aijaz Ahmad, "Jameson's rhetoric of otherness and the 'national allegory' ", in *The Post Colonial Studies Reader,* ed. Bill Ashcroft, Gareth Griffiths and Helen Tiffin (London and New York: Routledge, 1995), 78.

15. Barbara Christian, "The race for theory", in *The Post Colonial Studies Reader,* ed. Bill Ashcroft, Gareth Griffiths and Helen Tiffin (London and New York: Routledge, 1995), 458.

16. Ibid., 460.

17. Daniel Miller, Michael Rowlands and Christopher Tilley, Introduction to *Domination and Resistance,* ed. Daniel Miller, Michael Rowlands, and Christopher Tilley (London and New York: Routledge, 1989), 2.

18. James Scott, *Domination and the Arts of Resistance: Hidden Transcripts* (New Haven and London: Yale University Press, 1990), xi.

19. For a further discussion of the strengths and weaknesses in Scott's framework, see chapter 1, "The Henry Rebellion".

20. None of these 'findings', when unearthed in the texts, can of course be considered 'scientific'. In the end, they emerge from the artist's imagination. They do, however, provide us with second-level hypotheses that may be immeasurably rich precisely because of their freedom from the fetish of the footnote. Who can argue, for example, that Thelwell's *The Harder They Come* is less useful in evoking urban Jamaica in the 1960s than Carl Stone's *Class, Race and Political Behaviour in Urban Jamaica* (Mona, Jamaica: Institute of Social and Economic Research, 1973), or that Lovelace's *The Dragon Can't Dance* cuts less to the heart of Trinidadian sociopolitical life in the 1970s than Selwyn Ryan's *Race and Nationalism in Trinidad and Tobago* (Toronto: University of Toronto Press, 1972)?

21. Earl Lovelace, *The Dragon Can't Dance* (Harlow: Longman, 1979), henceforth referred to as *Dragon*; and Michael Thelwell, *The Harder They Come* (New York: Grove Press, 1980), henceforth referred to as *Harder*.

22. Other important Caribbean novels that cover similar territory include the following: V.S. Naipaul, *Guerrillas* (London: Penguin, 1975); Neville Dawes, *Interim* (Kingston, Jamaica: Institute of Jamaica, 1978); Orlando Patterson, *The Children of Sisyphus* (Essex: Longman Drumbeat, 1982); Andrew Salkey, *The Late Emancipation of Jerry Stover* (Essex: Longman, 1982); and Ralph deBoissiere, *Crown Jewel* (London: Picador, 1981). The novels by Dawes, Salkey and

deBoissiere are set in an earlier, pre-independence setting, but those of Patterson and, more so, Naipaul cover almost the exact same time and place as *Dragon* and provide a rich basis for future comparative research.

23. See, for example, Gordon Lewis, *The Growth of the Modern West Indies* (London: McGibbon and Kee, 1968); and Brian Meeks, *Radical Caribbean: From Black Power to Abu Bakr* (Kingston, Jamaica: The Press, University of the West Indies, 1996).

24. For an early discussion of style in the West Indian novel which argues in favour of the rich character sketches generated by Naipaul, Mittelholzer, Hearne and others, see Kamau Braithwaite, *Roots* (Ann Arbor: University of Michigan Press, 1993), 28–54.

25. Lovelace, *Dragon*, 27.

26. Thelwell, *Harder*, 8.

27. For one of the earliest and still best reviews of the film, see Gordon Rohlehr, "Once in a blue sun: Review of *The Harder They Come*", in *My Strangled City and Other Essays* (Port of Spain, Trinidad: Longman Trinidad, 1992), 95–106.

28. Lovelace, *Dragon*, 23.

29. Thelwell, *Harder*, 161.

30. Ibid., 165.

31. Lovelace, *Dragon*, 71.

32. Ibid., 247.

33. Ibid., 175.

34. Thelwell, *Harder*, 168.

35. Ibid., 172.

36. Ibid., 214

37. Lovelace, *Dragon*, 197.

38. I elsewhere explore these differences in relation to the 1990 coup attempt led by Abu-Bakr in Trinidad and Tobago. Reading that chapter, in which the point is first mooted that the Trinidadian state is less consolidated than that in Jamaica, and then rereading both *Dragon* and *Harder*, it is evident that there are rich hypotheses here worth further exploration. See Brian Meeks, "The Imam, the return of Napoleon and the end of history", in Meeks, *Radical Caribbean*, 83–100.

39. From 19–21 April 1999, following announced increases in the price of gasoline, Jamaica experienced islandwide demonstrations, including the blocking of roads and the burning of tyres. After two days of intense disturbances, the government eventually compromised, with a partial rollback in the gas price – see Introduction.

40. Wayne Brown, "The fire next time", *Sunday Observer*, 25 April 1999.

41. The term itself, derived from an African tribe, is used to connote backwardness and lack of sophistication.

42. Thelwell, *Harder*, 29.

43. Lovelace, *Dragon*, 91.

44. Ibid., 92.

45. Thelwell, *Harder*, 68.

46. See ibid., 110.

47. Lovelace, *Dragon*, 63.

48. Thelwell, *Harder*, 160

49. The focus in this chapter has been on a particular field of resistance, defined through the creation of space and style. There are other dimensions that need further elaboration. Thus, there is the older field of contested hierarchies of colour and shade, manifest, for example, in the tensions between Cleothilda, Olive and Caroline. And there is the centrally contested field of gender, evident in the relationship between Elsa and Ivan and captured graphically in Sylvia's story. For an important reading of gender in *Dragon*, see Linden Lewis, "Masculinity and the dance of the dragon: Reading Lovelace discursively", *Feminist Review*, no. 59 (June 1998): 164–85.

50. Lovelace, *Dragon*, 24.

51. See ibid., 25.

52. See ibid., 112.

53. See ibid., 172–73.

54. Thelwell, *Harder*, 201.

55. Dick Hebdige, "Subculture: The meaning of style", in *The Subcultures Reader*, ed. Ken Gelder and Sarah Thornton (London and New York: Routledge, 1997), 142. Hebdige paints a picture of subcultures constantly being co-opted and legitimized by commercial capitalism only to reemerge in new, spectacular and unsettling forms. The durability of Caribbean forms such as Rastafarianism, despite the evident process of commercialization, suggests that either a different definition of how subcultures function is required, there is a weaker commercial effect, or these movements cannot be seen as peripheral, subcultures at all.

56. Thelwell, *Harder*, 193.

57. Lovelace, *Dragon*, 138.

58. Anthony McNeil, *Reel from the Life Movie* (Kingston: Savacou, 1972).

59. Thelwell, *Harder*, 197.

60. Lovelace, *Dragon*, 66.

61. Ibid., 190.

62. Thelwell, *Harder*, 390.

63. Lovelace, *Dragon*, 55.

64. Ibid., 50.

65. Ibid., 71.

66. Thelwell, *Harder*, 110.

67. Ibid., 320.

68. Ibid., 321.

69. Lovelace, *Dragon,* 166.

70. Ibid., 178.

71. Ibid., 178.

72. Thelwell, *Harder,* 349.

73. Lovelace, *Dragon,* 189.

74. Benitez-Rojo, *Repeating Island,* 314.

75. Ibid.

76. Burton, *Afro-Creole,* 265–66.

Chapter 4

1. See Patsy Lewis, ed., *Jamaica: Preparing for the Twenty-first Century* (Kingston, Jamaica: Ian Randle Publishers, 1994), ix.

2. For recent examples, see Folke Lindahl, "Caribbean diversity and ideological conformism: The crisis of Marxism in the English-speaking Caribbean", *Social and Economic Studies* 43, no. 3 (September 1994): 57–74; Carlene J. Edie, *Democracy by Default: Dependency and Clientelism in Jamaica* (Boulder and London: Lynne Rienner; Kingston, Jamaica: Ian Randle Publishers, 1991); Obika Gray, *Radicalism and Social Change in Jamaica, 1960–1972* (Knoxville: University of Tennessee Press, 1991); and Obika Gray, "Discovering the social power of the poor", *Social and Economic Studies* 43, no. 3 (September 1994): 169–89.

3. See Carl Stone, *Class Race and Political Behaviour in Urban Jamaica* (Mona, Jamaica: Institute of Social and Economic Research, 1973).

4. For an excellent analysis of the sociopolitical currents in Kingston in the late sixties, see Rupert Lewis, "Walter Rodney: 1968 revisited", *Social and Economic Studies* 43, no. 3 (September 1994): 7–56.

5. See Carl Stone, *Democracy and Clientelism in Jamaica* (New Brunswick, NJ, and London: Transaction Books, 1983).

6. Aside from recent collections of his speeches and newspaper articles, Stone's last book was his hurriedly produced work on the 1989 Jamaican elections. See Carl Stone, *Politics Versus Economics: The 1989 Elections in Jamaica* (Kingston, Jamaica: Heinemann [Caribbean], 1989).

7. Stone probably comes very close to Edward Said's notion of the genuine intellectual as someone engaging in political affairs but with a degree of 'critical detachment', deriving from the recognition that the individual who is bankrolled by the government or the political movement will probably be compromised in his or her ability to represent the truth. Whether or not the university can provide a genuine space for critical detachment is, of course, the moot point, but it is wor-

thy of note that Stone was never able to join organizations. In the last years of his life, he became a member of the New Beginning Movement, an organization for political renewal in Jamaica, but he soon resigned out of the fear that some members were using it for their narrow political interests. See Edward Said, *Representations of the Intellectual: The 1993 Reith Lectures* (London: Vintage, 1994).

8. I thank Maurice St Pierre and Rupert Lewis for a stimulating discussion that led to this comment.

9. The term patron-clientelism owes its popular currency in the region primarily to Stone as does the concept of the 'garrison community' referring to the highly politicized and 'tribalized' communities of urban Jamaica where party loyalty is enforced, in the final count, by the gun.

10. See, for instance, Carl Stone, "An appraisal of the co-operative process in the Jamaican sugar industry", in *Perspectives on Jamaica in the Seventies,* ed. Carl Stone and Aggrey Brown (Kingston, Jamaica: Jamaica Publishing House, 1981), 437–62.

11. The difficulty of engaging in consistent academic research in the hot-house atmosphere of Jamaica – with multiple pressures coming from politics, crime, the economic system and the extended family – can be severe. That Carl Stone was able to sustain a career of prolific research, public intervention and publishing is quite remarkable. The price he paid, however, was often in drastically reduced time for reflection and reading, which academics in less intense environments take for granted. As a consequence, the depth of theoretical reading (though not the level of insight) to be found in *Class and Race* and *Democracy and Clientelism* is seldom replicated in his other books. For a sensitive picture of the academic environment at the UWI in the seventies and eighties, see Harry Goulbourne, "The institutional contribution of the University of the West Indies to the intellectual life of the anglophone Caribbean", in *Intellectuals in the Twentieth-Century Caribbean,* Volume 1, *Spectre of the New Class: The Commonwealth Caribbean,* ed. Alistair Hennessy, Warwick University Caribbean Studies Series (London and Basingstoke: Macmillan Caribbean, 1992), 21–49.

12. See Stone, *Class and Race,* 5.

13. See M.G. Smith, *The Plural Society in the British West Indies,* University of California Press, Los Angeles, 1965.

14. Stone, *Class and Race,* 8.

15. Ibid., 11.

16. Ibid., 16.

17. See ibid., 53.

18. In this, Stone borrows self-consciously from the then highly popular work of Ted Robert Gurr, who had yet to be criticized by Rod Aya, Jack Goldstone and

others, who argue, quite effectively, that there is no evidence that frustration necessarily leads to aggression and rebellion. See Ted Robert Gurr, *Why Men Rebel* (Princeton: Princeton University Press, 1970); and Rod Aya, *Rethinking Revolutions and Collective Violence: Studies on Concept, Theory and Method* (Amsterdam: Het Spinhuis, 1990).

19. See Stone, *Class and Race,* Figures 5.1 a, b, c and d, and Figures 5.2 a and b, 56–62.

20. Ibid., 63.

21. See ibid., 69.

22. Ibid., 166.

23. It is interesting to note Stone's reasons for the failure of an earlier third force, Millard Johnson's People's Progressive Party (PPP), which only received 0.86 percent of the popular vote in the 1962 general election. Stone argued that it lacked a populist leader; it emerged a decade before the conditions for its existence had ripened; but most importantly, it appeared primarily to race without integrating a treatment of class oppression. I am also convinced, although there is as yet no evidence to support it, that it was Stone's empirical work, identifying the social basis for a radical movement that inspired other young UWI-based intellectuals to form the Workers' Liberation League (WLL – later the WPJ). Trevor Munroe and other leaders of the new organization chose, however, to err on the other side, subordinating Stone's call for racial appeals to focus on class. See ibid., 166.

24. Ibid., 173.

25. This is equally apparent in his study of the 1972 general election, *Electoral Behaviour and Public Opinion in Jamaica* (Mona, Jamaica: Institute of Social and Economic Research), in which he states – in the face of the national euphoria which followed Michael Manley's electoral triumph in 1972:

It is in this perspective that the Jamaican electoral process must be seen as functioning primarily as a device to provide mass supports for governmental institutions which service primarily middle and upper class interests.

The fundamental emphasis is stability and the arresting and dampening of class and racial antagonism. Power has decidedly not passed to the people in 1972 as a genuinely populist approach to policy formation has been rejected by the new PNP government in the interests of stability, pragmatism and continuity. (98)

26. See Stone, *Democracy and Clientelism,* 253.

27. See, for example, Michael Kaufman, *Jamaica Under Manley: Dilemmas of Socialism and Democracy* (London: Zed Books, 1985).

28. Ibid., 7.

29. See ibid., 23.

30. Ibid., 22.

31. Trinidad and Tobago and Grenada are two examples of Caribbean states that have experienced, respectively, an army mutiny and attempted coup and a successful revolutionary overthrow. See Brian Meeks, "The Imam, the return of Napoleon and the end of history", in *Radical Caribbean: From Black Power to Abu Bakr* (Mona, Jamaica: The Press, University of the West Indies, 1996).

32. Stone, *Democracy and Clientelism*, 28.

33. Ibid., 82.

34. Ibid., 82. This is an important nuance in Stone's work because it illustrates his appreciation that the clients were not defenceless in the face of overwhelming odds. Unfortunately, this dimension is never developed adequately in his work. For further comment, see Gray, "Discovering the social power".

35. He compares his notion of patron-clientelism with James Scott's theory of 'machine politics', suggesting that, while Scott's thesis is relevant, it narrowly associates machine politics with getting votes; patron-clientelism, on the other hand, goes far beyond the purely electoral arena. He also criticized Scott's assertion that machine politics emerged where racial, ethnic or charismatic appeals were weak. He proposed that instead these elements may be seen as complementary to the patronage network and thus able to function alongside it. See James Scott, "Corruption, machine politics and political change", *American Political Science Review* (December 1969); and Stone, *Democracy and Clientelism*, 93.

36. Stone, *Democracy and Clientelism*, 94.

37. Ibid., 97–98.

38. Ibid., 259.

39. See Stone's seminal *Report of the Stone Committee Appointed to Advise the Jamaican Government on the Performance, Accountability and Responsibilities of Elected Parliamentarians* (Kingston, Jamaica: Bustamante Institute of Public and International Affairs, *c.* 1992).

40. See Carl Stone, "The Jamaican party system and political culture", in *Jamaica: Preparing for the Twenty-first Century*, ed. Patsy Lewis (Kingston, Jamaica: Ian Randle Publishers, 1994), 133.

41. Ibid., 144. There seems to be a contradiction between Stone's recognition of the continued dominance of the political parties by middle class persons and his demand that they should recruit more middle class members. Stone recognizes the central role that the professional strata have played in the formation of the patron-client system and wishes to end this, but equally wishes to strengthen the technical capability of the parties by having more trained and educated persons in the middle level leadership. He is also sensitive to the fact that the middle class – certainly its more independent members – are less entangled in the basic patronage system and therefore might help to undermine the increasingly ghetto-based, 'garrison' character of the parties. This tension is also never really resolved.

42. See ibid., 143–47.

43. Carl Stone, "Assessing our democracy: 1991 JLP's Central Clarendon dinner", in *Carl Stone Speaks on People, Politics and Development*, ed. Rosemarie Stone (Kingston, Jamaica 1995), 200.

44. Ibid., 197.

45. A similar point, though more closely related to Gramscian theoretical notions of hegemony, is made in my chapter on the 1994 political situation in Jamaica. See Brian Meeks, "The political moment in Jamaica: The dimensions of hegemonic dissolution", in *Radical Caribbean: From Black Power to Abu Bakr* (Mona, Jamaica: The Press, University of the West Indies, 1966), 124–43.

46. See Carl Stone, "Values, norms and personality development in Jamaica", in *Carl Stone Speaks on People, Politics and Development*, ed. Rosemarie Stone (Kingston, Jamaica: Rosemarie Stone, 1995), 232.

47. Ibid., 233–34.

48. See David Held, *Models of Democracy* (Cambridge: Polity Press, 1987).

49. See F.A. Hayek, *The Constitution of Liberty* (London: Routledge and Kegan Paul, 1973); and Robert Nozick, *Anarchy, State and Utopia* (Oxford: Basil Blackwell, 1974).

50. See C.B. Macpherson, *Democratic Theory: Essays in Retrieval* (Oxford: Clarendon Press, 1973); Carol Pateman, *Participation and Democratic Theory* (Cambridge: Cambridge University Press, 1970); and Nicos Poulantzas, *State, Power, Socialism* (London: Verso/NLB, 1980).

51. Held, *Models,* 269.

52. Ibid., 284.

53. Ibid., 285.

54. Gordon Lewis, *Main Currents in Caribbean Thought: The Historical Evolution of Caribbean Society in its Ideological Aspects: 1492–1900* (Kingston, Jamaica: Heinemann [Caribbean], 1983), 27.

55. For a good history of contemporary Caribbean political thought up to the early eighties, see Denis Benn, *The Growth and Development of Political Ideas in the Caribbean: 1774–1983* (Mona, Jamaica: Institute of Social and Economic Research, 1987). For a provocative set of essays on various themes in twentieth century Caribbean intellectual issues, see Hennessy, *Intellectuals,* Volume 1, *Spectre of the New Class.*

56. C.L.R. James' analysis of the social and political character of the West Indian middle classes remains, after four decades, as good a point as any to begin an examination of the character of the first generation of Caribbean political leaders. See C.L.R. James, "The middle classes", in *Consequences of Class and Color: West Indian Perspectives,* ed. David Lowenthal and Lambros Comitas (New York: Doubleday, 1973).

57. See for a recent attempt to rethink Williams' role in Trinidad politics, Selwyn Cudjoe's introduction to *Eric E. Williams Speaks: Essays on Colonialism and Independence,* ed. Selwyn Cudjoe (Wellesley: Calaloux, 1993).

58. See Magnus Blomstrum and Bjorn Hettne, *Development Theory in Transition: The Dependency Debate and Beyond, Third World Responses* (London: Zed Books, 1984).

59. For an important analysis of Rodney's role in Jamaica, see Rupert Lewis, "Walter Rodney".

60. For a comment on the political aftermath of Rodney's expulsion from Jamaica, see Ralph Gonsalves, "The Rodney affair", *Caribbean Quarterly* 25, no. 3 (1979): 1–24.

61. See, for a useful discussion of Hector, the Left and Antiguan politics, Paget Henry, "C.L.R. James and the Antiguan Left", in *C.L.R. James's Caribbean,* ed. Paget Henry and Paul Buhle (London and Basingstoke: Macmillan Caribbean, 1992), 225–62.

62. The WPA's post-Grenada critique, in its attempt to rethink a programme of democratic renewal for the Caribbean Left, remains a landmark document. See Working People's Alliance, "Draft programme of the democratic republic" (Mimeo, *c.* 1986).

63. For an important, if preliminary, examination of the political debate at Mona in the seventies, see Goulbourne, "The institutional contribution".

64. See, for example, Stone's article "Fighting crime" in which he lambastes "bleeding heart" lawyers in both the JLP and PNP for being unwilling to enforce the law on hanging. This is not to say that Stone did not have a sophisticated and sensitive grasp of the complex of factors that generated criminality in Jamaica over the past three decades. See Carl Stone, *The Stone Columns: The Last Year's Work* (Kingston, Jamaica: Sangster's), 130–32.

65. Stone, *Democracy and Clientelism,* 9.

Chapter 5

1. See Carl Stone, *The Political Opinions of the Jamaican People: 1976–1981* (Kingston, Jamaica: Blackett, 1982), 6, in which his own remarkably accurate polls indicate that the PNP had conceded its lead to the JLP from March 1978.

2. I thank Rachel Manley, Michael's eldest daughter, for her profound insights into the lives of her grandparents in her memoir of early childhood, *Drumblair: Memories of a Jamaican Childhood* (Kingston, Jamaica: Ian Randle Publishers, 1996).

3. In his insightful biography, Darryl Levi recognizes this restlessness, which he thinks, in part, might explain Manley's many marriages – a total of five in all. See *Michael Manley: The Making of a Leader* (London: André Deutsch, 1989).

4. Richard Hart, the Hill brothers, Ken and Frank, and Arthur Henry were the leading lights of the Left. For an interpretation of this period, see Trevor Munroe, *The Marxist Left in Jamaica: 1940–1950* (Mona, Jamaica: Institute of Social and Economic Research, 1977).

5. See Olive Senior, *The Message is Change* (Kingston, Jamaica: Kingston Publishers, 1972), for an examination of the themes of the 1972 general election.

6. See Michael Manley, *The Politics of Change: A Jamaican Testament* (London: André Deutsch, 1974).

7. Details on the PNP's programmes are to be found in a number of sources. See, for instance, Michael Kaufman, *Jamaica Under Manley* (London: Zed Books, 1985); Evelyne Huber Stephens and John D. Stephens, *Democratic Socialism in Jamaica: The Political Movement and Social Transformation in Dependent Capitalism* (London and Basingstoke: Macmillan, 1986); and Nelson W. Keith and Novella Z. Keith, *The Social Origins of Democratic Socialism in Jamaica* (Philadelphia: Temple University Press, 1982).

8. See Kari Levitt, *Jamaica: Lessons from the Manley Years,* Maroon Pamphlets no. 1 (Morant Bay, Jamaica: Maroon Publishing House, 1984), 5

9. See "The Michael Manley/ Kari Levitt exchange", *Small Axe,* no. 1 (1997): 81–115.

10. Ibid., 82

11. See Michael Manley, *Struggle in the Periphery* (London: Writers and Readers, 1982), 107–17.

12. See Levitt, *Jamaica: Lessons from the Manley Years,* 11; and Carl Stone, *Politics Versus Economics: The 1989 Elections in Jamaica* (Kingston, Jamaica: Heinemann [Caribbean], 1989), vii.

13. For the WPJ's interpretation of socialist orientation, see Workers' Party of Jamaica, *Programme: Workers' Party of Jamaica* (Kingston, Jamaica: Workers' Party of Jamaica, 1978).

14. I stand by this assessment, based on my first-hand observation, as a journalist working with the Jamaica Broadcasting Corporation (JBC), of many scenes of carnage shortly after violent attacks in 1980. Laurie Gunst in her recent study of Jamaican posses in the United States in the eighties comes to much the same conclusion. See Laurie Gunst, *Born fi Dead: A Journey Through the Jamaican Posse Underworld* (New York: Henry Holt, 1995).

15. "The Michael Manley/ Kari Levitt exchange", 101.

16. Ibid., 107

17. See Michael Manley, *A History of West Indies Cricket* (London: André Deutsch, 1989).

18. *Daily Observer,* 17 March 1997, 3.

19. *Jamaica Observer Weekly International Edition,* 21–27 March 1997, 5.

Chapter 6

1. Since this chapter was first written in 1998, the Jamaican government has embarked on an important new phase of transport reform. It includes the re-establishment of a centralized bus system, a new school bus initiative and plans for the reintroduction of a railway system for the outlying suburbs. It is notable, however, that all this is being done in the traditional bureaucratic manner, with limited popular intervention. The verdict is still out as to whether or not it will succeed, but the sequence of events described here still stands as a stark testament to the nature of Jamaican politics and society.

2. *Daily Gleaner*, 20 September 1995. I have tried to avoid the usual (*sic*) and left Jamaican vernacular and construction in place for authenticity. Where the language becomes difficult to comprehend for the monolingual English reader, an attempt at translation will be provided.

3. See "Traffic accidents, 1961–1995" (Document from the Office of the Senior Superintendent of Police for Traffic, Keith Gardner).

4. See Government of Jamaica, *Road Safety Project: Final Report Phase 1, December 1993* (Kingston, Jamaica: Ministry of Construction, 1994), 23.

5. For a discussion of uncivil societies, see John Keane, *Reflections on Violence* (London and New York: Verso, 1996).

6. "When truth is wilder than fiction", *Daily Observer*, 23 February 1996.

7. *Daily Gleaner*, 1 November 1997.

8. "It's a jungle on the roads", *Sunday Gleaner*, 5 October 1997.

9. "A plea for decent public transportation", *Daily Observer*, 3 October 1997.

10. "Traffic congestion: Too little planning", *Sunday Observer*, 19 October 1997.

11. "Transport solution", *Sunday Gleaner*, 1 October 1995.

12. I had a long interview with the new minister of transport, Peter Phillips, in March 1998. He was certainly aware of the urgency of the problem and understood the point, underlined in this paper, that the chaos on the roads could not be understood as a primarily technical phenomenon. While his proposals for reform spoke to sensible questions, such as road expansion and increased policing (though falling short of recognizing that the privatization of buses had been a complete disaster), there was little in them to suggest a recognition that if, indeed, the problem is in part a political one, then the solution may have to be, in part, political too. See Peter Phillips, interview with author, March 1998.

13. See "Traffic offenders owe over $70m", *Daily Gleaner*, 25 September 1997.

14. See Brian Meeks, "The political moment in Jamaica: The dimensions of hegemonic dissolution", in *Radical Caribbean: From Black Power to Abu Bakr* (Kingston, Jamaica: The Press, University of the West Indies, 1996), 124–43.

15. Karl Marx, "Manifesto of the Communist Party", in *The Marx-Engels Reader*, ed. Robert Tucker (New York and London: Norton, 1978), 474.

16. I thank Kari Levitt for this appropriate term drawn from an economic lexicon.

17. Jamaica is among the most rapidly urbanizing societies in the Western Hemisphere. In 1974, only 47 percent of the country was urban. Some twenty years later, the figure stood at 64 percent. See Inter-American Development Bank, *Social Progress Report, 1997* (Washington DC: Inter-American Development Bank, 1997).

18. Raphael Swaby, "Some problems of public utility regulations in a statutory board in Jamaica: The Jamaica Omnibus case", *Social and Economic Studies* 23, no. 2 (June 1974): 224.

19. Ibid., 246.

20. See Raphael Swaby, "The rationale for state ownership of public utilities in Jamaica", *Social and Economic Studies* 30, no. 1 (March 1981): 77.

21. See Swaby, "Some problems of public utility regulations", 251.

22. Ibid., 257.

23. See Patricia Anderson, *Minibus Ride: A Journey Through the Informal Sector of Kingston's Mass Transportation System* (Mona, Jamaica: Institute of Social and Economic Research, 1987), 23.

24. See ibid., 24.

25. See ibid., 26.

26. Carl Stone discusses what he saw as a relative policy convergence between the two main parties at length in his study of the 1989 Jamaican elections, *Politics Versus Economics: The 1989 Elections in Jamaica* (Kingston, Jamaica: Heinemann [Caribbean], 1989).

27. See Anderson, *Minibus Ride*, 28–29.

28. In a study of six package holders, Anderson found that 97.4 percent of the buses were single-person owned and that 95.9 percent were driven by the proprietor. See ibid., 39.

29. Ibid., 44.

30. Ibid., 48–49. This perception was still largely intact ten years later. In a survey carried out for Metropolitan Transport Management Holdings in May 1996, 77.4 percent of the respondents were either "somewhat dissatisfied", or "very dissatisfied" with the standard of bus service. The three most cited reasons for dissatisfaction were poor scheduling, overcrowding and the rude behaviour of the drivers and conductors. See "Draft final survey of the public transportation system" (Market Research Services Ltd, Kingston, 1996), 8–11.

31. See Anderson, *Minibus Ride*, 52–53.

32. For one assessment of Manley's 'transition', see David Panton, *Jamaica's Michael Manley: The Great Transformation, 1972–1992* (Kingston, Jamaica: Kingston Publishers, 1993).

33. See "Jamaica transport sector study: Draft final report, strategic transport plan for Jamaica, Wilbur Smith and Associates", Ministry of Water and Transport, Government of Jamaica, August 1993, 2–22.

34. For the comprehensive study that suggested and lay the basis for the subsequent reforms, see ibid.

35. The origin of the term lies in the name given to those Jamaicans who illegally migrated to the United States, were jailed for various criminal activities and subsequently deported to Jamaica. For many of those able to purchase the used cars, the term is both one of endearment, because the ability to escape from the confines and rigours of the bus is a source of liberation, and one that connects the used car to the culture and life of the poor and black who continually struggle, like the deportee, for a better life. But, like the original deportees who are blamed for everything that is wrong in the society, so too are the owners of the vehicles blamed for all the problems on the road, when they are but at the tip of the iceberg.

36. The social role of the 'deportee' is best summarized by the headline of an article in the *Sunday Gleaner,* 16 November 1997: it says simply "Deportees the best thing for Jamaica since emancipation".

37. Hilbourne Watson, Introduction, "The Caribbean and the techno-paradigm shift in global capitalism", in *The Caribbean in The Global Political Economy,* ed. Hilbourne Watson (Boulder and London: Lynne Rienner; and Kingston, Jamaica: Ian Randle Publishers, 1994), 4.

    There is a defeatist view that understands globalization as a process that has trumped sovereignty, at least for small, developing states. The inevitable conclusion, then, is to join the bandwagon of free trade, liberalization and privatization, on whatever terms are offered. This is certainly not my view, nor does it appear to be that of Watson. The alternative would be to recognize that states still retain the ability to manoeuvre within the interstices of a globalized system and there may even be room for redefining and expanding sovereignty, though at the regional level. See, for a more nuanced view on the state in the era of globalization, Linda Weiss, "Globalization and the myth of the powerless state", *New Left Review,* no. 225 (September/October 1997): 3–27.

38. Watson, "The Caribbean and the techno-paradigm shift", 5.

39. See, for example, Kari Levitt, *The Origins and Consequences of Jamaica's Debt Crisis: 1970–1990* (Mona, Jamaica: Consortium Graduate School of Social Sciences, 1990); and Elsie Le Franc, ed., *Consequences of Structural Adjustment: A Review of the Jamaican Experience* (Kingston, Jamaica: Canoe Press, 1994).

40. The power of a paradigm is perhaps manifest here, as there has been much in recent Jamaican history to shake the almost religious belief in the primacy of the market. For the last three years, the government has had to either take over or bail out most of the leading banks and financial institutions at massive expense to the public and future generations. Some of the reasons for their collapse is attributable to the high interest rate policy the government has pursued to mop up liquidity and stabilize the exchange rate. But much, it is now generally felt, has been due to mismanagement and incompetence. And there is also the experience of the privatized transport system. For the financial details of the entire bail-out exercise, see Minister of Finance Omar Davies' statement, "Davies explains restructuring", *Sunday Gleaner,* 26 April 1998.

41. See Carl Stone, *Democracy and Clientelism in Jamaica* (New Brunswick, NJ, and London: Transaction Books, 1983).

42. Hence, Stone notes, that even though the system of clientelism placed the "petty bourgeois" leadership firmly in control, this was by no means absolute: "On the other hand, the mass public is not without influence: this influence operates primarily through electoral politics" (ibid., 82).

43. See Anderson, *Minibus Ride,* 91–100.

44. Ibid., 101–2.

45. Literally, "make yourself smaller" to allow other passengers to fit.

46. Norbert Elias, *The Civilizing Process: The History of Manners and State Formation and Civilization* (Oxford and Cambridge, Mass.: Blackwell, 1994), 509.

47. A somewhat contradictory approach to Elias' position is to be fund in James Scott's work. Hegemony for Scott, if it exists at all, is always imperfect, contested, to the extent that nascent rebellion by the oppressed is always immanent. The danger in such an approach is that it fails to see degrees of nascent rebelliousness by not recognizing sufficiently degrees of hegemonial dominance. Its usefulness as an analytic tool is therefore compromised. See James Scott, *Domination and the Arts of Resistance: Hidden Transcripts* (New Haven and London: Yale University Press, 1990). For my comment on this question, see chapter 1, "The Henry Rebellion".

48. "Sick of bus sound systems", *Daily Observer,* 1997.

49. Senior Superintendent of Police Keith Gardener, interview with author, April 1998.

50. It might be useful to think of a stanza in Bob Marley's 1980 hit song "Bad card", which, although from an earlier period, suggests the same sense of loudness as not-so-hidden oppositional text:

I want to disturb my neighbour
'Cause I'm feeling so right
I want to turn up my disco

turn it up to full watts tonight
See Bob Marley, "Bad card", *Uprising* (Cayman Music 422–846 211–2)).

51. *Daily Observer,* 29 December 1997.

52. Ibid.

53. *Daily Gleaner,* 2 February 1998.

54. Jamaica's average annual growth rate between 1991 and 1997 has lagged behind all countries in the hemisphere, with the exception of Cuba and Haiti. This is a damning statistic, as Cuba has had the twin tragedies of the US blockade and the collapse of the Soviet Union, while Haiti, in the wake of its long night of dictatorship, was immediately plunged into further crisis with elected President Aristide's ouster from office in this period. Jamaica experienced no overt external or internal threat, but there is a crisis of hegemony that, in part, accounts for its record. See "Latin America and the Caribbean: Total gross domestic product" (Economic Commission for Latin America and the Caribbean, 1997).

55. A government team did travel to Buenos Aires in 1993 to see the system there, and they were impressed by the fact that it was both private and efficient. The difference, though, is that there are no single owner buses in Argentina. See "Report on visit to Buenos Aires to study and observe the transportation system – 25–30 September 1993" (Ministry of Water and Transport, Kingston, 1993).

56. I would suggest that Trinidad has both a long tradition of private route taxis and the absence of a moment of hegemonic dissolution to its advantage.

57. See Pierre Bourdieu, "A reasoned utopia and economic fatalism", *New Left Review,* no. 227 (January/February 1998).

58. The argument for local control hinges on the experience of the British Electric Traction (BET). Foreign investment may be a necessity, but the acceptance of foreign control in such a sensitive social and political sphere must, on the basis of history, be questioned.

59. I was disappointed with Minister Phillips' response to my mooting the possibility of community involvement in a reorganized transport system. He did not disagree in principle, but said that what was really required was for the elected representative to do his job. It would seem that an active and mobilized citizenry, monitoring and defending the public transport system, would immeasurably help the elected official in doing his job. See Phillips interview, 1998.

60. See Ellen Meiksins-Wood, *Democracy Against Capitalism: Renewing Historical Materialism* (Cambridge and New York: Cambridge University Press, 1996).

61. Don Robotham, *Vision and Voluntarism: Reviving Voluntarism in Jamaica,* Grace Kennedy Foundation Lecture (Kingston, Jamaica: Grace Kennedy, 1998).

62. Ibid., 5.

63. Ibid., 23.

64. Ibid., 37.

65. Ibid., 58.

66. See Scott, *Domination and the Arts of Resistance*, 128–34.

67. Ken Carter, *Why Workers Won't Work: The Worker in a Developing Economy: A Case Study of Jamaica* (London and Basingstoke: Macmillan Caribbean, 1997), 23. If the essence is to be captured, the woman is saying that she repays the hypocrisy and superiority of her managers by depositing spittle in their coffee each morning.

68. Ibid., 131–33.

Conclusion

1. Negative images of West Indians and the West Indies permeate the oeuvre of V.S. Naipaul. This quotation from *The Middle Passage* (Harmondsworth: Penguin Books, 1962) is, perhaps, as representative as any: "How can the history of West Indian futility be written? . . . History is built around achievement and creation, and nothing was created in the West Indies" (29). Yet, as both Brathwaite and Rohlehr suggest separately, Naipaul, precisely in his irony and contempt, is intimately engaged with the West Indian condition and, thus, very much West Indian. See Kamau Brathwaite, *Roots* (Ann Arbor: University of Michigan Press, 1993), 123; and Gordon Rohlehr, "The space between negations", *The Shape of that Hurt and Other Essays* (Port of Spain, Trinidad: Longman, 1992), 97–128.

2. This is an inversion of a comment made by Gordon Lewis. See Gordon K. Lewis, *Main Currents in Caribbean Thought: The Historical Evolution of Caribbean Society in its Ideological Aspects 1492–1900* (Kingston, Jamaica: Heinemann [Caribbean], 1983), 15.

3. See Elliott Abrams, "The Shiprider solution: Policing the Caribbean", *National Interest* (Spring 1996): 86–92. And, for two differing responses to Abrams, Patsy Lewis, "The Caribbean and the restructuring of the United Nations: Alternatives to Abrams' 'Shiprider solution' ", *Journal of Commonwealth and Comparative Politics* 34, no. 3 (November 1996): 235–47; and Holgar Henke, "The Shiprider solution and post-Cold War imperialism: Beyond ontologies of state/sovereignty in the Caribbean" (Mimeo, 1996).

4. See C.L.R. James, *The Black Jacobins: Toussaint L'Ouverture and the San Domingo Revolution* (New York: Vintage Books, 1989).

5. Jimmy Cliff, "The harder they come", *Jimmy Cliff: Reggae Greats* (Island 162–539 794–2)).

6. See George Beckford, Norman Girvan, Louis Lindsay, and Michael Witter, *Pathways to Progress: The People's Plan for Socialist Transformation, Jamaica, 1977–1978* (Morant Bay, Jamaica: Maroon Publishing House, 1985).

7. See Bernard Coard, *Grenada: Village and Workers, Women, Farmers and Youth Assemblies During the Grenada Revolution: Their Genesis and Significance*, Caribbean Labour Solidarity and the New Jewel Movement (London: Karia Press, 1989).

8. See David Close, *Nicaragua: Politics, Economics and Society* (London and New York: Pinter, 1988); and Brian Meeks, *Caribbean Revolutions and Revolutionary Theory: An Assessment of Cuba, Nicaragua and Grenada*, Warwick University Caribbean Studies Series (London and Basingstoke: Macmillan, 1993).

9. Francis Fukuyama, *The End of History and the Last Man* (New York: Avon Books, 1992).

10. See Jorge Dominguez, "The Caribbean question: Why has liberal democracy (surprisingly) flourished?", in *Democracy in the Caribbean: Political Economic and Social Perspectives*, ed. Jorge Dominguez, Robert A. Pastor and R. Delisle Worrell (Baltimore: Johns Hopkins University Press, 1993), 1–25.

11. See Selwyn Ryan, *The Muslimeen Grab for Power: Race, Religion and Revolution in Trinidad and Tobago* (Port of Spain: Inprint, 1991); and Brian Meeks, "The Imam, the return of Napoleon and the end of history", in *Radical Caribbean: From Black Power to Abu Bakr* (Kingston, Jamaica: The Press, University of the West Indies, 1996), 83–100.

12. See Roger Burbach, "Roots of the postmodern rebellion in Chiapas", *New Left Review*, no. 205 (May/June 1994).

13. See, for a critical analysis of the failure of the post-Duvalier neoliberal policies in Haiti that laid the basis for the growth of a popular movement and for an analysis of Aristide's rise, fall and return, Alex Dupuy, *Haiti in the New World Order: The Limits of the Democratic Revolution* (Boulder: Westview Press, 1997).

14. See Cynthia McClintock, "Peru's Sendero Luminoso rebellion: origins and trajectory", in *Power and Popular Protest: Latin American Social Movements*, ed. Susan Eckstein (Berkeley, Los Angeles and London: University of California Press, 1989), 61–101.

15. I wish to disagree, at least in emphasis, with Perry Mars' far more extensive concessions as to the ability of capitalism to resolve its own internal crises, as expressed in his recent study of the Caribbean Left. While many of his conclusions as to immediate strategy are echoed here, the underlying assumption is that the role of a radical Left is inevitably circumscribed by an overarching, confident and perhaps permanent system of global capitalism. This insufficiently appreciates the extent of the crisis in contemporary global capitalism and the political basis, therefore, for a radical resurgence. See Perry Mars, *Ideology and Change: The Transformation of the Caribbean Left* (Kingston, Jamaica: The Press, University of the West Indies; Detroit: Wayne State University Press, 1998), 165–75.

16. See Thomas S. Kuhn, *The Structure of Scientific Revolutions* (Chicago: University of Chicago Press, 1970).

17. The average daily listenership to the main talk radio programmes in Jamaica increased from some 471,000 persons in 1989 to 844,000 in 1996 in a total potential listenership in 1996 of some 1.7 million persons. See Trevor Munroe, *Renewing Democracy into the Millennium* (Kingston, Jamaica: The Press, University of the West Indies, 1999), 128.

18. See Patsy Lewis, "Not seizing the time: The consultative process in the OECS political union initiative", *Pensamiento Propio,* no. 8 (October/December 1998): 55–74.

19. See, for a detailed discussion, Livingstone Smith, "A comparison between the constitutional reform process of the 1940s and the 1990s in Jamaica" (Draft PhD diss., University of the West Indies, Mona, 1999).

20. See Kathy McAfee, *Storm Signals: Structural Adjustment and Development Alternatives in the Caribbean* (London and Boston: Zed/Oxfam America, 1991), 198–223.

21. For a vivid description of the UAWU's critical and historic breakthrough into the sugar sector, see Carl Feuer, *The Struggle for Workers' Rights at Hampden Sugar Estate* (Kingston, Jamaica: Social Action Centre, 1989).

22. This new axis is increasingly a matter of concern in Washington. In August 1999, for instance, the new US ambassador to the Eastern Caribbean accused Caribbean countries of "pandering" to Fidel Castro: "we feel that if the nations of the Caribbean would get together, and rather than cozy-up to Cuba, that they would tell the Castro regime that we mean business". See "US Envoy accuses CARICOM of pandering to Cuba" (*Weekend Observer,* 20 August 1999).

23. Among the most disturbing of recent developments in this contradictory conjuncture, is the increasing use of bleaching cream primarily among young women. In July 1999, the Jamaican government cracked down on the importation of bleaching cream due to the increase in the number of skin-related disorders reported at doctors' offices. See *Weekend Observer,* 16 July 1999. The reason for the increased demand is the result of an upsurge in the desire of darker skinned women to be fairer in order to attract boyfriends and ultimately attain a better life. See also "In Jamaica, shades of an identity crisis: Ignoring health risk, blacks increase use of skin lighteners", *Washington Post,* 5 August 1999.

24. This is my not uncontested argument as developed in *Caribbean Revolutions and Revolutionary Theory.*

25. C.L.R. James, *Notes on Dialectics: Hegel, Marx, Lenin* (Westport: Lawrence Hill, 1980), 16.

26. See, for example, Brian Meeks, "Social formation and People's Revolution: A Grenadian study" (PhD diss., University of the West Indies, Mona, 1988).

27. See Ann Hickling Hudson, "Towards communication praxis: reflections on the pedagogy of Paulo Freire and educational change in Grenada", *Journal of Education* 170, no. 2 (1988): 9–38.
28. See Meeks, *Caribbean Revolutions and Revolutionary Theory,* 165–79.
29. See ibid., 84–121.
30. For a discussion of what she describes as the conflict between the bureaucratic and emancipatory impulses within the Cuban Revolution, see Carolee Bengelsdorf, *The Problem of Democracy in Cuba: Between Vision and Reality* (New York and Oxford: Oxford University Press, 1994).
31. See Meeks, *Caribbean Revolutions and Revolutionary Theory,* 48–77.
32. Though it is true that the severe financial constraints of the post-Soviet 'special period' have seriously undermined the effectiveness of the vaunted Cuban health system. See "Critical case", *Newsweek,* 14 September 1998, 10–12.
33. See Close, *Nicaragua,* 139–43.
34. Growth rates in the recent period can neatly be divided between the smaller and the larger Caribbean territories, with both groups performing better in the pre-1980 phase and the smaller territories almost always performing better than the larger. In the 1980–93 period, the Dominican Republic, Jamaica and Trinidad all had negative rates of growth; St Kitts and Nevis and St Lucia, to use one example each from the Leewards and Windwards, had growth rates of 5.4 percent and 4.4 percent. See Norman Girvan, *Societies at Risk? The Caribbean and Global Change,* UNESCO Discussion Paper Series no. 17 (UNESCO, 1997), 33.
35. See Andres Serbin, *Sunset Over the Islands: The Caribbean in an Age of Global and Regional Challenges,* Warwick University Caribbean Studies Series (London and Basingstoke: Macmillan, 1998).
36. Girvan, *Societies at Risk,* 20.
37. See Brian Meeks, *Radical Caribbean.*
38. See, for instance, Ralph Miliband and Leo Panitch, eds, *Communist Regimes: The Aftermath,* Socialist Register 1991 (London: The Merlin Press, 1991); Robin Blackburn, ed., *After the Fall: The Failure of Communism* (London and New York: Verso, 1991); Alex Callinicos, *The Revenge of History: Marxism and the Eastern European Revolutions* (Cambridge: Polity Press, 1991); and David Miliband, ed., *Reinventing the Left* (Cambridge: Polity Press, 1994).
39. See Jorge Castaneda, *Utopia Unarmed: The Latin American Left after the Cold War* (New York: Alfred A. Knopf, 1993).
40. See ibid., especially 358–90.
41. Castaneda discusses the typical cyclic routine of populist governments in Latin America in chapter 13, "A Latin American dilemma". See ibid., 391–426.
42. See, for agreement with this, Mars, *Ideology and Change,* 170.
43. See Castaneda, *Utopia Unarmed,* 454.

44. See ibid., 437.
45. See Jay R. Mandle, "The crisis in and future of the Windward Islands banana industry" (Draft paper, Colgate University, August 1999).
46. See chapter 3, "The Harder Dragon".
47. See Mars, *Ideology and Change,* 171.
48. Though there are important signs that this is changing. See for instance, C.Y. Thomas, "On reconstructing a political economy of the Caribbean", and Maribel Aponte Garcia, "Caribbean and Latin American development theory and policy: An agenda for deconstruction-reconstruction", both papers presented at the conference New Currents in Caribbean Thought: Looking Towards the Twenty First Century, Michigan State University, 4–5 April 1997.
49. Perhaps the most important, for its pioneering character, is Alec Nove's *The Economics of Feasible Socialism* (London: Unwin Hyman, 1983); but other notable examples include Ralph Miliband, *Socialism for a Sceptical Age* (London and New York: Verso, 1994); Julian LeGrand and Saul Estrin, eds, *Market Socialism* (Oxford and New York: Oxford University Press, 1989); and John Roemer, *A Future for Socialism* (London, New York: Verso, 1994).
50. See, for an admirable attempt, Ellen Meiksins-Wood, *Democracy Against Capitalism: Renewing Historical Materialism* (Cambridge: Cambridge University Press, 1996).
51. The importance of this last point cannot be underestimated. This is the model pioneered by the Miami Cubans for different goals. It recognizes the relative flexibility and porosity of the US political system, as it does the potential power of millions of Caribbean migrants on the Eastern Seaboard. See, for a similar perspective, Anthony Payne, "Re-thinking US-Caribbean relations: Towards a new mode of trans-territorial governance in an era of globalization" (Paper presented at the seminar Coming in From the Cold: Small States Responses to Globalization, University of the West Indies, Mona, January 1999).
52. Serbin's discussion of the growing basis for a greater pan-Caribbean unity forged both from above, at the epistemic and at the popular levels, is persuasive and central to this proposal. See Serbin, *Sunset Over the Islands,* 86–98.
53. See Ralph Gonsalves, "Our Caribbean civilization: retrospect and prospect", *Journal of Eastern Caribbean Studies* 23, no. 1 (March 1998): 51–74.
54. See, for a similar argument, Samir Amin, *Capitalism in the Age of Globalization: The Management of Contemporary Society* (London and New York: Zed Books, 1997). The first serious volley in a new phase of resistance to globalization occurred in December 1999, at the meeting of the World Trade Organization (WTO) in Seattle. Some 40,000 activists, ranging from NGOs to religious organizations and trade unions, gathered, through an unprecedented mobilization on the World Wide Web, to protest the policy directions of the WTO. Issues

ranged across the entire gamut, from the loss of jobs in developed countries to cheaper labour sources in the South, the environmental degradation purportedly encouraged by neoliberal policies and the apparent undermining of sovereignty implied in binding and often punitive WTO rules. The activists on the street found ready support inside the conference from representatives of poor and developing countries, who felt themselves excluded from the hierarchical inner decision making bodies of the organization, with the resultant policies invariably in favour of the developed world. Despite the success of bringing the meeting to an abrupt and inconclusive end, the newly emerging global alliance is still fraught with contradictions. Thus, the demand from US unions for the retention of capital and jobs in the United States seems to run counter to the immediate call from many poor countries for a greater outflow of investment in order to boost local employment. Yet, even in this instance, there may be an underlying commonality. If the problem is not seen as one between countries, but is approached from the perspective of the interest of workers, then, neither those in the North nor the South desire exploitation in Dickensian sweatshops. From such a creative approach, there may yet be the basis for a more enduring long term alliance in the direction of envisioning an alternative, popular mode of globalization. See Kenneth Klee, "The siege of Seattle", *Newsweek*, 13 December 1999, 14–19.

55. Dupuy argues similarly on the need to deepen democracy and participation in order to counter the present structural tendency to transfer real power away from the citizenry to international institutions, even as 'democratization' is taking root. See Dupuy, chapter 1, "Meanings of the new world order", in *Haïti in the New World Order*, 1–20. And, for an alternative, if equally critical take on the meaning of the new world order for the Caribbean, see Thomas Klak, *Globalization and New-Liberalism: The Caribbean Context* (Lanham: Rowman and Littlefield, 1988).

56. Edward Kamau Brathwaite, "Negus", in *Third World Poems* (Harlow: Longman, 1983), 42–43.

Bibliography

Books and Articles

Abrams, Elliott. 1996. "The shiprider solution: Policing the Caribbean". *The National Interest* (Spring): 86–92.

Ahmad, Aijaz. 1995. "Jameson's rhetoric of otherness and the 'national allegory' ". In *The Post Colonial Studies Reader*, ed. Bill Ashcroft, Gareth Griffiths and Helen Tiffin, 77–82. London and New York: Routledge.

Amin, Samir. 1997. *Capitalism in the Age of Globalization: The Management of Contemporary Society*, Zed Books, London and New York, 1997.

Anderson, Patricia. 1987. *Minibus Ride: A Journey Through the Informal Sector of Kingston's Mass Transportation System*. Kingston, Jamaica: Institute of Social and Economic Research.

Anderson, Patricia, and Michael Witter. 1994. "Crisis, adjustment and social change: A case study of Jamaica". In *Consequences of Structural Adjustment: A Review of the Jamaican Experience*, ed. Elsie Le Franc, 1–55. Kingston, Jamaica: Canoe Press.

Aponte Garcia, Maribel. 1997. "Caribbean and Latin American development theory and policy: An agenda for deconstruction-reconstruction". Paper presented at the conference New Currents in Caribbean thought: Looking Towards the Twenty-first Century, Michigan State University, 4–5 April.

Aya, Rod. 1990. *Rethinking Revolutions and Collective Violence: Studies on Concept, Theory and Method*. Amsterdam: Het Spinhuis.

Bakan, Abigail. 1990. *Ideology and Class Conflict in Jamaica: The Politics of Rebellion*. Montreal and London: McGill-Queen's University Press.

Bakhtin, M. 1981. *The Dialogic Imagination*. Austin: University of Texas Press.

Barthes, Roland. 1972. *Mythologies*. London: Jonathan Cape.

Beckford, George, Norman Girvan, Louis Lindsay, and Michael Witter. 1985. *Pathways to Progress: The People's Production Plan for Socialist Transformation, Jamaica, 1977–1978*. Morant Bay, Jamaica: Maroon Publishing House.

Beckford, George, and Michael Witter. 1980. *Small Garden, Bitter Weed: Struggle and Change in Jamaica.* London: Zed Books; Morant Bay, Jamaica: Maroon Publishing House.

Bender, Frederic L., ed. 1998. *Karl Marx: The Communist Manifesto.* New York, London: Norton.

Bengelsdorf, Carolee. 1994. *The Problem of Democracy in Cuba: Between Vision and Reality.* New York and Oxford: Oxford University Press.

Benitez-Rojo, Antonio. 1996. *The Repeating Island: The Caribbean and the Postmodern Perspective.* Durham and London: Duke University Press.

Benn, Denis. 1987. *The Growth and Development of Political Ideas in the Caribbean: 1774–1983.* Mona, Jamaica: Institute of Social and Economic Research.

Berger, Mark. 1999. "Up from neo-liberalism: Free market mythologies and the coming crisis of global capitalism". *Third World Quarterly* 20, no. 2: 453–63.

Beverley, John. 1999. *Subalternity and Representation: Arguments in Cultural Theory.* Durham and London: Duke University Press.

Blackburn, Robin, ed. 1991. *After the Fall: The Failure of Communism.* London and New York: Verso.

Blomstrum, Magnus, and Bjorn Hettne. 1984. *Development Theory in Transition: The Dependency Debate and Beyond, Third World Perspectives.* London: Zed Books.

Bogues, Anthony. 1998. "Singing songs of freedom: Freedom and the black tradition in the Americas". Paper presented in a colloquium at the Afro-American Studies Program, 14 July, Brown University.

Bourdieu, Pierre. 1998. "A reasoned utopia and economic fatalism". *New Left Review,* no. 227 (January/February): 125–30.

Boyd, Derick. 1988. *Economic Management, Income Distribution and Poverty in Jamaica.* New York: Praeger.

Brathwaite, Edward Kamau. 1983. "Negus". *Third World Poems.* Harlow: Longman.

Brathwaite, Kamau. 1993. *Roots.* Ann Arbor: University of Michigan Press.

Burbach, Roger. 1994. "Roots of the postmodern rebellion in Chiapas". *New Left Review,* no. 205 (May/June).

Burton, Richard. 1997. *Afro-Creole: Power, Opposition and Play in the Caribbean.* Ithaca and London: Cornell University Press.

Callinicos, Alex. 1991. *The Revenge of History: Marxism and the Eastern European Revolutions.* Cambridge: Polity Press.

Campbell, Horace. 1987. *Rasta and Resistance: From Marcus Garvey to Walter Rodney.* Trenton: Africa World Press.

Carew, Jan. 1994. *Ghosts in Our Blood: With Malcolm X in Africa, England and the Caribbean.* Chicago: Lawrence Hill Books.

Carter, Ken. 1997. *Why Workers Won't Work: The Worker in a Developing Economy: A Case Study of Jamaica.* London and Basingstoke: Macmillan Caribbean.

Castaneda, Jorge. 1993. *Utopia Unarmed: The Latin American Left After the Cold War.* New York: Alfred A. Knopf.

Chevannes, Barry. 1976. "The repairer of the breach: Reverend Claudius Henry and Jamaican society". In *Ethnicity in the Americas,* ed. Frances Henry, 263–89. The Hague: Mouton Publishers.

Chevannes, Barry. 1995. *Rastafari, Roots and Ideology.* Syracuse: Syracuse University Press.

Christian, Barbara. 1995 "The Race for Theory". In *The Post Colonial Studies Reader,* ed. Bill Ashcroft, Gareth Griffiths and Helen Tiffin, 457–60. London and New York: Routledge.

Close, David. 1988. *Nicaragua: Politics, Economics and Society.* London and New York: Pinter.

Coard, Bernard. 1989. *Grenada: Village and Workers, Women, Farmers and Youth Assemblies During the Grenada Revolution: Their Genesis and Significance.* Caribbean Labour Solidarity and the New Jewel Movement. London: Karia Press.

Cohen, Albert K. 1997. "A general theory of sub-cultures". In *The Subcultures Reader,* ed. Ken Gelder and Sarah Thornton, 44–54. London and New York: Routledge.

Colburn, Forrest. 1994. *The Vogue of Revolution in Poor Countries.* Princeton: Princeton University Press.

Cooper, Carolyn, ed. 1998. Special issue on Reggae Studies. *Social and Economic Studies* 47, no. 1 (March).

Cooper, Carolyn, and Cecil Gutzmore. 1998. "Border clash: The politics of location in Jamaican popular culture". Paper presented at the conference African Diaspora Studies on the Eve of the Twenty-first Century, University of California, Berkeley, April.

Cooper, Fred. 1994. "Conflict and connecting: Rethinking African colonial history". *American Historical Review,* no. 99.

Cooper, Fred. 1996. *Decolonization and African Society: The Labor Question in French and British Africa.* Cambridge and New York: Cambridge University Press.

Craig, Susan. 1982. "Background to the 1970 Confrontation in Trinidad and Tobago". In *Contemporary Caribbean: A Sociological Reader,* ed. Susan Craig, 385–423 (Port of Spain, Trinidad: Susan Craig).

Cudjoe, Selwyn. 1993. Introduction. In *Eric E. Williams Speaks: Essays on Colonialism and Independence,* ed. Selwyn Cudjoe. Wellesley: Calaloux.

Dawes, Neville. 1978. *Interim.* Kingston, Jamaica: Institute of Jamaica.

DeBoissiere, Ralph. 1981. *Crown Jewel.* London: Picador.

Department of Government. 1998. *Welcome to the Department of Government.* Mona, Jamaica: University of the West Indies.

Director of Elections. 1998. *Report of the Director of Elections: General Elections 1997.* Kingston, Jamaica: Electoral Office of Jamaica.

Dominguez, Jorge. 1993. "The Caribbean question: Why has liberal democracy (surprisingly) flourished?" In *Democracy in the Caribbean: Political Economic and Social Perspectives,* ed. Jorge Dominguez, Robert A. Pastor, and R. Delisle Worrell, 1–25. Baltimore: Johns Hopkins University Press.

Dupuy, Alex. 1997. *Haiti in the New World Order: The Limits of the Democratic Revolution.* Boulder: Westview Press.

Economic Commission for Latin America and the Caribbean. 1997. "Latin America and the Caribbean: Total Gross Domestic Product". Typescript.

Edie, Carlene, J. 1991. *Democracy by Default: Dependency and Clientelism in Jamaica.* Boulder and London: Lynne Rienner; Kingston, Jamaica: Ian Randle Publishers.

Elias, Norbert. 1994. *The Civilizing Process: The History of Manners and State Formation and Civilization.* Oxford and Cambridge, Mass.: Blackwell.

Elliott, Michael. 1998. "Coming apart". *Newsweek,* 12 October.

Elster, John. 1985. *Making Sense of Marx.* Cambridge: Cambridge University Press.

Engels, Friederich. 1933. *Germany: Revolution and Counter-revolution.* Moscow: International Publishers.

Essien Udom, E.U. 1964. "The nationalist movements of Harlem". In *Harlem: A Community in Transition,* ed. John Henrik Clarke. New York: Citadel Press.

Farhi, Farideh. 1990. *States and Urban based Revolutions: Iran and Nicaragua.* Urbana and Chicago: University of Illinois Press.

Feuer, Carl. 1989. *The Struggle for Workers' Rights at Hampden Sugar Estate.* Kingston, Jamaica: Social Action Centre.

Foran, John, and Jeff Goodwin. 1993. "Revolutionary outcomes in Iran and Nicaragua: Coalition, fragmentation, war and the limits of social transformation". *Theory and Society* 22: 209–47.

Frankel, Boris. 1997. "Confronting neoliberal regimes: The post-Marxist embrace of populism and realpolitik". *New Left Review,* no. 226 (November/December): 57–92.

Fukuyama, Francis. 1992. *The End of History and the Last Man*. New York: Avon Books.

Gilroy, Paul. 1993. *The Black Atlantic: Modernity and Double Consciousness*. Cambridge, Mass.: Harvard University Press.

Girvan, Norman. 1997. *Societies at Risk? The Caribbean and Global Change*. UNESCO Discussion Paper Series no. 17 (UNESCO).

Girvan, Norman. 1998. " 'Not for sale': Three episodes in the life of democratic socialism". Paper presented for the symposium Jamaica in the Seventies, University of the West Indies, Mona, 24–26 August.

Girvan, Norman. 1998. "Social consensus, democratic socialism and the market economy". Paper delivered at the PNP Sixtieth Anniversary Symposium, 17 September, Kingston, Jamaica.

Girvan, Norman. 1999. "Reinterpreting the Caribbean". Typescript, University of the West Indies, Mona.

Gonsalves, Ralph. 1979. "The Rodney affair". *Caribbean Quarterly* 25, no. 3: 1–24.

Gonsalves, Ralph. 1998. "Our Caribbean civilization: Retrospect and prospect". *Journal of Eastern Caribbean Studies* 23, no. 1 (March): 51–74.

Goodwin, Jeff. 1992. "A theory of persistent insurgency: El Salvador, Guatemala and Peru in comparative perspective". Paper presented at the seventeenth Latin American Studies Association conference, September.

Goodwin, Jeff. Forthcoming. *State and Revolution in the Third World: A Comparative Analysis*. Berkeley and Los Angeles: University of California Press.

Goulbourne, Harry. 1992. "The institutional contribution of the University of the West Indies to the intellectual life of the anglophone Caribbean". In *Intellectuals in the Twentieth-Century Caribbean*. Volume 1, *Spectre of the New Class: The Commonwealth Caribbean,* ed. Alistair Hennessy, 21–49. Warwick University Caribbean Studies. London and Basingstoke: Macmillan Caribbean.

Government of Jamaica. 1993. "Jamaica transport sector study draft final report: Strategic transport plan for Jamaica". Wilbur Smith and Associates/Ministry of Water and Transport.

Government of Jamaica. 1993. "Report on visit to Buenos Aires to study and observe the transportation system, September 25–30, 1993". Ministry of Water and Transport, Kingston.

Government of Jamaica. 1994. *Road Safety Project, Final Report Phase 1, December 1993*. Kingston, Jamaica: Ministry of Construction.

Gramsci, Antonio. 1986. *Selections from Prison Notebooks*. London: Lawrence and Wishart.

Gray, John. 1998. *False Dawn: The Delusions of Global Capitalism*. New York: The New Press.

Gray, Judy, and Iain Densten. 1998. "Integrating quantitative and qualitative analysis using latent and manifest variables". *Quality and Quantity* 32, no. 4: 419–31.

Gray, Obika. 1991. *Radicalism and Social Change in Jamaica, 1960–1972*. Knoxville: University of Tennessee Press.

Gray, Obika. 1994. "Discovering the social power of the poor". *Social and Economic Studies* 43, no. 3 (September): 169–89.

Gray, Obika. 1999. "Global culture and the politics of moral deregulation in Jamaica". Paper presented to the Caribbean Studies Association Conference, Panama City, May.

Green, Cecilia. 1997. "Caribbean dependency theory revisited: A historical-materialist feminist revision". Paper presented at the conference New Currents in Caribbean Thought: Looking Towards the Twenty-first Century, Michigan State University, 4–5 April.

Gunst, Laurie. 1995. *Born fi Dead: A Journey Through the Jamaican Posse Underworld*. New York: Henry Holt.

Gurr, Ted Robert. 1970. *Why Men Rebel*. Princeton: Princeton University Press.

Hall, Stuart. 1988. "The toad in the garden: Thatcherism among the theorists". In *Marxism and the Interpretation of Culture*, ed. Cary Nelson and Lawrence Grossberg, 35–57. Urbana and Chicago: University of Illinois Press.

Hall, Stuart. 1993. "Encoding, decoding". In *The Cultural Studies Reader*, ed. Simon During, 90–103. London and New York: Routledge.

Harney, Stefano. 1996. *Nationalism and Identity: Culture and the Imagination in a Caribbean Diaspora*. Kingston, Jamaica: The Press, University of the West Indies; London: Zed Books.

Harris, Wilson. 1999. "History, fable and myth in the Caribbean and the Guianas". In *Selected Essays of Wilson Harris: The Unfinished Genesis of the Imagination*, ed. Andrew Bundy, 152–66. London and New York: Routledge.

Hawthorn, Geoffrey, Gayatri Spivak, Ron Aronson, and John Dunn. 1990. "The post-modern condition: The end of politics?" In *The Postcolonial Condition: Interviews, Strategies, Dialogues*, ed. G.C. Spivak, 17–34. London: Routledge.

Hayek, F.A. 1973. *The Constitution of Liberty*. London: Routledge and Kegan Paul.

Hebdige, Dick. 1997. "From culture to hegemony". In *The Cultural Studies Reader*, ed. Simon During, 357–67. London and New York: Routledge.

Hebdige, Dick. 1997. "Subculture: The meaning of style". In *The Subcultures Reader*, ed. Ken Gelder and Sarah Thornton, 130–42. London and New York: Routledge.

Held, David. 1987. *Models of Democracy*. Cambridge: Polity Press.

Henke, Holgar. 1996. "The Shiprider solution and post Cold War imperialism: Beyond ontologies of state/sovereignty in the Caribbean". Mimeo.

Hennessy, Alistair, ed. 1992. *Intellectuals in the Twentieth Century Caribbean*. Volume One, *Spectre of the New Class: The Commonwealth Caribbean*. Warwick University Caribbean Studies Series. London and Basingstoke: Macmillan.

Henry, Paget. 1992. "C.L.R. James and the Antiguan Left". In *C.L.R. James's Caribbean*, ed. Paget Henry and Paul Buhle, 225–62. London and Basingstoke: Macmillan Caribbean.

Hickling-Hudson, Ann. 1988. "Towards communication praxis: Reflections on the pedagogy of Paulo Freire and educational change in Grenada". *Journal of Education* 170, no. 2: 9–38.

Hintzen, Percy. 1989. *The Costs of Regime Survival: Racial Mobilization, Elite Domination and Control of the State in Guyana and Trinidad*. Cambridge: Cambridge University Press.

Hobsbawm, Eric. 1959. *Primitive Rebels: Studies in Archaic Forms of Social Movement in the Nineteenth and Twentieth Centuries*. New York: Praeger.

Huntington, Samuel. 1991. *The Third Wave: Democratization in the Late Twentieth Century*. Norman and London: University of Oklahoma Press.

Hutton, Clinton. 1998. "Notions of freedom in popular Jamaican music". Paper presented at the Caribbean Studies Association Conference, Antigua, May.

Hutton, Clinton. 1998. "GT 23M, Popular Jamaican Music 1962–1982: Roots lyrics as socio-political and philosophical text". Course outline, Department of Government, University of the West Indies, Mona.

Inter-American Development Bank. 1997. *Social Progress Report*. Washington, DC: Inter-American Development Bank.

Jackson, Robert H. 1990. *Quasi States: Sovereignty, International Relations and the Third World*. Cambridge: Cambridge University Press.

James, C.L.R. 1973. "The middle classes". In *Consequences of Class and Color: West Indian Perspectives*, ed. David Lowenthal and Lambros Comitas. New York: Doubleday.

James, C.L.R. 1980. *Notes on Dialectics: Hegel, Marx, Lenin*. Westport: Lawrence Hill.

James, C.L.R. 1984. *Beyond a Boundary*. New York: Pantheon Books.

James, C.L.R. 1989. *The Black Jacobins: Toussaint L'Ouverture and the San Domingo Revolution*. New York: Vintage Books.

James, Winston. 1998. *Holding Aloft the Banner of Ethiopia: Caribbean Radicalism in Early Twentieth Century America*. London and New York: Verso.

Jameson, Frederick. 1986. "Third World literature in the era of multinational capitalism". *Social Text* 15 (Fall).

Jarausch, Konrad, and Kenneth Hardy. 1991. *Quantitative Methods for Historians: A Guide to Research, Data and Statistics.* Chapel Hill and London: University of North Carolina Press.

Kaufman, Michael. 1985. *Jamaica under Manley: Dilemmas of Socialism and Democracy.* London: Zed Books.

Kaye, Harvey. 1988. Introduction. *The Face of the Crowd: Studies in Revolution, Ideology and Popular Protest: Selected Essays of George Rudé,* ed. Harvey Kaye. Atlantic Highlands, NJ: Humanities Press International.

Keane, John. 1996. *Reflections on Violence.* London and New York: Verso.

Keith, Nelson W., and Novella Z. Keith. 1982. *The Social Origins of Democratic Socialism in Jamaica.* Philadelphia: Temple University Press.

Klak, Thomas. 1988. *Globalization and Neo-Liberalism: The Caribbean Context.* Lanham, MD: Rowman and Littlefield.

Klee, Kenneth. 1999. "The siege of Seattle". *Newsweek,* 13 December.

Kuhn, Thomas S. 1970. *The Structure of Scientific Revolutions.* Chicago: University of Chicago Press.

Lacey, Terry. 1977. *Violence and Politics in Jamaica: 1960–1970.* Manchester: Manchester University Press.

LeFranc, Elsie, ed. 1994. *Consequences of Structural Adjustment: A Review of the Jamaican Experience.* Kingston, Jamaica: Canoe Press.

LeGrand, Julian, and Saul Estrin, eds. 1989. *Market Socialism.* Oxford and New York: Oxford University Press.

Levi, Darryl. 1989. *Michael Manley: The Making of a Leader.* London: André Deutsch.

Levitt, Kari. 1984. *Jamaica: Lessons from the Manley Years.* Maroon Pamphlets no. 1. Morant Bay, Jamaica: Maroon Publishing House.

Levitt, Kari. 1990. *The Origins and Consequences of Jamaica's Debt Crisis: 1970–1990.* Mona, Jamaica: Consortium Graduate School of the Social Sciences.

Levitt, Kari. 1998. "Lessons of the seventies for the nineties in international context". Paper presented at the symposium Jamaica in the Seventies, University of the West Indies, Mona, 24–26 August.

Levitt, Kari, and Michael Manley. 1997."The Michael Manley/Kari Levitt exchange". *Small Axe,* no. 1: 81–115.

Levitt, Kari, and Michael Witter, eds. 1997. *The Critical Tradition of Caribbean Political Economy: The Legacy of George Beckford.* Kingston, Jamaica: Ian Randle Publishers.

Lewis, Gordon, K. 1968. *The Growth of the Modern West Indies*. London: McGibbon and Kee.

Lewis, Gordon, K. 1983. *Main Currents in Caribbean Thought: The Historical Evolution of Caribbean Society in its Ideological Aspects, 1492–1900*. Kingston, Jamaica: Heinemann (Caribbean).

Lewis, Linden. 1998. "Masculinity and the dance of the dragon: reading Lovelace discursively". *Feminist Review*, no. 59 (June): 164–85.

Lewis, Patsy. 1996. "The Caribbean and the restructuring of the United Nations: Alternatives to Abrams' Shiprider solution". *Journal of Commonwealth and Comparative Politics*, 34, no. 3 (November): 235–47.

Lewis, Patsy. 1998. "Not seizing the time: The consultative process in the OECS political union initiative". *Pensamiento Propio*, no. 8 (October/December): 55–74.

Lewis, Patsy, ed. 1994. *Jamaica: Preparing for the Twenty-first Century*. Kingston, Jamaica: Ian Randle Publishers.

Lewis, Rupert. 1988. *Marcus Garvey: Anti-Colonial Champion*. Trenton: Africa World Press.

Lewis, Rupert. 1994. "Walter Rodney: 1968 revisited". *Social and Economic Studies* 43, no. 3 (September): 7–56.

Lewis, Rupert. 1999. *Walter Rodney's Intellectual and Political Thought*. Kingston, Jamaica: The Press, University of the West Indies; Detroit: Wayne State University Press.

Lindahl, Folke. 1994. "Caribbean diversity and ideological conformism: The crisis of Marxism in the English-speaking Caribbean". *Social and Economic Studies* 43, no. 3 (September): 54–74.

Lovelace, Earl. 1979. *The Dragon Can't Dance*. Harlow: Longman.

MacIntyre, Alasdair. 1973. "Ideology, social science and revolution". *Comparative Politics* 5, no. 3 (April): 321–42.

Macpherson, C.B. 1973. *Democratic Theory: Essays in Retrieval*. Oxford: Clarendon Press.

Madison, James. 1961. "Federalist Papers No. 10". In *The Federalist Papers*, Alexander Hamilton, James Madison and John Jay. New York: Mentor.

Mandel, Ernest. 1998. "Marx's theory of wages in 'The Communist manifesto' and subsequently". In *Karl Marx: The Communist Manifesto*, ed. Frederic Bender. New York and London: Norton.

Mandle, Jay R. 1999. "The crisis in and future of the Windward Islands banana industry". Draft paper, Colgate University, August.

Manley, Michael. 1972. *The Politics of Change: A Jamaican Testament*. London: André Deutsch.

Manley, Michael. 1982. *Struggle in the Periphery*. London: Writers and Readers.

Manley, Michael. 1989. *A History of West Indies Cricket*. London: André Deutsch.

Manley, Rachel. 1996. *Drumblair: Memories of a Jamaican Childhood*. Kingston, Jamaica: Ian Randle Publishers.

Market Research Services Ltd. 1996. "Draft final survey of the public transportation system". Typescript, Kingston.

Mars, Perry. 1998. *Ideology and Change: The Transformation of the Caribbean Left*. Kingston, Jamaica: The Press, University of the West Indies; Detroit: Wayne State University Press.

Marx, Karl. 1978. "Manifesto of the Communist Party". In *The Marx-Engels Reader*, ed. Robert Tucker, 469–500. New York and London: Norton.

McAfee, Kathy. 1991. *Storm Signals: Structural Adjustment and Development Alternatives in the Caribbean*. London and Boston: Zed/Oxfam America.

McClintock, Cynthia. 1989. "Peru's Sendero Luminoso rebellion: Origins and trajectory". In *Power and Popular Protest: Latin American Social Movements*, ed. Susan Eckstein, 61–101. Berkeley, Los Angeles and London: University of California Press.

McNeil, Anthony. 1972. *Reel From the Life Movie*. Kingston, Jamaica: Savacou.

Meeks, Brian. 1976. "The development of the 1970 revolution in Trinidad and Tobago". MSc thesis, University of the West Indies, Mona.

Meeks, Brian. 1988. "Social formation and People's Revolution: A Grenadian study". PhD diss., University of the West Indies, Mona.

Meeks, Brian. 1993. *Caribbean Revolutions and Revolutionary Theory: An Assessment of Cuba, Nicaragua and Grenada*. Warwick University Caribbean Studies Series. London and Basingstoke: Macmillan.

Meeks, Brian. 1994. "Re-reading *The Black Jacobins*: James, the dialectic and the revolutionary conjuncture". *Social and Economic Studies* 43, no. 3 (September): 75–103.

Meeks, Brian. 1996. *Radical Caribbean: From Black Power to Abu Bakr*. Kingston, Jamaica: The Press, University of the West Indies.

Meeks, Brian, ed. 1994. *New Currents in Caribbean Thought*. Special issue, *Social and Economic Studies* 43, no. 3 (September).

Meiksins-Wood, Ellen. 1996. *Democracy Against Capitalism: Renewing Historical Materialism*. Cambridge and New York: Cambridge University Press.

Miliband, David, ed. 1994. *Reinventing the Left*. Cambridge: Polity Press.

Miliband, Ralph. 1994. *Socialism for a Sceptical Age.* London and New York: Verso.

Miliband, Ralph, and Leo Panitch, eds. 1991. *Communist Regimes: The Aftermath.* Socialist Register 1991. London: The Merlin Press.

Miller, Daniel, Michael Rowlands, and Christopher Tilley, eds. 1989. *Domination and Resistance.* London and New York: Routledge.

Millette, David. 1995. "Guerrilla war in Trinidad 1970–1974". In *The Black Power Revolution 1970: A Retrospective,* ed. Selwyn Ryan and Taimoon Stewart, 625–60. St Augustine, Trinidad: Institute of Social and Economic Research.

Mills, Charles. 1994. "Getting out of the cave: Tension between democracy and elitism in Marx's theory of cognitive liberation". *Social and Economic Studies* 43, no. 3 (September): 1–50.

Mohammed, Pat, guest ed. 1998. *Feminist Review,* no. 59 (June).

Moore, Barrington. 1987. *Social Origins of Dictatorship and Democracy: Lord and Peasant in the Making of the Modern World.* Harmondsworth: Penguin.

Munroe, Trevor. 1977. *The Marxist Left in Jamaica: 1940–1950.* Mona, Jamaica: Institute of Social and Economic Research.

Munroe, Trevor. 1999. *Renewing Democracy into the Millennium: The Jamaican Experience in Perspective.* Kingston, Jamaica: The Press, University of the West Indies.

Naipaul, V.S. 1962. *The Middle Passage.* Harmondsworth: Penguin.

Naipaul, V.S. 1975. *Guerrillas.* Harmondsworth: Penguin.

Nettleford, Rex. 1970. *Mirror, Mirror: Identity, Race and Protest in Jamaica.* London: William Collins.

Nettleford, Rex. 1978. *Caribbean Cultural Identity: The Case of Jamaica.* Kingston, Jamaica: Institute of Jamaica.

Nettleford, Rex. 1993. *Inward Stretch: Outward Reach.* London: Macmillan.

Nove, Alec. 1983. *The Economics of Feasible Socialism.* London: Unwin Hyman.

Nozick, Robert. 1974. *Anarchy, State and Utopia.* Oxford: Basil Blackwell.

Panton, David. 1993. *Jamaica's Michael Manley: The Great Transformation, 1972–1992.* Kingston, Jamaica: Kingston Publishers.

Pateman, Carol. 1970. *Participation and Democratic Theory.* Cambridge: Cambridge University Press.

Patterson, Orlando. 1982. *The Children of Sisyphus.* Harlow: Longman Drumbeat.

Payne, Anthony. 1999. "Re-thinking US-Caribbean Relations: Towards a new mode of trans-territorial governance in an era of globalisation". Paper presented at the seminar Coming in from the Cold: Small States Responses to Globalisation, University of the West Indies, Mona, January.

Phillip, Anthony Emrold. 1996. *Life is a Stage: The Complete Calypsoes of Brother Valentino,* comp. Zeno Obi Constance. Port of Spain, Trinidad: Zeno Constance.

Planning Institute of Jamaica. 1998. *Economic and Social Survey: Jamaica 1997.* Kingston, Jamaica: Planning Institute of Jamaica.

Poulantzas, Nicos. 1980. *State, Power, Socialism.* London: Verso/NLB.

Premdas, Ralph. 1993. "Ethnic conflict in Trinidad and Tobago: Domination and reconciliation". In *Trinidad Ethnicity,* ed. Kevin Yelvington, 136–60. Warwick University Caribbean Studies Series. London and Basingstoke: Macmillan.

Robotham, Don. 1998. *Vision and Voluntarism: Reviving Voluntarism in Jamaica.* Grace Kennedy Foundation Lecture. Kingston, Jamaica: Grace Kennedy.

Rodney, Walter. 1981. *A History of the Guyanese Working People.* Baltimore: Johns Hopkins University Press.

Roemer, John. 1994. *A Future for Socialism.* London and New York: Verso.

Rohlehr, Gordon. 1992. *My Strangled City and Other Essays.* Port of Spain, Trinidad: Longman.

Rohlehr, Gordon. 1992. *The Shape of that Hurt and Other Essays.* Port of Spain, Trinidad: Longman.

Rudé, George. 1988. *The Face of the Crowd: Studies in Revolution, Ideology and Popular Protest: Selected Essays of George Rudé,* ed. Harvey Kaye. Atlantic Highlands, NJ: Humanities Press International.

Ryan, Selwyn. 1972. *Race and Nationalism in Trinidad and Tobago.* Toronto: University of Toronto Press.

Ryan, Selwyn. 1989. *Revolution and Reaction: Parties and Politics in Trinidad and Tobago, 1970–1981.* St Augustine, Trinidad: Institute of Social and Economic Research.

Ryan, Selwyn. 1991. *The Muslimeen Grab for Power: Race, Religion and Revolution in Trinidad and Tobago.* Port of Spain, Trinidad: Inprint.

Ryan, Selwyn, and Taimoon Stewart, eds. 1995. *The Black Power Revolution 1970: A Retrospective.* St Augustine, Trinidad: Institute of Social and Economic Research.

Said, Edward. 1994. *Representations of the Intellectual: The 1993 Reith Lectures.* London: Vintage.

Salkey, Andrew. 1982. *The Late Emancipation of Jerry Stover.* Harlow: Longman.

Samuelson, Robert. 1998. "A world meltdown?" *Newsweek,* 7 September.

Scott, David. 1995. "Revolution, theory, modernity: Notes on the cognitive-political crisis of our time". *Social and Economic Studies* 44, no. 3 (June): 1–25.

Scott, David. 1997. "The government of freedom". Paper presented at the conference New Currents in Caribbean: Looking Towards the Twenty First Century, Michigan State University, 4–5 April.

Scott, James. 1969. "Corruption, machine politics and political change". *American Political Science Review* (December).

Scott, James. 1985. *Weapons of the Weak: Everyday Forms of Peasant Resistance.* New Haven and London: Yale University Press.

Scott, James. 1990. *Domination and the Arts of Resistance: Hidden Transcripts.* New Haven and London: Yale University Press.

Senior, Olive. 1972. *The Message is Change: A Perspective on the 1972 General Elections.* Kingston, Jamaica: Kingston Publishers.

Serbin, Andres. 1998. *Sunset Over the Islands: The Caribbean in an age of Global and Regional Challenges.* Warwick University Caribbean Studies Series. London and Basingstoke: Macmillan.

Simpson, Louis. 1972. *North of Jamaica.* New York: Harper and Row, quoted in Douglas Hall, *Grace Kennedy and Company Limited: A Story of Jamaican Enterprise.* Kingston, Jamaica: Grace Kennedy, 1992.

Skocpol, Theda. 1994. *Social Revolutions in the Modern World.* Cambridge: Cambridge University Press.

Smith, Livingstone. 1999. "A comparison between the constitutional reform process of the 1940s and the 1990s in Jamaica". Draft PhD diss., University of the West Indies, Mona.

Smith, M.G. 1965. *The Plural Society in the British West Indies.* Los Angeles: University of California Press.

Soros, George. 1999. "The crisis of global capitalism". *Newsweek,* 1 February.

Spivak, G.C. 1990. *The Postcolonial Condition: Interviews, Strategies, Dialogues,* London: Routledge.

Spivak, Gayatri, and Ranajit Guha, eds. 1988. *Selected Subaltern Studies.* New York: Oxford University Press.

Stallybrass, Peter, and Allon White. 1986. *The Politics and Poetics of Transgression.* Ithaca: Cornell University Press.

Stephens, Evelyne Huber, and John D. Stephens. 1986. *Democratic Socialism in Jamaica: The Political Movement and Social Transformation in Dependent Capitalism.* London and Basingstoke: Macmillan.

Stone, Carl. 1973. *Class, Race and Political Behaviour in Urban Jamaica.* Mona, Jamaica: Institute of Social and Economic Research.

Stone, Carl. 1974. *Electoral Behaviour and Public Opinion in Jamaica.* Mona, Jamaica: Institute of Social and Economic Research.

Stone, Carl. 1981. "An appraisal of the co-operative process in the Jamaican sugar industry". In *Perspectives on Jamaica in the Seventies,* ed. Carl Stone and Aggrey Brown, 437–62. Kingston, Jamaica: Jamaica Publishing House.

Stone, Carl. 1982. *The Political Opinions of the Jamaican People: 1976–1981.* Kingston, Jamaica: Blackett.

Stone, Carl. 1983. *Democracy and Clientelism in Jamaica.* New Brunswick, NJ, and London: Transaction Books.

Stone, Carl. 1989. *Politics Versus Economics: The 1989 Elections in Jamaica.* Kingston, Jamaica: Heinemann Caribbean.

Stone, Carl. c. 1992. *Report of the Stone Committee Appointed to Advise the Jamaican Government on the Performance, Accountability and Responsibilities of Elected Parliamentarians.* Kingston, Jamaica: Bustamante Institute of Public and International Affairs.

Stone, Carl. 1994. "The Jamaican party system and political culture". In *Jamaica: Preparing for the Twenty-first Century,* ed. Patsy Lewis, 132–47. Kingston, Jamaica: Ian Randle Publishers.

Stone, Carl. 1994. *The Stone Columns: The Last Year's Work.* Kingston, Jamaica: Sangster's.

Stone, Carl. 1995. *Carl Stone Speaks on People, Politics and Development,* ed. Rosemarie Stone. Kingston, Jamaica: Rosemarie Stone.

Sutton, Paul. 1983. "Black Power in Trinidad and Tobago: The crisis of 1970". *Journal of Commonwealth and Comparative Politics* 21, no. 2 (July).

Swaby, Raphael. 1974. "Some problems of public utility regulations in a statutory board in Jamaica: The Jamaica Omnibus case". *Social and Economic Studies* 23, no. 2 (June): 242–63.

Swaby, Raphael. 1981. "The rationale for state ownership of public utilities in Jamaica". *Social and Economic Studies* 30, no. 1 (March): 75–107.

Thelwell, Michael. 1980. *The Harder They Come.* New York: Grove Press.

Thomas, C.Y. 1984. *The Rise of the Authoritarian State in Peripheral Societies.* New York: Monthly Review Press.

Thomas, C.Y. 1997. "On reconstructing a political economy of the Caribbean". Paper presented at the conference New Currents in Caribbean Thought: Looking Towards the Twenty-first Century, Michigan State University, 4–5 April.

Tilley, Charles. 1978. *From Mobilization to Revolution.* New York: Addison-Wesley.

"Traffic accidents, 1961–1995". Document from the office of senior superintendent of police Keith Gardener.

United Nations Development Programme. 1996. *UNDP Human Development Report, 1996.* New York and Oxford: Oxford University Press.

Wade, Robert, and Frank Veneroso. 1998. "The Asian crisis: The high debt model versus the Wall Street-Treasury-IMF complex". *New Left Review,* no. 228 (March/April): 3–24.

Wallerstein, Immanuel, Terrence Hopkins, and Giovanni Arrighi. 1989. *Antisystemic Movements.* London: Verso.

Watson, Hilbourne. 1994. Introduction: "The Caribbean and the techno-paradigm shift in global capitalism". In *The Caribbean in the Global Political Economy,* ed. Hilbourne Watson. Boulder and London: Lynn Rienner; Kingston, Jamaica: Ian Randle Publishers.

Watson, Hilbourne. 1997. "Themes in liberalism, modernity, Marxism, postmodernism and beyond: An interpretation and critique of Brian Meeks' 'Re-Reading *The Black Jacobins*: James, the dialectic and the revolutionary conjuncture' ". Paper presented at the conference New Currents in Caribbean Thought: Looking towards the Twenty-first Century, Michigan State University, 4–5 April.

Wedderburn, Judith, ed. 1991. *Rethinking Development.* Mona, Jamaica: The Consortium Graduate School of Social Sciences.

Weiss, Linda. 1997. "Globalization and the myth of the powerless state". *New Left Review,* no. 225 (September/October): 3–27.

Wickham-Crowley, Timothy. 1992. *Guerrillas and Revolution in Latin America: A Comparative Study of Insurgents and Regimes since 1956.* Princeton: Princeton University Press.

Widner, Jennifer. 1995. "States and statelessness in late twentieth century Africa". *Daedalus* 124, no. 3: 129–54.

Wolf, Eric. 1971. *Peasant Wars of the Twentieth Century.* London: Faber and Faber.

Workers' Party of Jamaica. 1978. *Programme: Workers' Party of Jamaica.* Kingston, Jamaica: Workers' Party of Jamaica.

Workers' Party of Jamaica. 1987. "Contribution to rethinking: issues in the Communist movement". Mimeo, Kingston.

Working People's Alliance. *c.* 1986. "Draft programme of the democratic republic". Mimeo.

World Bank. 1999. *World Bank World Development Report: Knowledge for Development 1998–9.* New York and Oxford: Oxford University Press.

Wright, Eric Olin, Andrew Levine, and Elliott Sober. 1992. *Reconstructing Marxism: Essays on Explanation and the Theory of History.* London and New York: Verso.

Yack, Bernard. 1994. *The Longing for Total Revolution.* Princeton: Princeton University Press.

Zakaria, Fareed. 1998. "So much for globalization". *Newsweek,* 7 September.

Zartman, William. 1995. *Collapsed States: The Disintegration and Restoration of Legitimate Authority.* Boulder: Lynne Rienner.

Interviews, Statements and Correspondence

Barnes, Stanley. Sworn statement, Huntley Munroe's file.

Christie, Adolphus. Cautioned statement, Huntley Munroe's file.

Damon, Titus. Cautioned statement, Huntley Munroe's file.

Gabbidon, Albert. Cautioned statement, Huntley Munroe's file.

Gardener, Keith. 1998. Interview with author. Kingston, Jamaica, April.

Harper, Donald. Cautioned statement, Huntley Munroe's file.

Haynes, Clem. 1996. Interview with author. Cocorite, Trinidad, 5 June.

Kernahan, Malcolm "Jai". 1996. Interview with author. Gonzalez, Port of Spain, Trinidad, 4 June.

Morgan, Eldred. Cautioned statement, Huntley Munroe's file.

Phillips, Peter. 1998. Interview with author. Kingston, March.

"Ronald Henry to Dad, Letter no. 1", Huntley Munroe's file.

"Ronald Henry to Dad, Letter no. 2", Huntley Munroe's file.

Thomas, Al. Cautioned statement, Huntley Munroe's file.

Thornhill, Terrence. 1996. Interview with author. Petit Valley, Trinidad, 20 December.

Newspapers

Sunday Observer (Jamaica)

Daily Observer (Jamaica)

Sunday Gleaner

Daily Gleaner

Daily Express (Trinidad)

Sunday Express (Trinidad)

Washington Post

Discography

Banton, Buju. 1994. "Love me brownin' ". *Mr Mention*. Polygram PH 1997.

Banton, Buju. 1995. "Til I'm laid to rest". *'Til Shiloh*. Polygram 314–524 119–2.

Cliff, Jimmy. 1984. "The harder they come". *Jimmy Cliff: Reggae Greats*. Island 162–539 754–2.

Culture. 1993. "Two sevens clash". *The Story of Jamaican Music*. Island CD 518 402–2.

Marley, Bob and the Wailers. 1980. "Bad card". *Uprising*. Cayman Music 422–846 211–2.

Mighty Diamonds. 1990. "Right time". *Go Seek Your Rights*. Virgin CDFL 9002.

Index